HOW TO
KEEP YOUR
DAUGHTER
FROM SLAMMING
THE DOOR

AN AWESOME MOM HANDBOOK

DEBORAH ANN DAVIS

HOW TO KEEP YOUR DAUGHTER FROM SLAMMING THE DOOR

How to Keep Your Daughter from Slamming the Door
An Awesome Mom Handbook

Published by D&D Universe, LLC

ISBN: 978-1-942009-09-2

Printed in the United States of America

FYI, the names and sometimes genders have been changed in some of the stories to protect the innocent (because sometimes anecdotes are not funny to the star of the anecdote).

Publisher's Cataloging-In-Publication Data
(Prepared by The Donohue Group, Inc.)

Names: Davis, Deborah Ann, 1957-
Title: How to keep your daughter from slamming the door / by Deborah Davis.
Description: [Colchester, Connecticut] : D&D Universe, LLC, [2018] | Series: An awesome
    mom handbook | Includes bibliographical references.
Identifiers: ISBN 9781942009092 | ISBN 9781942009108 (ebook)
Subjects: LCSH: Parent and teenager. | Mothers and daughters. | Teenage girls. |
    Parenting.
Classification: LCC HQ799.15 .D38 2018 (print) | LCC HQ799.15 (ebook) | DDC 649.125--dc23

Interior design and production: *Chapter One Book Production, Knebworth, UK*

Table of Contents

School's In Session: The Awesome Mom Philosophy

The 3 Rs… Rules. Responsibility. Rapport.

- ◆ **Are You an Awesome Mom?**
- ◆ **Why This Book is Different**
- ◆ **By The Time You Finish**
- ◆ **Your Own Mini-Pep Rally**

I love teenagers, with their flashes of brilliance, their occasional bravado, and the vulnerability that underlies it all. They are magnificent WIPs—Works In Progress—at a time when every emotion is magnified. Moment to moment, they vacillate between spectacular audacity, and freaking out over a pimple. Anyone's negative expression becomes a personal insult, whether it was directed at them, or not. Instant joy is just a word away. So is immediate devastation.

My name is Deborah Ann Davis and I'm a speaker, trainer and educator. Armed with a tenth-grade sense of humor, a M.Ed. in Supervision, a BS in Science, and a certificate in Personal Training, I taught grades 7-12 over 30 years, along with coaching basketball, cross country, and cheerleading.

Many times my role as a high school teacher felt like *School Mommy*, so I was completely blindsided when, as a new mom with ten years of teaching under my belt, I discovered that being a teacher and a mom were *not* the same thing. Faced with my tiny dynamo of a daughter, to my surprise—and distress—I realized I needed to shift gears. I was no longer the caring, but objective educator of teens; I was Mommy… and I was in way over my head. Thank goodness she learned to talk.

 I was Mommy… and I was in way over my head.

That's not to say I was totally helpless. After all, I had been juggling tweens and teens for a decade. Any given day provided the chance for unlimited emotional student combinations. As School Mommy, I had to draw upon all my experiences and creativity to provide the best setting, no matter who walked through that door, or how they were feeling that day: the shy and the boisterous; the bullies and the bullied; the academically proficient and the academically challenged; the calm in the eye of the storm and the loose cannon; the anxiety driven and the emotionally driven; the straight, gay and transgender; the artsy and the mathematical; the musical and the analytical… they all mattered.

Many of them lived with one parent, some with two, some with grandparents or relatives, some in foster care, and a few commuted from state institutions. Some of the kids had been together since kindergarten; some had arrived in town the day before. Some spoke one language (not always English), some spoke two, and a few spoke three. Although a couple felt entitled, too many felt unworthy. Some were hyper and, unfortunately, some were depressed. And some children bore burdens no child should be asked to bear. All of these different personalities and situations had to be considered if the students were going to thrive.

> And some children bore burdens no child should be asked to bear.

I worked very hard to break through emotional barriers, searching for resolutions to their academic problems. The students, parents, and I were a team. Together we kept the students on track, or helped get them back on track when they drifted.

Over time, I became very good at reading the children as they entered my classroom. They telegraphed things like, "Leave me alone" or "I'm having a bad morning," by the way they sat down, the way they interacted with other students, the direction they set their gaze—all of it gave me clues as to who needed more from me that day.

Through trial and error, plus a million conversations with teens hanging around my desk, I was able to flesh out what was going on with them, and learned how to give more to those who needed it without singling them out. If a strategy worked well with one kid on any particular day, I would try it on another kid later that week. I quickly accumulated a varied collection of tactics.

And, oh yeah, did I mention I taught them Science?

Are You an Awesome Mom?

Parenting, it turned out, was just as challenging as teaching. Needless to say, I could hardly wait to apply my tried-and-true school strategies on my daughter, but I had to wait (impatiently) for her to reach an age where I knew what I was doing. And because I was used to teaching high school kids, I wasn't prepared to handle everything that my tiny tot threw at me.

After a little over a decade of trial and error, my daughter *finally* caught up to my expertise: Teenagers. I had hit my parenting stride, and with, I might add, a much broader arsenal at my disposal than the average parent. Like any preteen, she was eager to imitate tween and teenage behavior, but I was ready for her little awesome self.

In retrospect, despite my constant misgivings, it turns out I had been an Awesome Mommy all along, even when I didn't know what I was doing. I just didn't know how to define it back then, but I do now.

Awesome Moms never stop trying when it comes to our children. When we don't know how to do it, we find someone who does, or we look it up. We collect stuff (recipes, articles, hand-me-down clothes, toys, books, lists of child-enhancing activities, pets, the neighborhood kids, etc.). That's what Awesome Moms do.

> We Awesome Moms aren't perfect. We're better than that. We are Awesome.

Yes, I was an Awesome Mommy, even on the days when the Tooth Fairy was a no-show, or when we sang *Happy Birthday* over a lit candle stuck into a Fig Newton because I forgot to pick up the cake, or after the preschool teacher called us in when our cheeky cherub executed a series of somersaults during Circle Time… and I made (unwelcomed) suggestions on how to restructure Circle Time so it wouldn't be so boring. We Awesome Moms aren't perfect. We're better than that. We are Awesome, with all of its awesome variety.

Our darling daughters are awesome for the same reasons moms are. They never stop trying when it comes to growing, learning, and maturing. But, just like you, they aren't perfect. They're better than that. They're Awesome. When they don't know how to do it, they find someone who does, or they look it up. They collect stuff (friends, knickknacks, electronic devices, toys, books, pets, memories, etc.). They keep trying. Every day they show up, despite whatever is going on internally. That's just what Awesome Daughters do.

Does the stress in your life make you feel less than awesome? Does your daughter's awesomeness escape her? Don't worry. The pressures of life don't actually erase your awesomeness, although they may obscure it. You are both still awesome, even when you don't feel it.

♦ Exhausted mothers who can't get off the couch are still Awesome Moms, but they are recharging. You need to take a moment for yourself so you'll be rejuvenated for the next round.

♦ Unhappy daughters who withdraw to their rooms are still Awesome Daughters, but they're in recovery mode. They, too, need to reboot before they face the world.

Because they both keep trying, eventually, Awesome Moms get off the couch and Awesome Daughters come out of their rooms, regardless of the sullen looks, the huffy sighs, the snarky comebacks, and the eye rolling (What? Did you think I was talking about your daughter?).

Your job is to make sure you don't get suckered into doubting your worth, and to make sure you don't allow your incredible daughter to doubt hers.

☑ **Do This**: How I'm Awesome

To help you recognize how awesome you are, here are the characteristics of an Awesome Mom. Circle the ones that apply to your situation.

♦ Awesome Moms create opportunities for their families.

♦ Awesome Moms seek knowledge, and implement it, which is powerful.

♦ Awesome Moms build daughters into women, and sons into men.

♦ Awesome Moms change the world one child at a time.

♦ Awesome Moms make mistakes, and then correct (most of) them.

♦ Awesome Moms try and try and try. Then they go to sleep, and in the morning they try again.

Her closed door may seem to punctuate an insurmountable barrier between you, but I guarantee that's the last thing either of you want. From your side of that door-knobbed divider, *you* want to figure out how to stop this from recurring; on the other side of it, *she* doesn't want to keep arguing with you, but neither of you know how to break out of the negative pattern.

Sound familiar?

When circumstances are overwhelming, everyone needs a plan to fall back on. Otherwise, temporary glitches interfere with our momentum. This handbook will provide you with tools and techniques to communicate with your daughter and strengthen your relationship. You no longer have to make it up as you go along, or worry about being unprepared if/when outside influences affect your relationship. ***How To Keep Your Daughter From Slamming the Door*** distills my career with teenagers into one place so *you* don't have to reinvent the wheel, and so you, too, can have a much broader arsenal at your disposal.

> When circumstances are overwhelming, everyone needs a plan to fall back on.

In my role as a teacher, I was in a position to guide the students. These kids knew me and trusted me to understand where they were coming from. Regardless of how they outwardly handled school, without exception, all of my students wanted:

- ◆ Unconditional love from their parents
- ◆ To be accepted
- ◆ To be admired
- ◆ To feel in control
- ◆ Help with unpredictable relationships
- ◆ For everything to just get better
- ◆ To replace their fear of failure with a feeling of confidence

Once the students' personal issues spilled over to their school performance, parents and students would find themselves sitting across from me in a conference. By the time we met, most parents were already frustrated with their teen.

Also, familiar?

Hey, if it were easy, everyone would have a great relationship with their teenagers, right? Don't give up hope. I helped those moms, and I can help you.

There was also a good reason why, in my role as a teacher, I was in a position to support the parents: They were fully aware their kids didn't dish it out at school the way they did at home. Because the students did my bidding, the parents were relying on me for solutions. What those parents wanted was very clear:

♦ Unconditional love from their child

♦ To be accepted

♦ To be admired

♦ To feel in control

♦ Help with their unpredictable relationship

♦ For everything to just get better

♦ To replace their fear of failure with a feeling of confidence

(Hmmm… Maybe the gap between you two isn't as big as it seems.)
Over the years I've met with hundreds of families trying to aid their children's efforts in school. Many of them were parenting teens for the first time and feeling mystified by the sudden dark clouds in their sunny relationship.

If you find yourself feeling like you're doing everything wrong, there are better days ahead. According to a Pennsylvania State University study on the ties between midlife-aged daughters and their elderly mothers, researcher Karen Fingerman, Ph.D. found that despite conflicts and complicated emotions, the mother-daughter bond is so strong that 80% to 90% of women at midlife reported good relationships with their mothers.

I'm guessing you don't want to wait that long for your relationship with your angel-turned-fiend to improve.

> **I make mistakes just like everyone else, but I try not to make them twice.**

After 30 years of teaching, eighteen of which overlapped with raising an incredible daughter (objectively speaking, of course), I can tell you with absolute certainty, your daughter doesn't need a perfect mom. She needs the Awesome Mom you already are. I'll be the first to tell you I'm not perfect (my daughter will be the second to tell you). I problem solve, and when I don't get it right, I fix it. I make mistakes just like everyone else, but I try not to make them twice. It takes dedication, time, and practice to be an Awesome Mom. Just ask my Awesome Daughter.

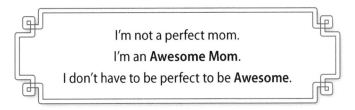

I'm not a perfect mom.
I'm an **Awesome Mom**.
I don't have to be perfect to be **Awesome**.

On the day your daughter was born, there was a very special moment when she first locked eyes with you. That was the first time she connected with her Number One Go-To Gal. She knew you were Awesome, and completely entrusted her fate to your hands.

Were you scared, and feeling ill-equipped and unprepared? I know I was.

That reminds me of a story …

Although the medical staff skillfully siphoned, swiped, and swaddled my delicate infant, I was appalled by their rough handling of something so small and fragile. However, it wasn't until they actually handed her to me that I feared for her very life. I didn't know what to do with that squalling bundle, and I was pretty sure they wouldn't take her back. Panicked, I spoke to her as if she was a frightened kitten… and miraculously, she peered at me and stopped crying.

That was our first moment. Neither of us noticed my husband and his camera, or the nurses and their equipment. For that instant, it was just us. In that moment, I took the time to apologize for all the mistakes I was going to make over the next couple of decades. She didn't seem too worried about what was to come, and my panic subsided. (Besides, we both really needed a nap.) Then, it was there on my chest where she fell into her first peaceful slumber.

We moms dealt with it anyway, didn't we? After all, like you, I knew more than a newborn, right? We're able to solve countless problems, dole out millions of hugs, and brace ourselves against buckets of tears. And, she's still thriving, despite the mistakes we made along the way.

As a mom, I've been through what you're going through. Today, my mission is to help you, Awesome Mom, re-discover the tools you already have inside; tools that will help you positively empower your teenage daughter as she develops into the strong, well-adjusted woman you want her to be.

> *"With all due respect, I often compare the mother-daughter relationship to being on a roller coaster, the big, scary kind that you're able to see from the next town over and whose passengers can be heard shrieking from miles away.*
>
> *Parts of that ride can certainly be thrilling and crazy fun, much like the way you may feel when you and your daughter are really getting along. There may be other stretches of that same ride that leave you feeling anxious, fearful, or nauseated—much like the way you may feel when you and your daughter are in the midst of an argument.*
>
> *There's one big difference, though, between these two rides. Unlike the experience at the amusement park, the ride you are on with your daughter will never come to a halt, automatically release its safety bar, and allow you to exit. No matter how scary or intolerable the ride may get with your daughter, there's not even a chance of getting off. This ride is forever."*
>
> Dr. Charles Sophy, author of *Side by Side: The Revolutionary Mother-Daughter Program for Conflict-Free Communication*, posted by MSNBC

If you're struggling with a strained relationship with your tween or teen girl, or you want to learn how to circumvent the drama before it rears its ugly head, keep reading. . . .

Why This Book Is Different

There are several wonderful books out there on parenting teens, many written by professionals in other fields (I've included some of my favorites in a handy *Answers at the Back of the Book* section), but my distinct perspective comes from the culmination of my years as a teacher and as a mom. Therapists, psychologists, social workers, and psychiatrists also work with the teen population, but I'm pretty sure they don't do it with 20+ teens at a time… in the same room… every day. It's a different skill set.

So is parenting.

But, of course, there is some overlap. My years of teaching experience make my approach to mother-daughter confrontations unique… and very helpful when it came to my own daughter. In my classroom, I had to know my students in order to effectively differentiate lessons to accommodate individual needs. From the first day of school, my mission was to figure out how to get 20+ pubescent bodies to do what I said, and when I said it, even though:

♦   they were usually bigger than my five-foot self, and

♦   they had no prior relationship with me.

I needed them to wade through that sea of phero-mones and cell phones so they could experience the feeling of success, even if the last thing they wanted to do was learn about science. My every word, every action, every raised eyebrow was designed to rein in the majority of the group, and to coax the outliers to come along for the ride. I was in charge, and they knew it.

> I needed them to wade through that sea of pheromones and cell phones so they could experience the feeling of success.

Each year, I began the first day of school in every class by putting my new students into a seating chart, which they did not like because they wanted to sit next to their friends (which *I* did not like). This strategy was important for two reasons:

♦   It established who was in control (me).

♦   While they worked on their first assignment, I could go about the business of memorizing their names and faces from my seating chart.

This first simple tussle of wills established my authority. I was requiring them to follow the rules I had set up, even though we were strangers. This process informed them who I was, and how I was going to conduct myself.

At the end of the first class, the fact that I could point to each one of them individually and get their names right (I studied!) demonstrated they mattered to me. It also let them know I was paying attention to them, so they had better not try anything.

And as long as I didn't surprise them by suddenly shifting my parameters, they trusted their expectations of me, and therefore trusted me, because they could predict:

♦   how I was going to act

♦   how I was going to treat them

♦   how I was going to respond to them

♦   how to obtain my approval

Your relationship with your daughter works the same way. The sooner any teacher (that's you) lets the student (that's your daughter) know what kind of teacher you are, the easier it is for her to behave properly. She needs to be able to predict your reactions and your behaviors. Before she can trust you with her innermost feelings and fears, there has to be a foundation in your everyday lives that says, "This is our typical, normal routine." It's a baseline that establishes trust between both of you, and makes it feel safer for her to confide in you.

> FYI, anger is the universal symbol of loss of control, so any gains your anger produces are fleeting at best.

If you don't establish the rules and parameters the way I did with my classroom, your relationship with your daughter will be like those uncomfortable schoolrooms where the teacher (usually a substitute) doesn't have control. You remember how it was. The students did not respect her, and continuously tried to see what they could get away with. The teacher's efforts to regain control were more punitive than disciplinary, and typically accompanied by anger.

FYI, anger is the universal symbol of loss of control, so any gains your anger produces are fleeting at best. Why? **Because they are not real gains**. They are just temporary attempts to avoid punishment.

That's the same situation you'll experience if you don't establish your authority, set limits, and enforce them in your home. Without that, your daughter won't know:

♦   how you are going to act

♦   how you are going to treat her

- ♦ how you are going to respond to her

- ♦ how she can obtain your approval

I just gave you a perfect metaphor for the importance of having control of your relationship with your child. That bears repeating:

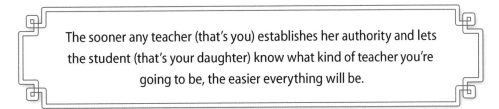

> The sooner any teacher (that's you) establishes her authority and lets the student (that's your daughter) know what kind of teacher you're going to be, the easier everything will be.

I can walk into a brand-new classroom knowing exactly what to do and what to say, but that comes with preparation and experience. Every Awesome Teacher has a learning curve, as does every Awesome Mom. Yes, as a novice, I goofed up at the beginning of my career, just like I blundered as a young mother. Did I learn from those mistakes? You bet I did, and I applied my newfound knowledge every chance I could. Being consistent, persistent, and insistent contributed to my success, as it will to yours.

Is it corny that as a teacher, I've set up this book to parody the school experience? Sure it is, but there's nothing wrong with corny. It paints a familiar picture for nearly all of us, no matter how we lived it. Why not capitalize on a time in our lives when our job was to learn, a time where you underwent the same period of maturation, vulnerability, and turmoil your daughter is experiencing right now? What better way to remind you of your child's day-to-day experiences, and to remember how you handled yours when you were her age?

Being consistent, persistent, and insistent contributed to my success, as it will to yours.

Do you remember the 3 Rs? *Reading, Writing, and Arithmetic?* (Does it bother anyone else that only one of those words actually begins with 'R'?) In keeping with tradition, each chapter in your handbook begins with its own set of the 3 Rs. I've loaded tons of information into each section, and scattered exercises throughout, with lots of areas for journaling. Expect a series of challenges accompanied by stories and examples to illustrate the major points. There will be clarifying quizzes, tactical tips and helpful hints, plus a chance to reflect at the end of each chapter. You will also find awesome resources in the ***Answers at the Back of the Book***.

Oh, and did I mention there would be Homework? As well as a Reading List, Field Trip suggestions, and Group Projects for you to do with your daughter?

Consider me your new secret weapon as I walk you through this refresher course on being an Awesome Mom. You're going back to school again, but this time around you'll actually have a clue.

By The Time You Finish

As soon as you started reading this *Awesome Mom Handbook*, you began a shift toward establishing balance in your relationship with your daughter. By the time you finish reading this book, you will understand the groundwork for *the relationship you want to have with your daughter for the rest of your lives*.

If you sprint through it, you will achieve some temporary changes in your strained relationship. Any token effort aimed at a quick fix will produce short-lived results. In the long run, it will also reduce your credibility with your daughter.

However, if you treat this journey to a better-quality relationship as the marathon it truly is, if you invest the necessary time, and consistently work hard on these challenges, you will see a vast improvement in how your daughter responds when you communicate with her. In the process, her attitude, and your attitude, will improve significantly.

And, why wouldn't it? You'll be exploring options, and experimenting with techniques, and she'll respond more and more readily to your overtures. Your commitment to the bond you share will reaffirm how important she is to you. Little by little, she will realize you can be entrusted with her innermost thoughts and problems, because you will have communicated your capacity for understanding her.

She will feel stronger and empowered. That will make her less vulnerable to negative influences from her peers. Her self-worth will grow as she successfully navigates her life. In turn, she

> **Good to Know**
>
> According to The 2016 U.S. Census Bureau, 9.6 million single parent families were headed by **single mothers**. These women are raising 1 out of every 4 children under the age of 18—by themselves. While this book applauds those fabulous fathers raising our next generation of empowered young women, the focus here is on the moms, and that particularly unique bond between mothers and daughters.

will be able to apply what she has learned from you to the ever-changing and tumultuous world of teenagers. Your trust in her ability to make good decisions will grow, and she will know it.

You will learn new strategies for dealing with your own issues, and the positive effects will trickle down to her. There will be more joy in your home as the burden and isolation of living under a strained relationship lifts. When your daughter cries, "Mom!" you won't tense up, wondering, "Oh, great. Now what?" Instead of expecting her to career into yet another argument, you will eagerly anticipate some tidbit from her life. Your heart will no longer clench when the door slams because it will just be from the wind.

The best way to use this book is to journal your progress. Use the blank spaces to track the issues and solutions unique to you and your daughter. Record your thoughts and reactions as you go along. Keep track of your daughter's reactions to your attempts to create change. Highlight and underline everything that helps you on your journey.

When you are feeling frustrated, and thinking that nothing you try works, the journal will:

♦ remind you of the incremental changes you recorded over the course of your marathon

♦ renew your hope, and

♦ refuel motivation to propel you forward

You will end up with an awesome record of your journey together, which can be used for years to come. Plus, your darling girl will love to go through the book when she has her own daughter.

If you commit to the process, and follow the path laid out in these pages, you're going to do great! And, you'll rock the final exam.

What?

Of course there's a final exam. I told you we were going back to school.

One last thing… if you have more than one daughter, read this book keeping only one of them in mind. I recommend waiting until you finish the book to apply the lessons and activities to your other daughter(s). Who do you start with? Whichever one is the walking teenage volcano. You might as well just jump in with both feet.

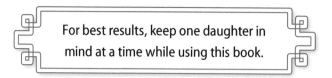

For best results, keep one daughter in
mind at a time while using this book.

Your Own Mini-Pep Rally

The purpose of a Pep Rally is to inspire enthusiasm, encouragement, and support before you sally forth. So, what better way to close the chapter?

Let's see what you got. Stand up and holler, "I'm an Awesome Mom!"

Would you like something more formal? Okay, here's your first cheer:

 Come on (Your Name),
You can do it!
Yell, "I'm Awesome!"
Put your heart into it!

So, what are you waiting for? Don't you miss the spunky tween who used to confide in you? Aren't you tired of the eye rolling and exasperated sighs that have replaced the winks and giggles? Wouldn't you like to not react when your daughter pushes buttons you didn't know you had?

It's all within your reach because you picked up *How To Keep Your Daughter From Slamming the Door.*

School is in session! And the warning bell for homeroom is about to ring. It's time to get to class.

Ready to cheer? All together now:

 H – U – S – T – L – E! Hustle! Hustle!
H – U – S – T – L – E! Hustle! Hustle!

Now, let's get started.

Chapter 1

The Warning Bell: Heeding the Signs Before It's Too Late

The 3 Rs… Recognize. Reduce. Reassess.

- **Pre-Assessment: The *Before* Part of Before-and-After**
  - Awesome Mom Pre-Assessment ◆ Homework: Awesome Daughter Pre-Assessment
- **External and Internal Pressures on Awesome Moms**
  - Part A: Awesome Mom External Pressures ◆ Part B: Awesome Mom Internal Pressures
  - Part C: Symptoms Manifested by Pressures on Awesome Moms
- **External and Internal Pressures on Awesome Daughters**
  - Part A: Awesome Daughter External Pressures ◆ Part B: Awesome Daughter Internal Pressures ◆ Part C: Symptoms Manifested by Pressures on Awesome Daughters
    - Homework: Unmasking Fast Food
- **Quick Fixes**
- **Now For Your Daughter**
  - Homework: Sharing Your Mission ◆ Homework: Identifying Pressures And Symptoms
- **Beating The Warning Bell: Myth Debunking 101**
  - Life Lesson #1: Eliminating Guilt ◆ Homework: Kicking HER Guilt to the Curb
  - Life Lesson #2: Debunking The Supermom Myth
  - Life Lesson #3: Confronting The Plenty-of-Time Myth
- **4 Unpopular (But Effective) Ways to Reduce the Pressures in Her**
- **10 Conversation Boosters for Your Tumultuous Teen**
- **Your Own Mini-Pep Rally**
- **How Did You Do?**

The dictionary defines pressure as "the use of persuasion, influence, or intimidation to make someone do something." Just like back in the day when the *Warning Bell* for homeroom signaled it was time to move it or lose it, you have all kinds of warnings telling you the same thing about your life, your daughter's life, and your relationship. The mounting pressures facing the two of you cannot be ignored.

In order for you to plan where you are going, you have to know where you are starting. Teachers use a *Pre-Assessment* and a *Post-Assessment* tool to determine where their students stand on a particular subject. By conducting the same assessment before and after the lesson, they can measure their students' progress.

I'm the teacher, so here's your assignment, your first step to preventing strain from building up between you and your precious child:

Pre-Assessment: The *Before* Part of Before-and-After

As part of a basic before-and-after tool, begin with the *Awesome Mom Pre-Assessment* found on the next page. This one is for you, but there is another one for your daughter on my website, **AwesomeMomTribe.com/Awesome-Pre-Assessment**, that you can download for free. And, yes, they are identical.

After you have read this book, completed the assignments, and practiced the things you learned, both you and your daughter will fill out all the same questions again in the *Post-Assessment*. When you compare them, your answers will clarify the changes in your relationship during your journey. This comparison will demonstrate the progress your relationship makes after today. And, trust me on this… the comparison will amaze you.

So, let's get to work!

DIRECTIONS: **Without sharing your answers,** both you and your daughter are to fill out your own *Pre-Assessment* tool. It describes the way your current relationship from your individual points of view. The *Awesome Mom Pre-Assessment* is on the next page, but you can download a free copy of the *Awesome Daughter Pre-Assessment* at **AwesomeMomTribe.com/Awesome-Pre-Assessment**.

Awesome Mom Pre-Assessment   Today's Date: _____

DIRECTIONS: Answer the questions but do not share them with your daughter today. Put them someplace where you won't lose them. You will be comparing them in the future after you both have done some work on your relationship.

How Do You Describe Your Relationship With Your Daughter?					
Write 5 words that describe your daughter's approach to life.					
Write 5 words that describe your relationship.					
Write 5 words that describe how you feel about your daughter.					
Write 5 words that describe how you feel about your relationship.					
Write 5 words that describe how you treat your daughter.					
Write 5 words that describe how your daughter treats you.					

Why do you think things are the way they are between you?

How does she contribute to the way things are between you?

How do you contribute to the way things are between you?

Additional Reactions, Reflections, and Ruminations

Any other thoughts?

_____

_____

_____

_____

_____

_____

_____

_____

_____

_____

_____

_____

_____

_____

_____

_____

_____

_____

_____

_____

_____

_____

Homework: Awesome Daughter Pre-Assessment

DIRECTIONS: Download the free *Awesome Daughter Pre-Assessment* at **AwesomeMomTribe.com/Awesome-Pre-Assessment** and print out a copy for your daughter.

Schedule time with your daughter to sit down and answer the questions, but do the work separately.

Say This: "I have a new project I'm working on, and I need 30 minutes of your time. I know you're really busy with school and (homework; sports; work; friends), so would it be better to help me out with this today or tomorrow?" (**Note**: Don't ask a question that can be answered with 'Yes' or 'No'.)

Then, show up prepared!

Tell her to answer the questions honestly since she will be the only one who sees them. That's right. *You don't get to read what she wrote.* She will not be sharing them with you. In the future, however, you will be discussing the changes after you both have done your homework, so have her put her pre-assessment someplace where she won't lose it.

At the end of this book you will find your *Awesome Mom Post-Assessment*. The matching *Awesome Daughter Post-Assessment* is also on my website, at **AwesomeMomTribe.com/Awesome-Post-Assessment**. Comparing them will allow you to chart your progress over the course of this handbook, but we'll discuss that later. For now, review your pre-assessment answers, and keep going.

External and Internal Pressures on Awesome Moms

Wow, where do I begin? *External and Internal Pressures on Awesome Moms* could be an entire book by itself.

You and your daughter live with a dazzling array of external and internal pressures, both positive and negative. All of these demands affect your relationship to varying degrees, and are complicated by a host of random contributing factors:

- ♦ the day of the week

- ♦ looming deadlines

- ♦ fluctuating hormones

- ♦ social obligations

- ♦ new assignments

- ♦ what you eat and drink

- ♦ outside relationships

You get the idea.

You've probably lived this way for so long, the stress level feels normal. Even the warning signs go unnoticed.

Part A: Awesome Mom External Pressures

Below is a starter list of common external pressures Awesome Moms face every day. **Circle** the ones you live with. On the next page, **add** the rest of the pressures specific to your situation… you know, the ones you obsess over when you are supposed to be asleep:

- paying mortgage or rent

- paying bills and reducing credit card debt

- living within your budget

- job pressures

- balancing your significant other/spousal relationship with work and kids

- meal planning, grocery shopping, etc.

- keeping on top of homework

- carpooling

- attending school functions

- doctor and dentist appointments

- attending your house of worship

- getting enough sleep

- housekeeping

- auto and home maintenance

- making sure your kids eat healthy every day

- making sure you eat healthy every day.

- getting enough exercise

- self-care

- peer pressure

- finding time for healthy sexual fulfillment

Your Additional External Pressures:

_____

_____

_____

_____

_____

_____

_____

_____

_____

_____

_____

_____

_____

_____

_____

Sometimes external pressure can come from very loving sources. Personally, I've experienced good-intentioned adult peer pressure from my adoring Italian grandmother. Her dinners were a loving torture. She was an absolutely fabulous cook, but after stuffing myself past the point of pain, I always had another helping. Why? To avoid her sorrowfully drooping shoulders as she'd mournfully return the pot to the stove, mumbling, "It's okay if you don't like it."

It didn't matter if it was your first or sixth helping… you had more. She did guilt really well.

Think about your present day adult world. How many times have your friends pushed an extra slice of pizza, or another piece of cake on you? Or, one last drink for the road? They don't feel comfortable indulging by themselves, and joiners make them feel validated. After all, they just want to fit in and be accepted, too.

Too bad no one pushes an extra helping of salad or veggies on us.

Part B: Awesome Mom Internal Pressures

Internal pressures are more insidious, and just as burdensome. You can only recognize them *after* you admit them to yourself. Below is a starter list of common internal pressures Awesome Moms like us face every day. **Circle** the ones you live with.

♦ negative self-image due to weight/body image/aging body

♦ self-criticism and self-bashing over mistakes or poor results

♦ guilt, guilt, and more guilt

♦ insecurity regarding your romantic/spousal relationship

♦ stagnation due to lack of time for creativity and pursuit of knowledge

♦ having to be on top of everything

♦ pressure to be perfect

♦ living up to the great homemakers, cooks, etc.

♦ comparing yourself to the mythical Supermom

♦ adult peer pressure (friends, co-workers, relatives, spouse)

♦ questioning self-worth/ability on the job

♦ providing proper guidance for your kids

♦ frustration over lack of Me-Time, i.e. for going to the gym, or meeting a friend for coffee

♦ feeling inadequate in general

♦ moodiness due to any and all pressures

Now, **add the rest** of the internal pressures specific to your situation. You know, the other ones you obsess over when you are supposed to be driving without distractions.

Your Additional Internal Pressures:

_____

_____

_____

_____

_____

_____

_____

_____

_____

_____

_____

_____

_____

_____

_____

_____

_____

_____

_____

_____

_____

_____

_____

How are you handling the pressures in your life? Ignoring them does not make them go away. If you don't figure out how to cope with them in a healthy way, they will morph into major unhealthy influences on your life. Has that happened to you yet? Keep reading to find out.

Part C: Symptoms Manifested by Pressures on Awesome Moms

Here's a starter list of typical physical and emotional symptoms created by unrelenting pressures. **Circle** the ones you experience.

Pay attention to these! *The warning bells are ringing.*

◆ Insomnia	◆ Nausea
◆ Depression	◆ Anxiety
◆ Anger	◆ Lack of Focus
◆ Isolation	◆ Crying Jags
◆ Panic Attacks	◆ Avoidance
◆ Heart Palpitations	◆ Dizziness
◆ High Blood Pressure	◆ IBS
◆ Self-Medicating Drug Use	◆ Cramps
◆ Sleep Disorders	◆ Irritability
◆ Nightmares	◆ Acid Reflux
◆ Headaches	◆ Sleeplessness
◆ Lethargy	◆ Frequent Colds
◆ Upset Stomach	◆ Withdrawal

Additional Symptoms:

How else are the demands of everyday life being expressed in your body? List them below.

_____

_____

_____

_____

_____

_____

_____

_____

_____

_____

_____

_____

_____

_____

_____

_____

_____

_____

_____

Ding, ding, ding!

The circled physical and emotional symptoms are warning you: *Your external and internal burdens must be addressed before your symptoms worsen.* Let me ask you something: What do you think your symptoms will look like this time next year if you don't deal with the source?

External and Internal Pressures on Awesome Daughters

Tears. Wailing. Stomping. Shouting.

Do you know why your darling daughter just exploded at you? It's not because of *The Chores Conflict*, although that might be what the two of you were just yelling about. It's never about *The Homework Hassle*, or even about *The What-To-Wear-To-School War*. The topic of your argument doesn't matter, although, at that moment, I'll bet it sure feels like it does.

No, the emotional bouts between you and your daughter are symptoms of a bigger issue: **Trust**. (Did you think I was going to say *pressure*? Yeah, well, I'm coming to that.)

Some old misunderstanding between the two of you, perhaps too minor for you to recall, but somehow significant to a tween, began chipping away at her trust. Who knows what it was. It could have been something as simple as you vetoing a trip to an overly violent movie after she told her friends she would go. When you didn't produce the expected response, for a youngster without a bigger picture to guide her, your reaction left her bewildered and wary. She may have felt like you questioned her maturity and didn't believe in her ability to handle things. Like I said, a minor incident for you, could have been a significant event to her.

No matter how the trust between you became weakened, with some work it can be improved. Your daughter wants to be able to trust you again. Regardless of how hard she pushes you away, you are the one she wants to confide in. She wants to feel that safety again.

While you try to figure out the best way to support her without being intrusive, she is trying to figure out how to balance her desire to please you with her own budding individuality. When she fails to attain either, her trust in you, and the rules you live by, decreases little by little with each confusing incident. Her feeling of helplessness grows, and her confidence in your

> **Good to Know**
> You'll find strategies for repairing trust throughout this book.

ability to understand diminishes. Insecurity abounds, and self-esteem evaporates, bit by bit, until she just can't handle it anymore. You ask her to feed the dog, and *BAM!* An epic meltdown ensues.

People only explode and lash out when they are at their wit's end, and don't have any other way to cope. Your daughter's pressures have backed her into a corner and she's

Regardless of how hard she pushes you away, you are the one she wants to confide in.

trying to survive. If she had another way to handle things, she would use it to deal with the situation. Instead, you get the infuriating rolling of the eyes, the annoying noisy exhalation, and the banging of the *almost* slammed door.

That's what my daughter used to do. It wasn't quite a slam, and immediately she'd crack it open and yell, "Sorry! I didn't mean that to be so loud," and then, she'd bang it shut again. When she was really frustrated, the second closing was as loud as the first, sometimes loud enough to prompt her to reopen the door to yell, "Didn't mean that, either."

Right. She wasn't fooling anyone. It felt *good* to almost slam that door with all those fight, flight, or freeze chemicals coursing through her veins. What better release when you don't know how to cope?

> That reminds me …
>
> I maintain the root of teen angst can be traced back to those worthless baby graphs where the pediatrician plots your newborn's height and weight to compare her with other babies.
>
> Why do they do that? You can already tell if she is big or little. Plus, my doctor said it doesn't mean anything anyway.
>
> Too late. That graph plants the seeds of uncertainty in the new mother. If you think about it, every Awesome Mom knows it's inappropriate for another baby's size to diminish her own baby's growth milestones. What sense does that make? I know it. You know it. The doctor knows it.
>
> But that doesn't stop us, does it? We end up comparing everything from size to first words, first crawl, first time standing, first steps, and on and on and on. We can't help it.
>
> No, peer pressure doesn't begin at school, my friends. It begins in the baby buggy.

Part A: Awesome Daughter External Pressures

Below is a starter list of common external pressures facing the average teen. **Put a star** next to the ones your daughter lives with. Don't be surprised if there are quite a few stars. After all, she is your daughter, and she's been modeling herself after you (just like every typical daughter does) ever since she first learned to say *Mama*.

- Negotiating Friendships and Crushes
- Getting Enough Sleep
- Juggling Daily Homework With Long-term Projects
- Writing Essays, Reports, Term Papers
- Studying For Quizzes, Tests, Exams
- School Club Meetings and Events
- Sports Practices and Games
- Extra Homework Help After School
- Group Projects and Lab Reports
- School Functions (Concerts, Games, Dances, Proms)

- Extracurricular Activities
- Scheduling Volunteer Work
- House of Worship Obligations
- Learning to Drive
- High School Rankings
- Holiday Celebrations and Performances
- College or Job Applications
- Cleaning Her Room, Household Chores, Pet Care
- Visiting Relatives
- Dating and Romance
- Working at an After School Job

Additional External Pressures on Her

Add any other pressures specific to your daughter's situation that are not listed above. You know… the other things you observe that she says she can handle.

_____

_____

_____

_____

_____

_____

_____

_____

_____

_____

_____

_____

_____

_____

_____

_____

_____

_____

_____

_____

_____

_____

Other kids go through similar drama, and have the same issues with their moms. (For that reason alone you should share this book with all the moms you know.) If your daughter surrounds herself with people struggling to figure out their own identity (i.e., best friends and schoolmates), social pressure can lead to making stupid decisions, including (but certainly not limited to):

- eating foods that will mess with her health

- vaping

- smoking

- drinking

- and, don't forget the two biggies that make every parent push the panic button: drugs and sex.

Just like bullies, friends who apply pressure actually feel uncomfortable with themselves. Whether this insecurity is about themselves or their actions, getting someone else to join in validates their decisions, even the bad ones.

It helps to reflect back on what you went through as a teen in order to empathize with your daughter's situation. It's a safe bet some of her internal angst stems from the familiar teenage issues you or your friends experienced.

> **It helps to reflect back on what you went through as a teen in order to empathize with your daughter's situation.**

Part B: Awesome Daughter Internal Pressures

Identifying internal pressures in your anxious offspring is problematic because you have to guess. Is she preoccupied with her body image and doesn't want to hear your views on it? Or, has she had a fight with her best friend and it's still too raw to discuss? Maybe she's agonizing over a crush and feels too embarrassed to share, or perhaps her teacher has assigned a group project with a couple of "Mean Girls." You never can tell.

This is a subjective task. Unless she actually tells you which internal demons bother her, it's not a fact; it's *your* assumption. In order for her to share them with you, first she must admit them to herself. And then, she must trust you enough to share.

Put a star next to any of the internal pressures listed below that *you believe* your daughter experiences. You know… the other ones you think she obsesses over when she's supposed to be doing her homework.

- Comparing herself to others (body image, weight, athleticism, intelligence)
- Obtaining a good high school rank (sports, academics, extracurricular activities)
- Pressure to please adults (parents, relatives, teachers, etc.)
- Fear of failure (group projects, overall grades, tests and exams, applying to colleges)
- Popularity and pressure to fit in (what to wear to school, how to act, who to bully)
- Friendship pressures (going along with what the others are doing versus doing what she feels is right for herself)
- Pressure to be sexual (dressing sexy, dating, sexting)
- Dealing with feelings of sexuality (crushes, romance)
- Pressure to be cool (illegal drugs, prescription drugs, alcohol, vaping, smoking)
- Reactions to her changing body and fluctuating self-esteem
- Pressure to be the perfect daughter
- Feeling unsafe and vulnerable

Additional Internal Pressures on Her

List any other internal pressures you believe affect your child.

_____

_____

_____

_____

_____

_____

_____

_____

_____

_____

_____

_____

_____

_____

_____

_____

_____

_____

_____

_____

_____

_____

_____

_____

_____

Part C: Symptoms Manifested by Pressures on Awesome Daughters

Here's your starter list of physical and emotional symptoms created by pressure.

Put a star next to the symptoms that affect your child. These are your warning bells that things have gone too far.

Circle the ones you exhibit.

- *Acid Reflux
- *Anger
- *Anxiety
- *Avoidance
- Breaking Curfew
- Bullying
- Comfort Eating
- *Cramps
- Crying Jags
- *Depression
- *Dizziness
- Exasperated Sighs
- *Frequent Colds
- *Headaches
- *Heart Palpitations
- *High Blood Pressure
- Hitting

- *IBS
- *Insomnia
- *Irritability
- *Isolation
- *Lack of Focus
- *Lethargy
- Lots of Sleeping
- Meanness
- *Nausea
- *Nightmares
- *Panic Attacks
- Passive Aggressive Behavior
- Physically Abusing Siblings
- Refusal To Participate
- Rolling Eyes

- Sarcasm
- *Self-Medicating (Pills, Alcohol, Nicotine, Drugs)
- Slamming Doors
- *Sleep Disorders
- *Sleeplessness
- Sneaking Out
- Stomping
- The Silent Treatment
- Threatening
- *Upset Stomach
- Verbally Abusing Siblings
- Whining
- Withdrawal
- Yelling

* This is not an exhaustive list of symptoms, but I selected these because in addition to being physical manifestations of internal emotional distress, which can be difficult to pinpoint and address, many indicators on this list can also be attributed to ingesting food coloring and food additives (sulfites, MSG, etc.) found in fast foods and snack foods, which can be easily identified and tackled. If you want to be able to tell the difference, clean up the nutrition in your household for three weeks, and see what happens to the both of you. After three weeks, your body will have had time to process out most of the junk you find in junk food. If her symptoms persist, that could indicate an underlying physical problem. Get your daughter allergy tested to rule out other physical causes.

Additional Physical and Emotional Symptoms

How else do you see the demands of everyday life being expressed in your daughter? List them below.

_____

_____

_____

_____

_____

_____

_____

_____

_____

_____

These symptoms are real warnings that you and your daughter have taken all you can take. Unless they are nutrition related, they do not represent responses to a bit of occasional pressure. These are full-blown reactions to either:

- really huge demands from only a few sources

- lots of little difficulties from a bazillion sources

- or both

When she doesn't trust you to understand her problems, she will not share them with you. If she hides her angst, you may not recognize the magnitude of her dilemmas.

If you recognize and interpret them correctly, you can head off trouble. Or, you can wait and see *what your daughter's symptoms will look like this time next year if you don't help her deal with the source now.*

Which are the most disturbing for you, overt emotional displays from your developing diva, or the nausea and headaches that represent her internalized turmoil? Personally, I prefer the eruptions. Your darling girl's flare-ups may push your buttons, but understand what is being signaled here. Her outbursts are blatant indicators that your daughter isn't coping well. When she keeps her anxiety to herself, you remain ignorant, and she remains beyond your help. Besides, believe it or not, her episodic eruptions have their good points.

- Each bout of tears removes her toxic chemicals before they can damage cells.

- Every slammed door or emotional outburst helps her depressurize.

If you do not deal with her issues in a healthy way, they will manifest in an unhealthy way. Unfortunately, the girl who holds it all in conceals her inner turbulence. That makes the identification of her problems much more elusive, even though they produce symptoms that indicate their presence. Ignoring the symptoms caused by her pressures does not get rid of them; neither does addressing the symptom. Treating the symptoms (i.e., with antacids, anxiety prescriptions, etc.), without resolving the underlying issues, will not fix anything permanently.

> **Good to Know**
> If you don't want to be blindsided by your daughter's problems, there are only two things you need to know:
>
> - What is going on with her
> - What is going on with you
>
> That's probably also the bad news.

I know of students who became too anxious to continue attending school, despite accommodations made for them, for fear they would become publically symptomatic (needing to rush to the bathroom, panic attacks, etc.). They ended up being home-schooled with tutors provided by the school system. In hindsight, the first symptoms were the seemingly random headaches, nausea and stomachaches, but the patterns were not recognized soon enough.

What you need is a way to connect with your daughter that will encourage her to open up. There are a lot of ways to approach this, but let's start with this one:

Homework: Unmasking Fast Food

Why treat the symptoms, when you can go after the source? Here's a great rainy day activity that can become the first step towards a positive lifestyle change. Turn it into a field trip by doing the research at your local library. While you're there, find a book you enjoyed at your daughter's age, and share it with her.

Pick a go-to processed snack or fast food both you and your daughter enjoy. Check the list of ingredients. Research the ones you can't pronounce by typing into your search engine, "Health Problems Associated With [Ingredient]." Find the symptoms you marked with a star or a circle that match that ingredient.

Now that you understand eliminating this go-to snack selection can lessen the symptom, discuss it with your daughter.

Say This: "I've been having [symptom], and I just read that [ingredient] causes it. Did you know it's in [favorite snack]? I want to find out if this is the cause. I read that you need to avoid it for three weeks to see if there's a difference. Who knows? The [ingredient] might not even be causing [symptom], but this way we can find out.

"I would really appreciate it if you would join me in this little experiment. Your support will help *me* stick to eliminating [favorite snack] for three weeks. It's going to be hard, so I need all the help I can get."

The daily pressures on your daughter are enormous, but the burden on you to help her resolve her issues is even greater. Not only are you dealing with *her* angst, but you still have to handle *your* daily pressures. Then, the rest piles on:

- ◆ your own memories of feeling awkward and insecure as an adolescent

- ◆ trying to remain calm in the face of your daughter's storm

- ◆ feeling guilty when you lose your temper

Trust me, the other Awesome Moms are dealing with the same stuff. It's a miracle that moms are still standing at the end of the day.

By the way…

♦ Everyone reacts to being emotionally attacked. What's important is how you respond to that clash.

♦ Everyone felt awkward and insecure when they were younger. They still do if they bought into the image-damaging drivel from the media, and from their equally damaging awkward, insecure peers.

♦ Not everyone allows guilt and blame to fester inside them. **Your guilt** for not knowing how to prevent your angsty adolescent's meltdowns **is misplaced and unwarranted**.

♦ *Self-blame* is a waste of your time. *Self-awareness* is what you should be focusing on.

Not to mention, you should be congratulating yourself for picking up this book so you can make a difference. You're an Awesome Mom!

Here's the real kicker. Whichever way you react to the pressures in your life, you can expect your teen will do the same because:

♦ most likely you're genetically related

♦ she lives in your household where she copies your habits and coping solutions

Your guilt for not knowing how to prevent your angsty adolescent's meltdowns is misplaced and unwarranted.

This is not the time to negatively judge yourself or your daughter. This is the time for objective assessment. Look at it this way: If you both have the same color eyes, or if she laughs the way you do, you don't judge. You observe. Similarly, you should not judge how either of you handle pressure. This is *not* about placing blame or feeling guilt. Instead, observe, listen, and learn to read the signs.

Quick Fixes

It's time to do a quick check-in. Are you feeling a bit uneasy right about now? After focusing on your daughter's pressures and symptoms, and looking at your own, I wouldn't be surprised if your tension, and a bit of anxiety, have jumped a notch or two.

While you're getting a handle on this, here are four helpful tools you can use right now to relieve some of that anxiety building up inside. These practices are good for your body, they're the perfect way to steal a little Me Time, *and* they're free!

Quick Fix #1: Fake Smiling

1. Clench your teeth and stretch your lips as far as you can.

2. Hold for 5 seconds, and relax.

3. Pretend to smile, no matter what your mood is.

Do this now. It's important. Your body cannot tell the difference between a real smile and a fake one. By pretending to smile, you trigger the production of your happy hormones, which will make you feel better.

Quick Fix #2: Mindful Breathing

1. Draw your shoulders back.

2. Listen as you take a slow deep breath through your nose.

3. Listen as you slowly exhale through your relaxed mouth. Relax as you exhale.

4. Repeat for a total of five deep breaths, although in a pinch, three will do.

Do this now. It's important. By the way, yawning is good. It indicates an energy shift.

Do *Mindful Breathing* five or more times daily. Do it:

♦   when you are driving

♦   before you get out of bed

- after your head hits the pillow
- before and after every meal
- prior to a meeting at work, and definitely after one.

Do **Mindful Breathing** whenever you feel tense, and whenever you think of it. Make this part of your daily routine, like brushing your teeth. Mindful, slow, deep breathing has several benefits:

- It moves your lymph through your lymphatic system (which basically moves when you do).
- It massages your organs.
- It adds more oxygen to your blood.
- It increases your blood flow to your brain, which—let's face it—can always use some extra oxygen.
- It leads to yawning, an indication of a positive change.

Quick Fix #3: The Zip-Up

1. Sit up straight.
2. Take a deep calming breath.
3. Place your fist at your navel as if you are zipping up your sweatshirt.
4. Zip yourself up all the way to below your lip.
5. Twist/lock your imaginary zipper in place.
6. Reach your hand over your shoulder like you are going to scratch your back.
7. Grasp an imaginary blanket, and pull it up over your head, and down to below your nose.
8. Twist/lock it to the imaginary zipper.

Do this now. It's important. You have now energetically zipped yourself up. This blocks the negative energy from people around you, and keeps it from entering your energy field.

Do *The Zip-Up*:

- before you interact with your daughter
- when you deal with a grumpy person
- while you are sitting in traffic
- prior to tackling an issue

This technique will help you feel fortified. Even if you don't believe in this type of solution, it doesn't matter. You get the benefits just by going through the motions. It can't hurt, right?

Quick Fix #4: The Heart-Brain Connection

1.   Place your right palm on your right temple, and your left palm over your heart. Relax and breathe normally until you have to sigh or yawn.

2.   Keeping your left palm over your heart, shift your right palm to your forehead. Relax and breathe normally until you have to sigh or yawn.

3.   Place your right palm over your heart, and place your left palm over your left temple. Relax and breathe normally until you have to sigh or yawn.

4.   Keeping your right palm over your heart, shift your left palm over to the back of your head. Cover the bulge at the base of your skull (the occipital lobe). Relax and breathe normally until you have to sigh or yawn.

Do this now. It's important. This practice helps center and calm you. The sighing and yawning are signs that your energy has shifted. With luck, your yawn will make your eyes water, which releases toxic chemicals. The more you practice this, the faster the yawn will come.

Do you realize that at this point, you have already taken four Me Moments for yourself? Continue this several times a day, and you'll see a difference.

Now For Your Daughter

If you can find a way to reduce the pressures your daughter is swimming in, her life will be so much saner, which in turn will quiet your life. Letting her know your intentions up front gives her a lifeline to reach for.

Homework: Sharing Your Mission

If your relationship will allow it, share your intentions with your teachable teen. It will help orient her, and keep her from being surprised, and possibly alarmed.

 Say This: "I am on a mission to reduce the pressures in our lives so we can both be happier and healthier." Show her the lists of symptoms from this chapter, and the symbols you made on them. Ask her what she would like to add or contradict, but don't argue with her opinions. She's entitled to them. *Just listen*.

> Don't argue with her opinions. She's entitled to them. *Just listen*.

Note: If you show her this book, she is going to want to flip through it. Don't let her curiosity distract you from your mission. Tell her, "I'll give you the book to look at after we talk, but I want to stay focused on this right now."

Showing her your lists will convey your current awareness of her burdens. Giving her a chance to contribute to the lists invites her to make you aware of the others. That will help alleviate some tension in her because you're showing her support, even if you are simply listening.

Hints For a Smoother Conversation:

The following tips should be shared before she starts in order to make sure you are both on the same page.

♦ As she adds things to the list, don't interrupt her to offer solutions, no matter how much you want to. She needs the opportunity to purge her pressures. You can problem solve later.

♦ If she brings up something that belongs on your own list, quietly write it down for later. Discussing your pressures at this moment will only add to hers.

♦ Don't comment, protest or argue about anything she reveals.

♦ Let the conversation flow where it will.

♦ Listen objectively. This is about raising awareness in you and in her, and not about placing blame.

♦ Don't take it personally if she wants to add things to your list.

♦ Don't take it personally if she puts you or your actions on her list (more on that later).

♦ There is no place for guilt here. Guilt is an unfortunate habitual—and highly inappropriate and unproductive—reaction to your daughter's distress. This process starts the first of the four steps for eliminating guilt (more to come on that shortly).

Once you are both clear on her issues (at least the ones she shares with you), you can reassure her that together you'll help her get through them.

Say This: "If I don't know the answer to any of these issues, I will find someone who does."

If the strain on your relationship makes it uncomfortable for you to approach her, especially if you anticipate she will reject your efforts,

Say This: "I'm working on a way to reduce the pressures in our lives, and I want to bounce something off you. Do you have about ten minutes to sit with me now, or would tonight after supper be better?"

This script provides several advantages:

♦ It gives her a choice, and therefore some power.

♦ It clues her in about the topic.

♦ It raises curiosity about what your new idea is.

♦ *Ten minutes* sounds like a short enough amount of time to keep damage from occurring.

♦ By giving her a choice of *now* or *later*, there is no opportunity for a "No" response.

> Using noncommital responses will keep the conversation flowing.

You can also try approaching from the side door.

Say This: "How do you think your best friend is handling the pressure of _____? I think her mother is worried about her." This gives her the chance to share her opinions on emotional topics without feeling like she's in the hot seat.

Whatever you do, **don't disagree with her opinions**. Again, they are *her* opinions, and she is entitled to them. Besides, for a teenager, opinions can change as quickly as the weather in Connecticut.

Using noncommittal responses will keep the conversation flowing.

Say This:

♦ "That's an interesting way to look at it."

♦ "I understand what you are saying."

♦ "What does your best friend think about that?"

♦ "Did you feel that way when you were younger?"

Homework: Identifying Pressures and Symptoms

Using one of the approaches from this section, invite your daughter to make a private list of **10 Internal Pressures** she lives with. Tell her she doesn't have to share them with you if she doesn't want to.

Then show her the list of physical symptoms in this book and ask her if she is feeling any of them. Explain that some symptoms are caused by pressure, like the ones in her life. Discuss them with her and emphasize your commitment to helping her reduce and resolve those symptoms. Reinforce that you want her to feel better, and you will help her in any way you can.

☑ Do This: Share the Love

Don't forget to share the two *Quick Fixes* with her. *Mindful Breathing* and *The Zip-Up* are good for everybody. She'll most likely get a kick out of *Fake Smiling*.

⊷◆⊶

Beating the Warning Bell: Myth Debunking 101

The airlines got it right. On every flight, they instruct you to first cover your face with the oxygen mask, and then put the mask on your child. The same applies when you are outside the plane. You have to take care of *you* before you can take care of your daughter. If you are not managing your pressures, you will not be able to handle your darling daughter's outbursts, nor will you be able to help her deal with her stressors.

Before you can steer your daughter toward the healthy direction, you have to take control of your life. Because everyone's situations vary, I'm going to limit the next discussion to three huge, pressure-building issues facing Awesome Moms:

♦ **The Guilt Myth**

♦ **The Supermom Myth**

♦ **The Plenty-of-Time Myth**

Take a deep breath. It's a marathon, not a sprint, remember? For that matter, take five slow deep, mindful breaths because we're about to tackle a big *Life Lesson: Eliminating Guilt*.

Life Lesson #1: Eliminating Guilt

Somehow our society has nurtured a disproportionate respect for Guilt. I'm not saying there is no place for Guilt. New Guilt actually has one constructive purpose. Are you ready for it?

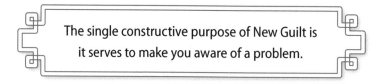

The single constructive purpose of New Guilt is it serves to make you aware of a problem.

That's it. There's nothing else. Once you are aware of the problem, your guilt has served its purpose. It's done. Let it go!

If you are like the rest of us, your personal life might have a few previously-ignored items that need tending to. Sometimes we allow those issues to generate guilty feelings. Occasionally, we allow an incident to produce the overwhelming, incapacitating Guilt that makes it impossible to think clearly.

If you are one of the hordes carrying Old Guilt like it's a badge of (dis)honor, stop it! Old Guilt doesn't do you any good. It contributes stress chemicals to your bloodstream that wreak havoc with your body on a cellular level (which is the basis for all diseases). It does nothing to improve the situation. It doesn't help you in any way. It's time to release it.

Here are the four steps for eliminating Old Guilt (or New Guilt) over a situation you have caused.

1. Do whatever is necessary to make sure the situation does not get worse.

2. Make any repairs you can to the situation.

3. Ask for forgiveness from anyone negatively impacted from the situation.

    ♦   If they forgive you… Great!

    ♦   But if they do not forgive you, move on. You have done everything you could to stop the situation from getting worse, and to set the situation right. If they decide to hold on to a grudge, that's all on them. That's no longer you. Your role in the situation is concluded. You are not responsible for their grudges. You are responsible for you, and your journey.

4.   This final step is the hardest of the four, but *you must forgive yourself* for the situation. If you could have done better at the time, you would have. Cut yourself some slack when you err. Just make sure you learn from your mistakes so the situation is not repeated.

I'm no stranger to Old Guilt. As the eldest child, I felt responsible when my parents split up. With the naivety of a typical nineteen-year-old, I somehow believed if I had uttered the right line, or done the right thing, I could have helped them muddle through their differences, and thus saved their marriage.

Instead, I continued to attend college, and did not return home to fix their marriage. In my eyes, I selfishly had not rescued our family unit. I had abandoned them all. The fact that I had no prior experience in marital counseling seemed irrelevant. Only to myself did I secretly admit my shameful role in the destruction of our family. Honestly, I carried that useless Old Guilt, for not rising to the occasion when they needed me most, well into my thirties.

> Honestly, I carried that useless Old Guilt, for not rising to the occasion when they needed me most, well into my thirties.

It's probably obvious to you, as it now is to me, that their marriage was my parents' journey, not mine. How they handled it was their responsibility, and my carrying that Old Guilt for more than a couple of decades was inappropriate. It wasn't until I learned how to eliminate Old and New Guilt that I finally let it go.

Their divorce was long ago, and both of my parents were happily remarried to other people by the time I dealt with the issue, so the first step in eliminating my guilt was irrelevant. But I did sit individually with my parents and my sisters to acknowledge how I had abandoned them and ask their forgiveness. I received a variety of responses, but ultimately, I realized two things.

♦   Although my younger sisters had felt abandoned by me, they understood my not quitting college to come home.

♦ *No one* agreed the nineteen-year-old child I was could have saved the marriage.

Do I still feel guilty about it? Nope, not anymore. I forgave my nineteen-year-old self for believing she could change the way two forty-year-olds were interacting. I erased my concept of being responsible for things I was not responsible for. And, I forgave my adult self for hanging on to such an obvious misconception for so many years. Yes sir, I kicked that Old Guilt to the curb!

This Old Guilt situation was caused by a particular incident, and then internalized and hoarded for years until I eliminated it. The physical manifestation for me was the onset of migraines. Is it a coincidence that my migraines have all but disappeared since I resolved my Old Guilt? I think not.

I hope my story illustrates the utter worthlessness of Old Guilt. If it comes from without, at best it's punitive. Whether it's internal or external, it's always damaging. Nobody's life is enhanced by Old Guilt. No problems are solved by Old Guilt. The people inflicting Old Guilt don't actually feel better. They merely avoid resolving their own issues by pointing a finger at someone else.

It's time to eliminate your Old Guilt. Believe me, it feels great! Join me in kicking Old Guilt to the curb. Take action by nipping New Guilt in the bud. You deserve a Guilt-Free existence, and your family deserves a Guilt-Free You.

☑ Do This: Kicking Guilt to the Curb

Think about a specific, guilt-ridden episode in your life. It's okay to let those negative feelings wash over you because this will be the last time it will happen.

1. Ask yourself, "Is there something I can do to keep the situation from getting worse?" Be honest. If there is, be brave and **do it**!

2. Ask yourself, "Is there something I can do to repair the damage?" If there is, take the time to **fix it**!

3. Contact (go visit; call on the phone; write a letter; send a card) the individuals negatively impacted by your part in the situation, and ask for their forgiveness. **Put the book down and go do it right now!** Don't be

afraid. Either they will forgive you, or they won't, but either way, you will have done your part.

4. Now, **forgive yourself**. No one died and made you Judge (ignore that if you actually are a judge) so stop punishing yourself. *Let The Guilt Go!* This was the most difficult step for me. I had lived with guilt for so long, it didn't feel normal—or responsible—for me to let it go.

<—◆—>

Releasing my feelings of guilt was the greatest gift I have given myself. Now I take responsibility for my actions without self-blame. When I'm wrong, I say I'm wrong, and just as importantly, I don't allow others to blame me or try to make me feel guilty. Instead, if I make a mistake, or do something I regret, I make sure the situation is contained and can't worsen. I see if I can fix the situation. I apologize for my contribution to the situation. And, I forgive myself for my involvement in the problem, even if the others don't forgive me. Then, I make sure I never make that mistake again.

Taking responsibility makes me feel empowered and straightforward, not victimized and defensive. It's a wonderful way to interact with the world.

Are you still having difficulty releasing the guilt? That comes as no surprise if you've been holding on to it for a long time. It probably feels like a part of you. Perhaps it would be easier for you to see the unsuitability of guilt when you consider your child.

If she were feeling inappropriate guilt over something she had done, you would want to relieve her of that emotional burden, without removing the responsibility of her deeds. Instead of leaving her awash with guilt, you'd prefer to help her learn from her actions, and grow as a person.

Use that same compassion and clarity you have for your precious child to help reorient

---

Good to Know

By the way, did you know that the surge of power that comes from letting go of guilt is actually your brain spurting out happy chemicals to reward you for doing something good for your survival? (Did I mention I'm a Science Geek?) For one, dopamine energizes you when you find a way to meet a need. Each of the four steps for *Kicking Guilt to the Curb* produces its own individual "I can achieve it" rush. *And*, once you forgive yourself and get your dopamine reward, your brain will remember, so when the next guilt-saga release happens, it already knows what to do, and rewards you that much faster.

your precious self. Don't wallow in that worthless guilt. Dropping the guilt lifts emotional burdens from your heart. Get back to the business of living a full life.

Kicking Guilt to the Curb is one of the most important Life Lessons you can model for your daughter. Tell her what you are attempting to do, and why. Explain what the benefits will be for you. Help her understand that electing to accept responsibility for your actions, choosing to ask for forgiveness, and deciding to forgive yourself, is not for sissies. These are powerful actions. She needs to know you are about the business of empowering yourself so she will have a strong positive role model.

Homework: Kicking HER Guilt to the Curb

If your relationship will allow it, ask your daughter about an incident that makes her feel guilty so she can go through the four steps to guilt elimination.

Say This: "When I was younger, I felt guilty about the dumbest things, like _____ . How long do you think someone should feel guilty over something that's not earth-shattering? That's a lot of wasted energy, right? Everyone holds on to guilt if they don't know better. Well, I decided not to be like everybody else, and get rid of my guilt. I've been carrying around _____ guilt all this time, but now I'm done with it. I followed these four steps, and *poof*, I feel so much lighter and free!

"I want you to feel that way, too. With your permission, I'd like to walk you through the steps with something you feel guilty about. You don't even have to tell me what it is for this to work."

If she can, she should start small, with an incident that is not overwhelming. She may not feel comfortable sharing her residual-guilt incident for fear it will lessen her in your eyes, or result in punishment. That's okay. You don't need to know what it is.

☑ Do This: Asking For Forgiveness

1. Have her privately write the incident on a slip of paper so you can't see it.

2. Walk her through the four steps one at a time, while she writes down the answers.

3. When it comes to asking forgiveness, have her make a list of the people she needs to contact. Again, you don't have to see it.

4. Direct her to find their contact info right at that moment. Discourage apologizing through email or texting because it is so easy for intentions to be misinterpreted through those media.

5. Help her write a script, and then rehearse what she wants to say. It's her choice whether to reveal it to you, so expect to coach her in general terms. She also doesn't have to share the incident while she practices the script.

6. Step out of the room so she can call the people. Or, have her schedule when she will talk to them.

7. Follow up with her about how the people were impacted, their reactions, and how your daughter now feels. You may have to walk her through the four steps again, especially if someone decides to hold a grudge and not forgive her.

⬥

What if your adolescent is too anxious try, and says "No" to your overture? She may not feel comfortable enough to face her hidden guilt herself, or for her to trust you with it.

☑ Do This: Backing Off Graciously

Before you approach her, write the steps to *Kicking Guilt to the Curb* on a piece of paper. Have it handy in case she refuses to go through the exercise with you.

💬 **Say This:** "That's fine. I love you no matter what. There's no pressure here for you to do this with me. Here are the steps for getting rid of Old Guilt. [Give her the paper.] I want you to have them so you will understand what I'm trying to do in my life. I love you."

This is a wonderful behavior to model. There are countless benefits to your teenager seeing you forgive yourself for mistakes, but here are five of my favorites.

1. She will think it appropriate for her to forgive herself for her mistakes.

2. She won't feel unforgivable if she makes mistakes.

3. She won't live her life under the cloak of guilt.

4. Her brain will produce happy chemicals, which will encourage her to drop other guilt issues, which in turn will become a healthy habit for her.

5. She will come to forgive you instead of blaming you for mistakes you may make. (Yes, Awesome Moms do make mistakes.)

Be patient with yourself, and become a student of the process so you can better teach it to your darling daughter. Believe me, she watches everything you do (it's those tiny mirror neurons you'll learn about in *Chapter 3: Science Class*).

Here's the irony of the situation. If all she experiences in life is success (which, of course, is all we really want for our adolescent angels), she won't be prepared to cope with problems as an adult. So, treat your failures as what they are: *Life Lessons* that afford you the opportunity to learn how to grow into the empowered adult we all want to be. Embrace blame-free transparency, and claim your Awesome Mom status.

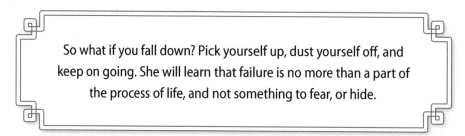

So what if you fall down? Pick yourself up, dust yourself off, and keep on going. She will learn that failure is no more than a part of the process of life, and not something to fear, or hide.

☑ Do This: Fully Claim Your Awesomeness

Right now, declare aloud: **"I'm an Awesome Mom!"** Now, stand up and declare, loud and proud: "I don't need to be perfect because I'm *Awesome*!" (How's that for a Conversation Starter?)

Did that make you uncomfortable? Or perhaps it doesn't feel like the truth?

Let me clear this up for you. You *are* an Awesome Mom.

How can I say that without knowing you? Because you are reading this book right now. That makes you the kind of mom who tries to find a better way for your beloved children. Regardless of how busy you are, or how overwhelming your life is, you are taking the time to seek solutions. That's Awesome! And, so are *You*. Now, go back and say it again, but be louder this time.

Post it on your refrigerator, and on your bathroom mirror. Read it loudly every time your see it. Welcome to the new world.

> You deserve a Guilt-Free existence, and your family deserves a Guilt-Free You.

Don't confuse being an Awesome Mom with being a Perfect Mom. First of all, Perfect Moms don't exist. Second of all, no one needs you to be perfect. Your family needs you to be Awesome and happy, to always pursue the best situation for them, to continually learn and grow.

Life Lesson #2: Debunking The Supermom Myth

While we're at it, let's trash a second widespread ridiculous belief. Our society conveys an inappropriate image of Mommy as Superwoman. You don't want to confuse being an Awesome Mom with being Supermom, either. According to the myth, Supermoms are supposed to single-handedly juggle jobs/careers, families, and spouses/significant others perfectly, while tending to our own self-development and growth.

In case you've been sucked into believing this fairy tale, let me get rid of that pressure for you right now. That's a big fat myth. Don't buy into it. Don't let the media seduce you into buying into it, and definitely don't let other people guilt you into believing it. It's a fallacy. Supermoms don't exist. Period.

I promise if you look closely at anyone who appears to be doing it all on her own, you'll find "Supermom" actually has help… a husband, daycare, housekeeper, older siblings helping younger siblings, relatives, a personal assistant, a staff at work, a nanny, a virtual assistant, public transportation, food delivery service, restaurants, babysitters, accountant, advisors, teachers, books, carpoolers… the list goes on and on. No one does it all by themselves, not without sacrificing something, like time with your family. Or sleep.

Everybody needs help to juggle the responsibilities of a family. There are only so many hours in a day, and some of them must be devoted to you. If not, bit by bit you will begin to lose yourself. If you allow yourself to be completely used up, you will no longer be any good to anybody, including your daughter.

Say This: Shout it out right now: **"Who needs Supermom? I'm *Awesome Mom*!"**

Did you shout? Try it again, this time throwing your shoulders back and planting your fists on your hips.

In my life, the woman who came closest to being Supermom was my mother-in-law. The woman gave birth to fifteen healthy children and raised them at their family-owned resort. She attended every sports event for each and every kid. There was dinner on the table every night, freshly laundered clothes, and conversation in the kitchen for anyone who cared to attend.

I, on the other hand, had one small baby, who didn't even cry that much, but I felt as overwhelmed as if she was quintuplets. I also had two sisters-in-law with new babies who seemed to be taking everything in stride. I just couldn't seem to get myself organized outside of my classroom. Why was it that everyone else was Supermom, while I couldn't decide on cloth or disposable diapers? And how in the world did my mother-in-law manage with more than one? Or, more than a dozen?

Because she didn't do it alone. That's what made her such an Awesome Mom. She recognized and tapped into the people who could relieve her load, including teaching the older siblings to help the younger ones. The girls cooked and cleaned, and the boys kept the grounds and the buildings. Her husband taught all of them business skills, and everyone helped with the resort events.

> I promise if you look closely at anyone who appears to be doing it all on her own, you'll find "Supermom" actually has help.

My awesome mother-in-law also included the community in her Support Team. She knew the teachers at the schools. She encouraged bible study sessions to be held at their place so her children could easily attend. Over the years, the children shadowed the various construction contractors and wedding planners who came in, studying how to handle the tricks and tools of their respective trades. She supervised everyone and kept her family running smoothly until the last one grew up and moved out. By that time, she had graduated to being an Awesome Grandmother.

> I had one small baby who didn't even cry much, but I felt as overwhelmed as if she was quintuplets.

Those Supermom paragons are illusions. In reality, they are Awesome Moms who have figured out how to maximize their Support Team. It's too bad I didn't understand back then that no one does it alone. Instead, I tried to hide how much I was struggling with the baby-husband-job juggle because I had completely bought into the *Supermom* Myth. I hid behind a cheery façade, secretly ashamed of my shortcomings. I wanted my family, especially my husband, to admire how effortlessly I was handling everything. If the truth be told, I wasn't even close.

Looking back, I see how ridiculous my belief in Supermom was. Of course I needed support! What new mom doesn't? I wish someone had told me how awesome it would be to take advantage of the Support Team that already existed. I could've been capitalizing on established resources instead of overwhelming and exhausting myself.

In case you, like me, convinced yourself that you aren't Awesome, let me repeat: **You are an Awesome Mom!** *No one does it alone*, especially if you have school-age kids.

☑ Do This: Generate Your Support Team

If you haven't done so already, look around and see how you can shift some of your responsibilities to your Support Team. Write your ideas here:

_____

_____

_____

_____

_____

_____

Life Lesson #3: Confronting The Plenty-of-Time Myth

The last of the big evil threesome is Plenty-of-Time (or the lack thereof). Both you and your daughter feel the pressure of Time. It starts in the morning, when you both have to get ready for the day, eat breakfast, collect your belongings, check schoolbags, and make sure you have everything you need, including lunches. She goes off to school, leaving you to spend about eight hours working at home, or working outside the home, or attending school, or recuperating; and then you both rendezvous at home for your evening obligations.

The problem with *The Plenty-Of-Time Myth* is that Plenty-Of-Time doesn't exist.

It all fits on that nifty calendar stuck to the fridge, or shrunken to cellphone size, but it doesn't necessarily translate so well to real life. What happens when something out of the ordinary comes along, like an invitation, or a new opportunity, or exams? Or, when something bad comes around, like an unconscious washing machine, or the flu? Do you shift things around so you can squeeze in the new time-suck, or do you drop one of the other time-draining activities to make room?

Most Supermom Wannabes believe in the *Plenty-of-Time Myth*, and try to squeeze it all in, adding all kinds of new pressures to their lives. You do it. I do it (when I'm not paying attention). We all do it.

The family adjusts to the overcrowded schedule. Before long, a new normal is reached, and we think, "See? I fit it all in. No problem!" The new pressures become part of the daily grind, and the increased pressure becomes routine… until the next golden opportunity or sick pet squeezes everything over to make more room.

The Plenty-of-Time Myth makes your daughter believe she can say *yes* to everything, too, which adds more bulk to her personal schedule. Believe me, I know. When I was a teen, at one point a teacher told my parents my grades were dropping in her class, a classic sign that I was having difficulty fitting it all in. Their solution? They told me I should drop the last thing I added to my plate, my adored dance class.

Of course that was the correct response, but I wasn't having it. I made a deal with them that included bringing my grades up while keeping everything else. After that, I continued to hide my struggle, dance class and all, behind better grades. The lesson I learned was as long as my grades were good, my folks couldn't tell I was having difficulty managing my life. Meanwhile, I was one stressed-out teenager!

It would benefit both you and your daughter to periodically discuss her time constraints before her attempts to juggle her schedule backfire. As a matter of fact, it would benefit you both to seasonally discuss your schedules. Compare them and find out where the "stressful" issues lie. You can then decide if adjustments need to be made. You may elect to let something go, or to postpone it to a later time.

If your angelic adolescent believes in *The Plenty-Of-Time Myth*, it's because *you* buy into it… or because your attempts to do it all make it *appear* like you believe it. The problem with **The Plenty-Of-Time Myth** is that Plenty-Of-Time doesn't exist. You only have 24 hours in a day. Roughly divided, that's 8 hours for sleep, 8 hours for school/work, and 8 hours for everything else.

Everything else? How minimalist does that sound?

Those everything-else eight hours are what you and your daughter have to tame. *Everything else* includes:

♦ 2 hours for sports

♦ 1 hour for dinner

♦ 2-3 hours of regular homework

… which leaves only 2 hours for *everything else*:

♦ school projects

♦ relationship interactions

♦ getting cleaned up for bed

♦ household chores

♦ hobbies

♦ TV and social media, etc.

When do you find time for yourself?

If you don't take time for yourself, or, if you do but it's not apparent to your daughter, it's vital you break the Plenty-of-Time cycle now. Communication is the key. Impress upon your daughter how important self-care and Me Time are, with words, and through actions by taking care of yourself. It would behoove you both to make sure she not only gets the point, but also buys into it with her choices. The last thing you want is for either of you to get so worn down, you get sick.

So, when is the best time to discuss how to balance school obligations and fun? I vote for during the summer, or on a holiday, when you both have a bit more time. If she is in high school, begin by revisiting the previous year's final exam session. *Don't discuss her grades*. Instead, ask her about the *process*. Dig out the nail polish and chat with her while you two do your toes.

Say This:

- "On a scale of 1 to 10, how stressed were you for the first exam? What about the last exam?"
- "In retrospect, did you give yourself enough time to study?"
- "What would you do differently if you could go back in time?"

From there, ask her to apply her answers to upcoming midyear exams in January, May's AP Exams, or June's final exams. Then, work your way backwards.

- "When should the studying begin?"
- "How many projects and tests did you have last December?"
- "How easily did (sports/concerts/recitals) fit into your schedule last year?"

———◆———

I strongly recommend having these conversations before the school year starts. It's much easier to have the chat when the outcome doesn't hang in the balance. Once school starts, the excitement of new extracurricular opportunities overwhelms her common sense.

The alternative is to realize midway that your daughter's schedule can't accommodate her being on the school Math Team, on an AAU (Amateur Athletic Union) sports team, on the Prom Committee, and president of the Library Club, while balancing three AP (Advanced Placement) courses. When her grades or health suffer, you may try to relieve some of the pressure by suggesting she drop something, but she will swear she can do it all. Then *Slam!* Suddenly she's fuming on one side of the door, and you're steaming on the other. Why? Because your daughter thinks you don't believe in her anymore, and now she doesn't know how to deal with the feeling of isolation being produced.

I can't even begin to tell you how planning ahead can reduce the pressures in your lives. Year after year I watched the same problem develop with my students. From Day 1, they juggled homework with as many other extracurricular activities as they could cram in. With every minute filled, there was no time for anything else… until the holiday season approached. Suddenly, there was Plenty-of-Time to squeeze in more obligations—concerts, playoffs, parties, last-minute tests and quizzes before the winter break, projects and presentations, shopping, decorating, performances, and visits with relatives.

That high-stress period concluded with the holiday break, followed by the eagerly anticipated return to school—and Mid-Year Exams—in January (okay, maybe *eagerly* is not the right word).

And you thought December sounded nerve-wracking.

☑ Do This: Un-Frazzle the Holidays

You know, just because it's classic for everyone to be frazzled over the holidays doesn't mean it's a requirement.

Solution:

1. About a month prior to major holidays, draft your daughter into helping you make a plan.

2. Make a commitment to each other to keep to specific limitations on your time obligations.

3. Pledge to not take on anything new unless you drop something current.

4. Treat your time like the sacred commodity it is, and you will reduce the pressure it exerts on your lives.

If you do this, you can calm down your household from November to February (Veterans Day, Report Cards, Thanksgiving, Hanukkah, Christmas, Kwanzaa, New Year's Eve, New Year's Day, Three Kings Day, Mid-Term Exams, Valentine's Day). Subsequently, you'll only have four more months of school left to depressurize before summertime arrives. Yay!

4 Unpopular (But Effective) Ways to Reduce the Pressures on Her

The difference between how you handle clutch situations, and how your daughter handles herself, is based on your respective brains. Your adult brain, with its fully developed functioning forebrain—the center for logic and reasoning—is capable of a good decision, despite the good-natured pressure from your friends.

Unfortunately for your daughter (and for you), her forebrain is the last part of her brain to fully develop. However, the risk-taking and immediate-gratification parts of the brain

> Unfortunately for your daughter (and for you), her forebrain is the last part of her brain to fully develop.

kick in at a very early age. When she compares the risk of getting in trouble for having a beer to the risk of trashing her popularity if she doesn't, that little bit of forebrain logic she has developed deserts her. (I'm saving the rest of this topic for your *Science Class*.)

The objective is to protect your challenging cherub by reducing the pressure on her during this confusing time. Here are four strategies that may not make you the most popular mom at the moment, but will up your awesome factor tenfold.

1. **Set rules and *enforce* them.**

    The quickest route to unpopularity in your home is to establish consequences for a rule you've set, and then to follow through if she breaks the rule. However, you must suck it up for the sake of your daughter. Kids who don't understand how to live within established limitations at home, also don't know how to do it in the real world. Figuring out how to navigate life without a clear understanding of abiding by the rules creates an enormous pressure. However, facing consequences teaches them cause-and-effect, and ultimately makes life easier to understand.

2. **Remove Party Pressure**

    The best way to reduce peer pressure in her life is to not let her be subjected to situations where she will be faced with expected risky behavior, i.e., teenage parties. If you never attended a teenage party yourself, you can watch any of the movie classics featuring a plethora of bad decisions being made in a short period of time by a multitude of pre-frontal brain teens. (May I suggest a John Hughes marathon?)

My advice? *Don't let her go to parties.* Most likely there will be alcohol and drugs, so why put her into a situation designed for her to fail? Here's some advice for when she angrily retires to her room the night of the party she's not attending:

Say This: "I'm sorry this is so difficult for you, but I love you too much to be pressured into letting you go. I'll come up to check on you later." That last bit should keep her from entertaining the idea of sneaking out.

----◆----

School dances may be a safer option because at least they are loosely chaperoned. If your daughter is mature enough to handle the situations that may arise there, prepare her with strategies to stay within the limits you set. As much as you would like her to be able to stand up for herself, and be strong enough to go against the tide, the advice you give her needs to align with her personal desire to fit in.

3. **Share Conversation Strategies**

Arm her with humor to help her deflect peer pressure graciously. The last thing your daughter wants is to say or do something that will make her feel more like an outsider. Putting her friends at ease with humor makes them feel accepted instead of opposed, and reduces the pressure being brought to bear.

For example, if alcohol is snuck into the dance, she can:

Say This:

- "I don't want to stunt my growth."
- "I hate the way beer tastes. Do you have anything hamburger flavored?"
- "No thanks. If I'm going to do something I shouldn't, it's going to be chocolate."
- "No way. The only way I got to come tonight is my mom's going to meet me at the door with a Breathalyzer."

----◆----

Can you see how planning strategies can help relieve the pressure on her? Don't be put off when she rolls her eyes about this one. She's listening.

4.   **Communication Is The Key.**

Communication will forever be the key to bridging the gap between you and your daughter. Your connection will help her manage the pressures in her life. You are still the adult in charge who makes the important life decisions, but conversations help minimize the disappointment when you have to tell her "No" for her own good.

Speaking of which, the discussion on attending parties, dances, and proms should come up *way before* they are even scheduled. Get her used to the parameters you set before they have to be enforced. Hearing the rules the week she hears about a party will make her feel ambushed, and she will lash out accordingly.

If your relationship is already strained, you may feel a bit wary broaching potentially touchy subjects with her, especially if there is a chance of being rebuffed.

Go for it anyway.

Say This: "Last year there was a Back-To-School Party that you weren't allowed to attend. We should talk about this before it comes up again. Is today or tomorrow better for you?"

Or, "You're going to be faced with different situations this year. I'd sure like to help keep some of the pressure off you. How is your BFF handling things like parties?"

Even if she rejects your attempt, it doesn't erase the fact that you tried… and she knows it. Sometimes it feels like a test to see if you'll give up. The only way around that one is to put yourself into the line of fire again.

And again.

And again.

You will find a variety of strategies throughout this book, but in general, keep your approach focused on the positive. Here are some real-life topics you can use to enhance your communications. Meanwhile, listen carefully and watch to make sure your teen isn't overloaded by life.

10 Conversation Boosters for Your Tumultuous Teen

1. Get a teen magazine and flip through it with her, sharing how different her world is from when you were a teen. Ask her about how today's ads impact her. Talk about the racial makeup of the models today and back then. Ask her who the people are in one of the photos to generate a discussion about how they are living their lives as compared to your realities. Ask her, if she could make her own magazine, what would she change? Ask whether her best friend agrees with her on these points.

2. Reach out. Encourage other adults (coaches, older sibling, relatives, etc.) to be active in your teen's life by setting up a cookout, a bonfire on the beach, or similar informal event. Invite her best friend and her parents so you can learn about their family dynamics. You need to know who and what your darling daughter is being exposed to.

3. By discussing the dynamics in her group projects, clubs, and teams, you can help her develop strategies for impasses. This indirectly teaches your teen to be an individual or a leader, and not a follower. It also teaches her how to work with others with a common goal.

Focus on the positive instead of criticizing. If you don't do it, she won't do it.

4. Focus on the positive instead of criticizing. If you don't do it, she won't do it. Praise her special talents to others, and then take the time to share their positive reactions with her. Nurture her interests by helping her connect with others of the same ilk. Remind yourself of what you admire in her. She'll sense it.

5. Unless they live under a rock, entertainment and advertising have a HUGE influence on teens when it comes to substance use, sexual behavior, body image, and gender roles… more than your daughter realizes. (Don't underestimate its influence on *you*.) Discuss how advertising affects you and your purchasing. Research how to deal with scammers, spammers, liars, and con artists. Share the info with her.

6. Talk to her about what you like and what frustrates you about Facebook, Twitter, and other social media. Ask her what she likes/dislikes about the social media she uses. Research together what would be a good amount of time to spend on social media, and how both of you can work on cultivating positive social friends and contacts.

7. Set and enforce limits on her media use and discuss your reasons. If she disagrees, invite her to research reputable sources that support her point of view for you to take into consideration. Research sources that support your view point and offer them for her consideration. Devise a compromise based on what the research shows you both.

> It's all about self-development as a Lifelong Learner, how to move yourself further along the continuum of life.

8. Focus on your daughter's health instead of her appearance. Share things you are doing to enhance your own health. This is not about fixing yourselves because nothing is broken. It's all about self-development as a Lifelong Learner, how to move yourselves further along the continuum of life. Invite her to be your Praise Pal on your health journey so she'll learn the importance of encouragement. Offer to do the same for her so she'll embrace her own self-development, just like her mom.

9. Encourage independence and integrity by discussing controversial decisions in the movies and books you both love. Use everyday opportunities, such as watching a program together, whether it's *The Gilmore Girls*, *Blackish*, or a reality TV show, to generate dialogues about crushes, friends, hurt feelings, partying, sex… you get the idea. Communicate your values and expectations, and talk about the risks. Use the plots to better connect and discuss the messages they send about body image and other expectations.

> Life has a way of muting new advancements unless you actively promote them.

10. Model and teach positive stress management and coping skills. (Whew! That's a big one!) Tell her what you are doing so she will notice. Encourage her to alert you about the positive changes she is making so you can be on the lookout for them. Cheer on her endeavors. Life has a way of muting new advancements unless you actively promote them.

You won't be able to implement all these ideas at once. Permanent change will be gradual, and new habits will have to be cultivated to replace the old. Until then, you will have to deal with the strain on your relationship, and the pressure that's been building because of it, but now you'll have a plan.

Your Own Mini-Pep Rally

Now that you can identify the pressures on you both, you are in a better position to understand your situation. It's time to attack some of these concerns. Dealing with the issues will be like opening the relief valve on a pressurized tank—a huge *whoosh*, followed by a gradual leveling out until everything feels normal. It's going to be awesome!

Stand up and roar:

Extra, extra!
Read all about it.
This Mom is Awesome.
There's no doubt about it!

How Did You Do?

To reflect how you feel about the outcome, put one of the following emojis next to each task you undertook.

Assigned Task	Results	Assigned Task	Results
Awesome Mom Pre-Assessment		Identifying Pressures and Symptoms	
Awesome Daughter Pre-Assessment		Share the Love	
Awesome Mom External Pressures		Kicking Guilt to the Curb	
Awesome Mom Internal Pressures		Kicking HER Guilt to the Curb	
Awesome Mom Symptoms		Asking For Forgiveness	
Awesome Daughter External Pressures		Backing Off Graciously	
Awesome Daughter Internal Pressures		Fully Claim Your Awesomeness	
Awesome Daughter Symptoms		Generate Your Support Team	
Unmasking Fast Food		Un-Frazzle the Holidays	
Quick Fixes		4 Unpopular (But Effective) Ways to Reduce the Pressures on Her	
Sharing Your Mission		10 Conversation Boosters With Your Tumultuous Teen	

Chapter 2

History Class: Why Are My Mother's Words Coming Out Of My Mouth?

The 3 Rs… Reminisce. Reevaluate. Refashion.

- ◆ Life With Mom Versus Life As Mom
- ◆ Life As *Pre*-Mom Versus Life As Mom
- ◆ Kick the Bad Habits and Change the Course of Your History
- ◆ Button Pushing: How Did I Get Here?
- ◆ Early Communication Is the Key
- ◆ When Envelope Stretching Sneaks Up On You
- ◆ Tips To Setting Consequences
- ◆ What To Change First
- ◆ Your Own Mini-Pep Rally
- ◆ How Did You Do?

The dictionary defines *history* as the whole series of past events connected with someone or something. That means your history is your story.

They say Einstein defined *insanity* as doing the same thing over and over again, but expecting a different outcome.

So, if history repeats itself, does that mean if your mother drove you crazy, then you are destined to drive your daughter crazy?

Hmmm…

Life With Mom Versus Life As Mom

If you have a daughter, you are probably sandwiched between two mother-daughter relationships, one with her, and one with your own mother. Of course, these relationships are two completely different entities, but, in case you are confused, don't expect your mother's treatment of your daughter to resemble the way she raised you. Your child's relationship with your mother will never be like your relationship with your mother.

The standard grandma is not responsible for her grandbaby. She is free to indulge and shower her grandchild with love and affection, free of discipline and consequences.

> I want to take my hat off to acknowledge the thousands of non-standard grandmothers who are going through it all again, this time raising their grandkids.
> You are doubly awesome.

Even in a perfect world, your mother could not have had that kind of relationship with you as her child. She was responsible for you, which meant combining love and affection with discipline and consequences.

You are the sum total of all your experiences, as is your mother, and as is your daughter. This includes the good and the bad decisions, the positive and negative events. The trick is to make your history work for you regardless. Everything can be a learning experience… if you decide to view it that way. We're going to look at your learning experiences, a.k.a., your history, as we take a stroll down Memory Lane.

Remember yourself at your daughter's age? Your brain was changing. Your body was changing. Your feelings were changing. Things you hadn't noticed before were suddenly vitally important. You were evolving to understand the difference between obediently following rules, and the ethics of rules. I'll bet you remember the first day your period made its unwelcomed debut. My poor daughter got her period, glasses, and braces one right after another.

Remember when clothes became more than just something to keep you from being naked in public? You were ready for it all (although your mother didn't necessarily agree): makeup, perfume, hairstyles… all of it. You knew how you were supposed to look because the magazines told you how you were supposed to look. Teen movies and boy bands backed them up, setting an imaginary standard you could not possibly achieve.

♦ Were you happy with your weight? Maybe, if it matched the swimsuit model on the cover of *Sports Illustrated*.

♦ Were you happy with your hair? Only if you could make it look like your favorite celebrity, or that pretty girl in your school.

♦ Were you happy with your complexion? Not if your body was trying to expel the chemical additives found in fast food and junk food. (How could candy be bad for you if it was being advertised on TV?) We call that acne.

♦ Were your feelings hurt easily? Did you wrestle with the concept of popularity? Had you experienced your first crush yet? Or mean girls?

If you were like me, nothing your mother said could dissuade you from defining the media hype as your measuring stick, a comparison that would always leave your awesome self feeling less than awesome.

When your mom tried to help you embrace what was uniquely you, it probably felt like she just didn't get it, which made you feel somewhat disconnected from her. On top of that, as you got older, it seemed like your mother was inexplicably changing. Suddenly, she didn't understand you anymore. She became annoying and unreasonable, even though every now and then she still exhibited flashes of brilliance that made you proud to call her Mom.

> Your typical teenage daughter is about as tuned-in to you as your typical teenage self was tuned-in to your mom.

Your typical teenage daughter is about as tuned-in to you as your typical teenage self was tuned-in to your mom. It was all about you back then; and today, in your daughter's world, it's all about her.

Yes, that's right. Your mother was going through back *then* what you are going through *now*. I think it's some kind of cosmic payback.

☑ **Do This:** Me and Mom
Write out the answers to these questions:

A. How much of your present-day situation with your daughter matches the one your mother had with you? Was your mom the one you went to for advice? Or, did you turn to other hormonal teenage girls to explain life to you? How well did your mother understand you when you were your daughter's age? Did you feel like your parents were accessible? What did they do to make you feel that way? Or, did you confide in your pet because pets don't judge?

B. What does your daughter do? Is the drama your daughter puts you through in any way similar to the episodes your mom had to deal with?

_____

_____

_____

_____

_____

_____

_____

_____

_____

_____

_____

_____

_____

_____

_____

_____

_____

_____

You may not have realized it, but back then you were standing with an army of insecure teenagers. To varying degrees, every single one of your peers was going through what you were going through, even those enviable kids who seemed to have it all together.

Meanwhile, as you were doing the teenager thing, your mother was trying to figure out how to parent a teenage girl. Just like your daughter watches and imitates you, so did you with your mother... as did your mother with her mother. You and your mom are both the product of the parenting you experienced.

Do you remember being angry with your mother when you were in high school, and saying, "I will never do *that* when I'm grown up!" or "I'll *never* treat my children like *that*"?

How's that working out for you? If you modeled your mother's behavior, is it so farfetched to think you might be modeling her parenting strategies, too? Could it be that maybe more than one of your current go-to parenting habits comes courtesy of your mom?

Perhaps history does repeat itself after all.

Have you started annoying or embarrassing your daughter the way your mother used to annoy and embarrass you? Are there other times when you spectacularly save the day... like your mother occasionally did? A lot of that can be traced back to your upbringing, and to your relationship with your mother, whether you want to emulate her... or be the complete and total opposite of her.

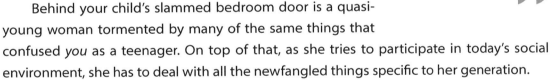

> You and your mom are both the product of the parenting you experienced.

Behind your child's slammed bedroom door is a quasi-young woman tormented by many of the same things that confused *you* as a teenager. On top of that, as she tries to participate in today's social environment, she has to deal with all the newfangled things specific to her generation.

You know what Mini-You is trying to do behind that wooden rectangle with the *Do Not Disturb* sign hanging from the doorknob, because you were there at some point during your teenage life. She's trying to regroup and recharge so she can venture forth again... right after she makes sure she hasn't ruined her connection to you with that last door slam.

Delving Deeper: Where She Stops and Where I Begin

Part 1: Take a moment to examine your relationship with your mother. What did you walk away with from your childhood?

  A. **Make a list** of the things she did that had a positive impact on you… her outstanding practices, her ideas and solutions, what she did to help create the Awesome Daughter you turned out to be:

_____

_____

_____

_____

_____

_____

_____

_____

_____

_____

_____

_____

_____

_____

  B. Go back through the list and **circle** the ones you have incorporated into your life.

Congratulations on mastering these formal and informal Life Lessons from your mom.

C. What about the items that are not circled? These great ideas may have gotten lost over the years. If they worked for your mom, perhaps they can work for you, too.

Why not start incorporating them into your current life? **Pick one** that you can start today, and write it here:

_____

_____

_____

_____

_____

_____

_____

_____

_____

Part 2: **Start a second list**, this time for the things your mother did/does that you don't approve of, or that had a negative impact on you:

_____

_____

_____

_____

_____

_____

_____

_____

_____

_____

A. This time, go back and **write** "I Don't" next to the habits you have managed to avoid in your life, and then circle them.

Congratulations for not letting history repeat itself.

B. Now **take a look** at the ones you did *not* circle. These are the less-than-stellar habits you've inadvertently inherited from your mother, the ones you don't really want. If you truly don't approve of them, now would be a good time to look at how you can eliminate them, and thereby change the negative impact they have on your relationship with your charming cherub.

C. **Choose *one*** habit to target for elimination. To make yourself accountable, tell your daughter and your family what you are attempting to do. Even if they are not able to actively support you, their awareness can keep them from accidently sabotaging you. Write it here:

_____

_____

_____

_____

_____

_____

_____

_____

_____

_____

_____

_____

_____

_____

☑ **Do This:** Enhance Your Awesome Foundation

Go back and look at the things you circled in both lists. This foundation of your Awesomeness is the product of your Mother/Daughter Relationship. Foundations are meant to be built upon, so, figure out which item in your list you would like to work on next during the upcoming week.

1. **Write it** into the space below.

2. Until it becomes a habit, enter a **daily reminder** in your calendar for the next month, and then a couple of weekly reminders after that.

3. **Post a sticky note reminder** on the refrigerator and on your bathroom mirror to help maintain your focus.

Good luck and have fun with it! You're Awesome!

_____

_____

_____

_____

_____

_____

_____

_____

_____

_____

_____

_____

_____

_____

_____

Life As *Pre*-Mom Versus Life As Mom

Sex. Now that I have your attention, having sex, whether planned or spontaneous, is the action of a female who may have to shove her current life into the background, and bring a child into the foreground. Conceiving a baby becomes a possibility, whether you intentionally accept that responsibility or not. It doesn't matter whether you use birth control or if you are trying to get pregnant. You are putting yourself into an emotional, psychological, and physical situation where that one in a million sperm can find that monthly egg… a scenario, which by default, includes making room for a baby in your life.

As adults, *we* understand that. Too bad the teenage brain can't pre-register the impact of their actions. Oh well. The brain of a teen is not biologically equipped to do that on its own. (More on that later.)

Your role as Mom began with that first missed period. (Cue the Awesome Mom music.) Once you realized you were with child, your Support Team expanded to include an OB-GYN, who helped you create the best possible environment for the baby you carried. Your OB-GYN told you what to do:

Take your vitamins.	**Nix the cigarettes.**
Stop the alcohol.	**Balance the nutrition.**
Get plenty of sleep.	**Get regular exercise.**
Eliminate the drugs.	**Watch your stress levels.**

Did you maintain those good habits after your daughter arrived, accompanied by her eighteen-year guarantee your life wasn't going to belong to just you anymore? Have you been setting a good example by walking the walk and talking the talk? Or have you been preaching "Do as I say, not as I do" for more than a decade?

Do you have any idea what your original OB-GYN would say if she saw you now? I do:

Take your vitamins.	**Nix the cigarettes.**
Stop the alcohol.	**Balance the nutrition.**
Get plenty of sleep.	**Get regular exercise.**
Eliminate the drugs.	**Watch your stress levels.**

Well? Are you?

Delving Deeper: Life As Mom

Compare your prenatal self-care to your current self-care. How are you doing? Write your updates in the space provided.

- **Are you still taking vitamins? _____ Which vitamins are you taking?**

_____

_____

_____

A recent Gallup Poll shows 54% of American women take vitamins but usually not until they are in their 50s.

- **How much alcohol do you drink weekly? _____ In which situations do you take a drink?**

_____

_____

_____

Did you know that women who consume eight or more drinks per week are defined as *excessive* drinkers?

- **Are you getting plenty of sleep? _____ How many hours of sleep do you get a week?**

_____

_____

_____

Sleep-deprived moms have extra risk of depression, heart disease, and blood clots that can lead to strokes, *and* they experience more hostility and anger.

♦ **Are your prescription drugs under control? _____ What are you taking, and when will you be done with it?**

_____

_____

_____

According to Parents.com, ten years ago more than 18 million women ages 26 and older reported abusing prescription medications (using Xanax, Ritalin, Vicodin, OxyContin for unintended uses). That number was up by almost a million addicts from the previous year, *which makes moms part of the most rapidly growing group of drug abusers in America.*

♦ **Are you *still* smoking cigarettes? _____ What are your views on your daughter smoking?**

_____

_____

_____

The overall mortality rate among female smokers in the United States is about three times higher than nonsmokers. Have you made a plan for who is going to take care of your daughter if you become a statistic? Or, are you going to eliminate your smoking habit once and for all?

♦ **How balanced is your nutrition? _____ What kind of eating patterns would you like your daughter to have?**

_____

_____

_____

The average American mother does not take in balanced nutrition. *CBS* reported about 57% of black women are obese, as are 47% of Hispanic women, 38% of Caucasian women, and 12% of Asian women. *Obesity maims and kills.* One of my relatives had to have her foot amputated a couple of years before she died of obesity-related causes. Obesity not only messes with energy levels and physical mobility, carrying extra pounds increases a woman's risk for diabetes, heart disease, stroke, and cancer.

> ◆ **Are you modeling how to live an active life by regularly incorporating movement into your day? _____ How does your daughter's activity level compare to your activity level when you were her age?**

_____

_____

If you value activity, so will your daughter. If you don't, no matter how active she is in her youth, she is destined to become a permanent couch fixture in the future, especially when her academic obligations increase.

Good to Know

Remember: In terms of upping your activity, the objective is not to get to the gym. The objective is to get out of the gym so you can go live life actively. The gym is a tool for getting stronger and increasing your coordination. The true objective is to go outside and play with your daughter—ping pong, badminton, tag, tennis, hiking, skating, rollerblading, dancing, etc. *Get going!*

Whether your daughter is yours biologically, or you welcomed her into your family from elsewhere, your job is to nurture and raise her, to help her reach all her potential and glory. She can't move forward without help. The question is, from where will that help come? From her teenage world? Or, are you ready to take your place as her guide and mentor?

If you've been living a healthy lifestyle, most likely your daughter

> If you want your daughter to live a strong, healthy life, then guess what? *You* have to live a strong and healthy life, too.

embraces a healthy lifestyle, too. If not, most likely you are part of the more than 70% of the American workforce that *USA Workplace Wellness Alliance* says are struggling with one *or more* chronic health conditions; **and your daughter is destined to become part of the more than 70% of school-age kids who will develop one *or more* chronic health conditions**.

Listen up, Mom. Your unborn baby girl depended on you to keep your body and mind healthy. Nothing has changed. You still need to keep yourself healthy for her, now that she's a teenager, unless of course, you're ready to relinquish your motherhood role to somebody else… like to the state, a guardian, foster care, or an orphanage.

Don't let that happen to you *or* your Awesome Daughter.

Sounds harsh? *Good.* I would not be serving you well if I didn't hold up a mirror to you. You are the one who decides if you like what you see. My mission is to help your relationship with your teenage daughter, not to help you preserve the status quo. Tough love goes both ways. If you want your daughter to live a strong, healthy life, then guess what? *You* have to live a strong and healthy life, too.

Your daughter needs you to *thrive*, not just survive. How else can she learn to thrive, and flourish, and grow, and bloom? Isn't that what you want for her? How can she do that if your life choices are ruining your health?

She needs you to be there to rescue her when her emotions back her into a corner. She needs you to show her the way back if she takes a wrong turn. She needs you to take the higher road when all reason abandons her. Only one of you gets to be a teenager at a time, and right now, it's *not* your turn.

> Only one of you gets to be a teenager at a time, and right now, it's *not* your turn.

But, it is your turn to be the wise, sage-like adult, even when you are standing on the other side of her slammed door, wondering why your own life is a moving target.

What do you do?

Take a deep breath. (Take three. They're free.) Accept your responsibility. It is what it is. No self-blame, just understanding. Stop succumbing to the anxiety caused by any inappropriate guilt.

The way I see it, you have two mindsets to choose from:

1. **Accept Responsibility**. This is what accepting responsibility looks like: "My action caused this reaction. I have the power to stop this from happening again by changing my action. I'm in charge of me."

Or,

2. **Accept Blame**. "My action caused this reaction. It's all my fault. I'm to blame. Bad me! I deserve to be a victim of guilt." (Note: This is *not* what accepting responsibility looks like.)

FYI, I vote for feeling empowered by #1. (Big surprise?)

Those apprehensive feelings from #2 are not concrete things. They are only symptoms generated by guilt and self-blame, mere fabrications of your emotions. They aren't true manifestations of your life. They aren't tangible things. So, cut yourself some slack.

There are two types of Awesome Moms:

1. Awesome Moms who have made mistakes.

2. Awesome Moms who have not made mistakes... yet.

Have you ever made a mistake? So, what! You made a mistake. Get over it.

Accept it... Fix it... Improve the situation... Ask forgiveness... Forgive yourself... And move on. That's all there is to it. Decide how you want to respond to situations, and respond that way. It's time to place your feet on a different emotional path and follow it.

> Make it an awesome ride, filled with love, mistakes and solutions.

And, by the way, if you look over your shoulder, you'll find your daughter right there with you, following the same path. Like it or not, you're bringing your darling girl along for the ride. The trick is to make it an awesome ride, filled with love, mistakes, and solutions.

☑ **Do This:** Take a Me-Moment

Right now, at this very moment, using your love to help focus and center yourself, take three slow deep breaths and get centered. No one will notice. (If you need a refresher course, review in *Chapter 1* about how to derail pressures that derail you.)

Use the *Mindful Breathing Quick Fix* all day long. Make it a habit throughout the day:

- ♦ When you wake up
- ♦ Before you fall asleep
- ♦ Exercising
- ♦ Driving
- ♦ Ironing

- ♦ Chopping veggies for that yummy stir-fry
- ♦ Playing on social media
- ♦ Zoning out on the couch
- ♦ Now

———◆———

Complete any of the previous exercises you may have skipped. Experiment using different strategies and conversations with your daughter. And, keep reading this book…

Kick the Bad Habits and Change the Course of Your History

Every Awesome Mom, including you, is the sum total of all her experiences, the good and the not so good. Your current habits, the beneficial habits and the not-so-wonderful habits, are so ingrained in your very existence, that you don't notice them (which, of course, is the basic definition of a habit). Over the years, you've made choices in response to the external pressures from peers, work, family, and the media. If, at this stage, there is an area of your life that needs a bit of sprucing up, or something you need to flat-out change, it will take considerable effort to alter the course of your history.

But the point is, **you absolutely *can* change it**. Your past does not define you. You define you.

Start with accepting responsibility for being where you are now. I'm talking about Guilt-Free, Blame-Free Responsibility, not that other weird kind that makes you feel badly, and then overwhelms your decision-making capability.

> ❝
> Your past does not define you. You define you.
> ❞

> Accepting responsibility puts you in a position of power

Accepting responsibility puts you in a position of power because **YOU** are the one deciding how you are going to view things. Historically, guilt and self-blame only served to make you a victim. Who needs that? Not you!

Accept responsibility if it was yours, **evaluate how you contributed** to the situation, and **see if there is a better solution**, but do this while **kicking any blame to the curb**. Learn from your previous decisions without getting negative toward yourself. If you could have done better at the time, you would have, so no need to harp on it. Move forward and leave it in the past. Use your new understanding to make the next decisions more advantageous.

Example: Once again, you don't have the time to cook, so you bundle everyone into the car and head to a fast-food joint. Everyone orders a fat cell's dream meal: burgers, fries, soda, and dessert. Later, on the way home, you feel badly about not making a traditional family dinner, for letting your fatigue overrule your better judgment, for not providing any veggies, and for allowing dessert and sodas.

Solution:

A. **Reject the guilt**: Kick that inappropriate guilt to the curb! This was your decision to make, and you made it. Based on the circumstances, you decided what to feed your family.

B. **Understand your contribution to the situation**: When you're tired and looking for a quick fix for dinner, your sweet tooth wields more power. Guilt creates a need to make up for not making dinner yourself, thus justifying the sweets.

C. **Find an alternative**: While you are recharging during supper, brainstorm with your family how to organize things so you can make dinner at home. For example, try taking the family out to a grocery store that has a salad bar. Let your daughter prepare her own salad. Pick up a precooked chicken and bring the feast back home to eat.

Easy, right? All you need to do is replace that inactive self-blame with positive self-action. The power is in your hands. With this better solution, you:

- substitute a fast-food dinner with salad and baked chicken

- replace a meal in the car with a dinner at home

- lower temptation by supplanting the overwhelmingly beautiful dessert ads at the fast-food joint with a view of the fresh produce section of the grocery store

- accommodate the exhaustion of a long day by not having to cook

- model the behavior you would like your daughter to embrace

- are guilt-free and blame-free and feeling empowered by your choices

Note: If you need a refresher course, review the section about purging useless guilt in *Chapter 1* so you can better derail the pressures that derail you.

> **Good to Know:**
> Here's a little secret. Every time you accept responsibility and reject the beguiling power of guilt and blame, you will feel a *zing* of empowerment course through you. Be on the lookout for it.

Crazy, isn't it? **With just your mind**, you can choose to be either a game-changer, or a bogged-down victim, purely by taking responsibility for your actions.

Welcome to your new world; your fresh, empowered world; the world where you recognize you're an Awesome Mom.

Boost your new direction by intentionally surrounding yourself with strong women who accept responsibility for their actions. Limit your time with people who try to assign blame or inflict guilt. You know the type—the neighbor who starts every conversation by complaining about her kids; the sibling who turns one-upmanship into a hobby; the friend who gossips about mutual friends.

These people are toxic, and their presence in your life needs to be limited or eliminated altogether. Even if you aren't the focus of their stories, after a while, repeated exposure to guilt-producing stories makes judgmental behavior sound normal, and therefore harder to differentiate in your own life. When guilt seems appropriate, people both accept guilt and cast guilt all too readily. They become victims, and they create victims. That's not what healthy relationships are supposed to be about.

Until you reclaim your power by eliminating your own worthless guilt and pointless self-blame stemming from your undesirable habits, your beloved daughter may also be heaving blame and guilt in your direction. Amidst the stomping around your home, the sigh heaving, and the door slamming, you may hear these classics:

♦ "You're ruining my life!"

♦ "You can't understand what I'm going through!"

♦ "You don't care!"

♦ "You never listen to what I say!"

♦ _____ (fill-in-the-blank)

My advice is to just hang in there. As you learn and grow, so will she. Teach her about the steps you are following to purge inappropriate guilt. Verbally take her through the four stages each time a situation arises. This modeling will stay with her, and without being told, she will understand you are reclaiming your power.

As an added bonus, your determined example will empower her to shed her own victim status. She will learn to release her own little torments, the things that she doesn't tell you about, but which plague her with guilt and blame. **As your darling girl eliminates her victim standing, she will become less vulnerable to peer suggestions**.

That's HUGE.

Like any good habit, getting to the point where you *automatically* accept responsibility (but not the blame or guilt) will be a true game-changer. Altering your lifestyle will take time, but all your existing habits, even the mundane ones, were all acquired the same way: through repetition. Do you have to post reminders so you will remember to fix your hair? No. And, why not? Because it's automatic, a.k.a., it's a habit.

But here's the kicker: if you are dissatisfied with a current habit—let's call it XYZ— it's not enough to be motivated to change it. Nope. You have to *replace* it with something else. Concentrating on *Not Doing XYZ* becomes the same thing as *Focusing On XYZ*. That's obsessing. You'll never get out from under XYZ that way.

But, if you *replace* XYZ with something else, your focus will be on accomplishing your new task. It also provides a more positive bent than denying yourself your old habit.

☑ **Do This:** New For You

Pick a habit you want to change. Write it here:

_____

_____

After you read *Everything Old Is New Again*, the box on substituting a strategy specific for creating a new habit, come back and write the new habit you are going to substitute below, along with the first strategy you are going to use:

_____

_____

———◆———

Good to Know: *Everything Old Is New Again*

Here is an example of substituting an old habit for a new one: When smokers try to quit smoking, they are challenged by both the grip of the nicotine addiction *and* their physical habit of reaching for a cigarette. The nicotine can actually leave your blood in about three days, although for some it can take up to two weeks for the withdrawal symptoms to subside. Meanwhile, you have to break the physical habit *while* your brain chemistry returns to normal.

Smoking is a habit that involves using your hands, so replace it with another habit that also uses your hands. Wear several bangles on the wrist of the hand opposite your "smoking" hand. Every time you feel like reaching for a smoke, move one of the bracelets from one wrist to the other. When the first arm is bare, you treat yourself to a monetary deposit in your piggy bank (the change in your pocket, a dollar, a five-dollar bill, etc.), a reward for resisting the old habit. Keep shifting the trinkets back and forth when necessary.

When you make it through the first day without a cigarette, you owe yourself another bracelet. At the end of two months, when you no longer reach for the cigarette out of habit, and your brain chemistry is close to being free of the nicotine, break out the piggy bank and treat yourself to a manicure (the kind that comes with a massage).

To give your new habit a fighting chance of succeeding, make yourself accountable. Tell someone what you are trying to do, and ask her to be your Accountability Partner. Check back with her periodically (Daily? Weekly? At the end of one month? At two months?) to show how you're doing. Be transparent. Knowing you're accountable keeps you motivated when your intention sags.

If your new habit will positively impact your health, *tell your daughter about your intention*. Whether she has faith in your ability to change or not, she will internalize your efforts in a positive way and she may even join in herself.

To be clear, an Accountability Partner is not responsible for what you do, your success, or your motivation. That's all on you. An Accountability Partner serves as that mirror we hold up to view ourselves, and to keep us honest. Your Accountability Partner wants renewed resolve, not excuses, should your efforts sag.

> **Good to Know:**
> Although your daughter could support the efforts of your Accountability Partner, she should not be the one who holds you accountable. As your child, that puts undue stress on her. If you don't think your daughter's concerns about you contribute strain to your relationship, you are sadly mistaken. Our children assess our situations through adolescent eyes, and they come up with adolescent conclusions, many of which you are not privy to. We can anticipate a few, but some are completely unexpected.
>
> Don't be surprised if her concern and anxieties about you influence your daughter's progress at school, or her flare-ups at home. Worry can easily be translated into exasperation and a waspish attitude. She may know how to push your buttons, but you inadvertently push hers, and contribute to her volatility, when she frets about you.
>
> Do share your journey with her, but don't ask her to keep you accountable.

Button Pushing: How Did I Get Here?

The first time you bribed your toddler with sweets to head off a tantrum, you handed her a little of your power. She probably didn't understand that she had control over you. At that age, she understood screaming and thrashing produced a treat. It might have seemed like a lot of effort on her part, but, hey… it worked. Your beautiful baby had discovered your first button.

And how to push it.

Of course, for you, by the time you were going on your third year of sleep-interrupted, household-juggling, baby-bag-carrying Mommydom, that innocent sweet/bribe only represented a brief moment of blessed relief. You had quieted down your tearful toddler successfully and controlled the situation.

Or, had you?

Although this strategy may prevent a meltdown every time, the child never learns how to handle the word, "No." Eventually, the lack of that one vital coping skill produces all those tween-age emotion-laden battles about homework, skirt length, curfews, necklines, junk food, appropriate movies/books, etc. Hearing a "No" is confusing and upsetting to her when you've trained her to expect "Mom will say *Yes*."

That reminds me of a story …

I remember when my cherished cherub threw her first public tantrum. We were at Sears, and I had promised her we would stop at the toy section before we left. Unfortunately, we ran out of time. I tried to explain the situation to her, but her almost-three-year-old self was not having it.

Right before we reached the store exit, she flung herself backwards into a circular clothing rack, screaming and kicking her feet. The women's clothing display completely hid her body. All you could see were her little legs thrashing in the aisle, and the swaying of the size ten dresses hanging on the rack.

While she carried on, a steady stream of witnesses to my parenting skills (or lack thereof) passed in and out the doors, but there was nothing I could do. There was no way to retrieve her without getting kicked in the face.

I stood there, horrified and embarrassed, wringing my hands, wondering what to do, heart thumping with a rivulet of cold sweat trickling down my sides.

An elderly woman patted me on the shoulder. "Don't you give in, dearie. You're doing the right thing. She'll tire herself out." She winked as she walked by. "And you'll thank your lucky stars later."

"Th—thank you," I called after her, grateful for her kindness.

Although I still couldn't see the small wailing face, to my immense relief, my churlish cherub seemed to be pausing for a breath. "Are you done?" I asked.

"NO!" Her shriek rattled my teeth as she launched into Round Two.

Oh no. I should have grabbed her while she was catching her breath. Now, it was too late. The only part of her I could reach was those flailing legs.

She paused again.

I could hear her panting somewhere in the midst of the women's dresses. "Are you done yet?"

"No!" More kicking. More screaming. More people staring. But strangely, I was feeling calmer. I knew how this was going to play out. My baby girl had a lot of energy, but even *she* was going to wear down eventually. I was getting used to feeling embarrassed, so I hung in there, and outwaited her. I was the one in control.

She paused to catch her breath again.

"Are you done yet?" Now, I was grinning and rolling my eyes at the passersby, who responded with expressions of sympathy.

"No." This response sounded more like a grunt. She launched into a less enthusiastic Round 4, which ended after a few moments.

"Are you done yet?"

Pant. Pant. "Yes."

"Okay. Let's go home." I helped her out of the clothes rack, took her hand, and triumphantly sailed out of the store.

Based on what I had observed of other moms with their bellowing broods in the grocery store aisles, I expected a repeat performance from my precious progeny, but now I was ready for it. However, she never tried it again. I guess it wasn't worth the effort.

So it turned out that my darling daughter's only public tantrum provided an important Life Lesson for both of us. To this day, I do thank my lucky stars that I wasn't able to pluck her out of that clothes rack before she stopped screaming. If I had been able to reach her, I would have tried to quiet her to prevent my own embarrassment, and I never would've learned that timeless lesson—**Don't Give In To Tantrums**! My public humiliation was a trade-off for me learning the value of saying "no" and the importance of standing my ground.

Don't Give In To Tantrums!

My glorious girl also learned a couple of valuable lesson that day:

♦   A tantrum doesn't produce diddlysquat.

♦   No matter how interesting they look when other kids do them, tantrums are exhausting!

Everybody wins!

Even if you were not fortunate enough to have the help of a circular clothing rack during your charming cherub's first public meltdown, I have two important points for you to remember now that she's a tumultuous teen.

♦   Every decision we make models a behavior. If you manage to hold out for 45 minutes while your teen/tween is blowing up, but then give way at Minute #46, you teach her that tantrums need to last 46 minutes. If she carries on like a banshee for 90 minutes, but gets no results, she will give up, or try a different (quieter) tactic. It's not worth the energy to her. After all, she could've been spending that 90 minutes figuring out a different strategy.

♦   It is so worth it to hold the line with your turbulent teenager. If you can be courageous and withstand the brunt of her adolescent anger, the light at the end of the tunnel is magnificent. Instead of becoming a battle, your disagreements will become conversations.

You can pave the way to a relationship based on mutual respect and love, one where she trusts her expectations of you, and you understand her better. She will feel closer to you and confide in you. The big bonus is that she'll enter the next stage of her life with a poise and self-possession that will serve her well going forward.

"But my daughter isn't a toddler. Is it too late? What can I do now?" If that's you speaking, there is no *easy way* to undo years of bad habits. However, there is a *simple way*.

☑ Do This: Surviving the Teen Tantrum

It may be twelve years late, but let her throw her tantrum, and don't give in. It will be loud and painful, but holding the line will be effective. She'll learn a new tactic if you are consistent.

This is not an instruction for you to sit there and take it. Protect yourself from her angry energy.

- Do *The Zip Up* to shield yourself energetically.

- Do your deep *Mindful Breathing*.

- Listen to your heartbeat. Center yourself on you.

- Picture your energy force field deflecting her words, allowing you to remain calm.

Be strong. Don't cave in to stop the tantrum, no matter what she says, or how sorry you feel for her.

Say This: If she demands that you engage with her, tell her you can't concentrate on her words while she is so upset, and it would be a waste of both your time... but you love her, and will be happy to discuss it later when she feels better.

> Remember, her opinions are her opinions, not yours, and she is entitled to them.

If her frustration has escalated to her throwing objects, remove yourself from the room. Make sure she can't hurt anyone else, and wait for her to calm down. Calm yourself down, and take that time to decide what would be an appropriate consequence. Come from a place of love, not a place of anger. Your darling diva is in pain and needs you to rescue her. If you don't feel equipped to help her, find someone from your Support Team who can assist you.

As with any explosion, that initial energetic burst is not sustainable. *Once she calms down*, inform her that any violent act leads to an automatic loss of privileges. Ask her what she thinks is an appropriate consequence. It will clue you in to how she perceives the magnitude of her actions. Remember, her opinions are her opinions, not yours, and she is entitled to them. Having said that, you are only soliciting her opinion to gather intel. Just because you asked for it doesn't mean you're going to follow it.

Once she calms down, it's time to have a discussion.

Say This: "Let's figure out a better way for you to handle your anger when you feel like you are not being heard. Would you like to talk now, or after supper?"

♦ If she chooses now, begin the conversation with, "I love you, no matter what." Tell her what the consequences of her actions are (her punishment), and then remind her again that you love her, no matter what. Then, begin your discussion.

♦ If she chooses later, schedule a time to talk. Tell her you love her, and then tell her what the consequences of her actions are. Repeat that you love her, excuse yourself, and leave the room. When you have the discussion later, begin by saying, "I love you, no matter what."

———◆◆◆———

Once your protocols are established, let the games begin!

Sometimes the adolescent brain short circuits, causing your loving daughter to blurt out nonsensical statements. Even though they are the products of frustration, they still can hurt if you aren't prepared to take them in stride. Here are a few strategies for common buttons she might push.

Button Pusher #1: *"You're ruining my life!"* Translation: "I can't figure out how to change your mind." You aren't really going to ruin her life unless you present a weak front. That will create a mean girl, who will turn into a mean adult. Now *that* will ruin her life.

Button Pusher #2: *"I hate you!"* That's code for "I'm at the end of my rope and don't know what else to do." It means she feels betrayed by your sudden philosophic flip-flop and hates how unsure she is of her position.

Button Pusher #3: *"You would if you loved me!"* Clarification: "I'm resorting to emotional blackmail to get you to do what I want." Even if you were fooled by this one when you were a teen, you don't have to get duped by it now. Since when does someone else get to define when and how you love? You know you love her, no matter how your decisions may appear to her... and she knows it, too. That's why she can risk having a meltdown. She knows you'll still be there when the dust settles.

Early Communication Is the Key

Do Not Spring This, Or Any Other New Change On Her! If historically you've been giving in to placate her temper, her teenage brain won't understand your sudden decision to hold the line. She may feel like something has gone horribly wrong with your relationship. She may even wonder if something is wrong with you. Since she hasn't developed coping tools, her behavior will reflect her desperation and fear.

Solution: Have the conversation early.

Choose a calm, unrelated moment, and explain to her what the new rules are going to be. Let her know what the new consequences are. (Make sure you pick consequences you can live with, i.e., don't take away the car if you will need her to drive to the grocery store.)

 Say This: "Now that you are more mature, we're going to approach our discussions on a more grown level because you can handle them now. I would like to explain the changes to you. Do you have some time today to talk, or would you rather talk tomorrow night?"

If she gives you negative attitude, tell her, "Look, I love you, and I know what's best for you. But, I see how upset you are over a request to talk. Maybe you're not ready for this discussion yet. Why don't we continue this tomorrow night? I love you." Then go into another room.

This process will subtly model that you are not going to accept her outbursts and negative attitudes. It also removes you from her verbal line of fire.

> Choose a calm, unrelated moment, and explain to her what the new rules are going to be.

When you bring it up again, emphasize two things:

- ◆ You love her, no matter what.

- ◆ She is old enough to learn to cope with not getting her own way.

What if your attempt at early communication in a neutral setting backfires, and she gets upset? How do you cope when she directs her angst toward you?

We all know when a first grader cries, "I hate you!" it's easier to not take it personally because it's obviously her frustration. But from a middle schooler, it can hurt more. Over the years, we lose sight of our objectivity, and her angry statements become very personal. If your daughter resorts to mean and spiteful verbalization to vent her frustration, **Leave The Room**. You don't deserve to be on the receiving end of her rant, and it will eventually wear you down. Plus, all that negative energy affects your mind and body, and you need to nip it in the bud.

Say This: "I love you. I do not treat you with such meanness and disrespect (Or, "I've decided I am no longer going to dump my frustration on you"), and you are no longer allowed to treat me with meanness and disrespect. We can talk when you calm down. I love you." Then, walk into another room.

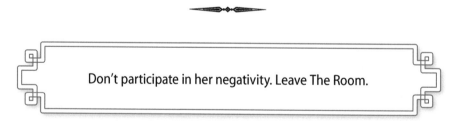

Don't participate in her negativity. Leave The Room.

If she follows you, still going at it, stop, and turn around. Calmly repeat what you said. Then keep walking. You can go into another room, or step outside, but do not let her keep at you.

If she doesn't stop, say, "Look, yelling at me is not going to make me change my mind. Get used to it. I love you, but we are not discussing this until you calm down. I'm closing this door right now, but feel free to come back when you want to talk *with* me, not yell *at* me. I love you, no matter what."

GENTLY close the door. It will interrupt the flow of words and emotions.

Be ready to fling it open again when she controls her voice. Hug her, and say, "I knew you could do it. What do you want me to hear? I can understand you so much better without the yelling."

Just keep holding firm with your daughter. Consistency will lead to the relationship every Awesome Mom wants, filled with trust, camaraderie, and communication.

Good to Know

When my daughter was growing up, I always reminded her of something that every parent needs to say to their kids: "Sometimes you get your way, and sometimes you don't. This is one of the times where you *don't* get your way. However, you will get your way on another day. It doesn't mean I love you any less."

To drive the point home, when one of those other occasions occurred, my goal was to notice it and say, "This is one of those times you get your way." It's important that you help her notice both.

When Envelope Stretching Sneaks Up On You

Do you remember trying to see how far you could bend your parents' rules when you were a kid? Aren't you glad your progeny doesn't try to stretch the envelope?

I'm just kidding. Of course they do.

Don't take it personally, and don't be surprised. It's what they are supposed to do on their journey to master their world. They've been exploring their environment and trying new things since they figured out how to suck on their toes. Part of that is the identification of their limits, which they constantly have to test because they, as people, are changing relative to those limits. The other part is the curiosity and excitement generated by anything new.

There's an old parable told by one of my science professors about changing the temperature around a frog. If you put a frog into hot water, the sudden change in temperature will make it jump right out. However, if you put a frog in cold water, and slowly heat it, the frog will perish without ever trying to escape.

Why? The big temperature difference is impactful enough to make the frog change its environment, but tiny incremental changes lull the frog into a feeling of security.

Actually, this is a tale about you and the limits you set for your daughter. You are the frog, and your daughter's envelope pushing is the rising level of heat. Small incremental changes lull you into a false security that you are maintaining control, until one day you realize how hot it's gotten.

But, you're not a frog. You're an Awesome Mom. Once you are aware, you *can* change your environment.

You are now aware.

That reminds me of a story…

My friend Marlene set a new curfew of 10:00 p.m. for her daughter, Jussandra. One night her daughter arrived home by 10:05 p.m. Marlene did not reset the curfew back to 9:30 p.m., the consequence she had originally established for being late, but instead let the teenager off with a warning. After all, her daughter was a good girl, and five minutes was not that big of a deal.

What message do you think Jussandra received from her mom's response? Getting home *close* to ten o'clock was acceptable, and being five minutes late was reasonable. Over the next few months, Jussandra began pushing the curfew envelope a few minutes more and a few minutes more, without any consequences. 10:05 p.m. turned into 10:10 p.m., and 10:10 turned into 10:15, etc.

Until one night, Jussandra walked in at 10:53 p.m. Marlene had been fuming for 49 minutes. Her anger was fueled by her recognition of the impotency of her rule enforcement, and the realization that little by little she had somehow relinquished her power.

When she angrily confronted her daughter, Jussandra was shocked and confused, so she reacted with an emotional explosion. From her point of view, she had been respecting the boundaries close enough as she understood them. After all, she and her friend had really needed to finish their school project for tomorrow. Besides, she was only five minutes later than she had come in the previous weekend. Her mother's behavior felt unpredictable and blown way out of proportion for a five-minute difference.

Good communication could have prevented this entire scenario. Jussandra could have called her mother and requested permission to stay out later for her project. Or, Marlene could have reminded her daughter about her curfew before she left for the evening. She also could have called her daughter twenty minutes before she was due to come home to remind her it was time to finish up.

Instead, they both remained in their own little "She Knows What I Mean" bubbles, and as a result, an unnecessary strain on their relationship developed. Combine that with a good student's stress of whether her project was ready to turn in, and you can guess what followed... tears, yelling, accusations, stomping, and slamming.

Jussandra felt blindsided and wrongly accused.

Marlene felt ineffectual, frustrated, and ultimately guilt-ridden for upsetting her daughter who was already under enough pressure.

Both felt disrespected and betrayed by this person who was supposed to love her and have her back.

Picture what this night could have looked like if only a little conversation had been applied the first time Jussandra was late, when that envelop was first stretched? Most likely the teenager would have understood the importance of maintaining her curfew as her mother saw it. When faced with her project's deadline, she would have known to call her mother to get permission to stay later. Mom's expectations of her would have been crystal clear, and Jussandra would have been able to trust her expectations of her mother's reactions. Marlene would have felt relieved and still empowered because her daughter would have understood what was allowed and was following the rules.

Sometimes your daughter's envelope pushing feels like eternal discontent, and naturally that wears on you emotionally. The second she detects a crack in your veneer, she views it as her adjusted limit.

This is not some evil plot being hatched by your daughter. This is your child trying to make sense of her constantly changing self within her constantly changing domain. Your unceasing vigilance is required as a parent, and it *is* exhausting, especially if you are going it alone.

But, it's necessary. She's not ready to do it on her own.

Discuss the rules and curfew for the new school year during the summer (when the pressure isn't as intense.) Talk about where and when she can go with her friends, but do it while on a family vacation away from them. Every year starting in fifth grade, casually chat about dating and crushes. The rules will change each year as she gets older, so be

Good to Know

You can prepare for *The Inevitables*, those unavoidable, looming envelopes just begging to be stretched:

- ♦ Dating
- ♦ Extending curfew
- ♦ Parties
- ♦ Going out with friends

The Inevitables, are coming, make no mistake about it. It's just a matter of time. How do you prep for them?

Early communication, Awesome Mom. Early communication.

forthcoming with your expectations.

Should an incident arise, she'll be prepared for the consequences because she will know the drill.

Say This: "When we discussed the household rules, we talked about what would happen in this situation. Do you remember what I told you, or would you prefer I remind you?"

That reminds me of a story…

Several times a year, I orchestrated heart-to-heart chats with my daughter about dating. I purposefully chose a relaxed setting where I "casually" brought it up. Since there was nothing hanging in the balance, she was always open to the conversation. I also planted seeds for the future. Toward the end of our talk, I'd sigh and say with a smile, "I hope you get out of high school a virgin."

My little tween would grin back and reply, "Oh, don't worry, Mom. I will!"

Until her freshman year.

A popular senior was getting pretty friendly, so our talk lasted longer than in past years. "I hope you graduate a virgin," I eventually said.

She sighed and slumped in her chair. "Oh, so do I, Mom. So do I."

Obviously, my growing girl's world was changing, so I made our discussions more frequent. Early communication made it easier to have our dialogues.

Was it always smooth sailing?

Nope.

Sometimes she was denied getting her way, and of course she'd get upset. Sometimes my casual approach felt invasive, causing her to snarl a bit. And, even though on those rare occasions when she accused me of ruining her life,

♦ in hindsight, I didn't actually ruin her life, although sometimes I worried that I might.

♦ today, she doesn't even remember thinking that.

So, what do you do when your growling gal sets her heart on going to a party in the next town, which, to her, appears to fall within your guidelines? Because she has created a scenario in her mind where it makes sense, your "No" is confusing to her and feels arbitrary. She can't form a clear picture of what to truly expect, which whittles away at her trust in you, and therefore in your relationship.

The Result: If you've been consistently communicating, expect a boiling teapot. If you haven't, you'll get to witness your own personal Pompeii-sized eruption.

When moms establish rules, and then bend them to avoid conflict, they teach their children to initiate conflict in order to get their way. If the limits you set fly out the window when you try to keep peace in the house, you're training your daughter to keep pushing the envelope until she finds your *true* boundaries—not the ones you state and she pretends to honor. Why does she do that? Because she needs to understand where the edges are so she doesn't fall off.

> When moms establish rules, and then bend them to avoid conflict, they teach their children to initiate conflict in order to get their way.

In the beginning, those volatile reactions to previously unenforced limits are not because the walking volcano doesn't agree with your rules, or because the rules are inconvenient. Each time you change your mind, your ambiguity baffles and unbalances her. (Will you say *yes* this time? Why not, if you said *yes* the last time?).

However, as time goes by, her outbursts are no longer due to confusion and shock over the rules. Your daughter simply doesn't agree with your policies, or the rules are inconvenient for her plans. She blows up at you because she knows eventually she *will* get her way. Her outbursts have morphed into a controlling behavior, which quite frankly, is akin to bullying you.

Warning: When her emotional explosion influences the limits you set by making you change your mind, the lesson you teach her is:

Loud + Aggressive = Getting Your Own Way

Look past your own discomfort to the bigger picture—the one where she interacts with people outside your home. If she uses this type of bullying behavior with you because it's all she knows, she will use it with other relationships. When she cannot cope with being told "No" by other kids, she will throw tantrums and bully them until she gets her way. She will not cooperate with her teachers. And, she will continue to embarrass you in public.

For your daughter's sake, and for the sake of your relationship, stick to your guns! You set those limits for a reason, and her manipulation doesn't alter that reason. The key to effective limits is to hold to them until *you* intellectually—not emotionally—decide to set different limits. At that point, you…

 Say This: "You seem ready to handle a few changes. Is now a good time to talk, or would you rather wait until your homework is done?"

Tell her how it is going to be. She can contribute to the conversation, but remind her at the outset that as the ranking adult in the room, the decision is yours, and yours alone. Clearly describe the parameters for her expected behavior, and be equally as clear about the consequences for crossing the line.

> She can contribute to the conversation, but remind her at the outset that as the ranking adult in the room, the decision is yours.

And then *you hold to those limits.* She may not like the new rules, but as long as *you* abide by them, you won't baffle her since she will know what to expect.

Tips To Setting Consequences

The trick to enforcing the limits you set is to pick a consequence that:

♦ is determined ahead of time

♦ fits the crime

♦ you are willing to enforce

♦ is not decided in anger

If you impulsively dole out punishment when you are angry, you may accidently lay down a penalty that messes with *your* day. I know parents who decreed they were taking away their kids' cell phones for a week, and then had to reverse their declaration after one day. Why? Because they still needed to be able to stay in contact with their kids.

Yes, that punishment was as ineffectual as it sounds.

Alternatives anyone?

♦ Get a prepaid phone for your kids to carry. After school the kids return the phone and the parents can check usage.

♦ Allow phone use outside of the home only (school, library, school-related activities like band practice or sports) but as soon as the kids get home, they have to turn in their phones.

Voila! Consequences for kids without inconveniencing the parents.

Other parents take away the car, but in doing so, remove the offspring's ability to get to practice, work, etc. The parents end up thinking they have to adjust their schedules to get their kids to where they're supposed to be.

Exactly who is being punished here? The minor inconvenience for the child is actually a royal pain in the butt for the parents.

The alternative?

♦ Take away the driving privilege, and do *not* substitute your services. Part of the consequence has to be for *her* to figure out how to get where she's going, not *you*, **via a mom-approved method**. If the consequences of her actions mean she misses her obligations, she will feel the impact of her decision even more keenly. Bonus: If she understands this ahead of time, it will deter her from pushing the envelope too far.

♦ Take away the driving privilege, but not the driving obligations. Driving chores that aid you (i.e., trips to the dry cleaners or grocery store) are allowed at your request, but nothing else.

The point here is that if you establish the limits ahead of time, and decide on consequences best suited to you, you can plan ahead so your life is less disrupted.

Delving Deeper: Define Your Limits

Think back to a clash between you and your daughter over something she wanted to do that you did not deem appropriate. Or, if you two haven't been down that path yet, pick one of *The Inevitables*, mentioned earlier in this chapter. One of them is bound to be a potential sore subject. Describe it here:

_____

_____

_____

_____

_____

_____

_____

_____

_____

_____

_____

_____

_____

_____

_____

_____

_____

_____

What's the rule/limit at the center of the conflict?

_____

_____

_____

_____

_____

_____

_____

_____

_____

_____

_____

_____

_____

_____

_____

Fill out the chart below, and be absurdly clear on how you define that rule. Then, create 2 or 3 appropriate consequences if this rule is not observed. Take into consideration how her punishment will affect your life and schedule.

Rule:	
Consequence:	Impact on my life
Consequence:	Impact on my life

Let's say she pulls some shenanigans tonight before you have time to clarify things. While it's impossible for me to know the specifics of your situation, I'm going to make the assumption that you're going to feel upset. So, do the obvious:

When you are upset, **tell her you are upset**.

Tell her that due to your emotional state, you are going to take the night to decide how you are going to handle her punishment.

💬 **Say This:** "I love you too much to do this out of anger."

—◆—

When you are alone, first calm yourself down with (*Mindful Breathing* and *The Heart-Brain Connection* (see Chapter 1), and then figure out how to provide effective consequences that won't interrupt your flow. Reach out to your Support Team to brainstorm suggestions, but don't get sucked in to commiserating. If their teens are "worse" than yours, the feeling of relief may dilute your intention to reinforce your limits, and thereby mess with your consistency.

> "
> I love you too much to do this out of anger.
> "

On the other hand, stories about their perfect parenting can make you self-doubt, especially when you're already stressed.

Once you figure out a punishment to fit the crime, write it down on a piece of paper. You will need it for the upcoming technique when you and she have your discussion.

Remember, even though you have significant influence on your teenager's decisions, so does her undeveloped brain, *and* the undeveloped brains of her friends. Plus, you understand about making mistakes because you used to be a teenager. Tomorrow,

💬 **Say This:** "I love you so much and I'm so pleased with how far you've come. However, you have done something inappropriate, so of course there are consequences to your actions, right? But, that does not change my love for you, or how proud I am of you.

"Before I tell you your punishment, are you capable of telling me why you did what you did? I promise to listen quietly until you are done."

—◆—

Guess what you do next?

That's right! You listen quietly until she is done. Then,

Say This: "If you could go back in time to before [the incident], what would you do differently?"

———◆———

Listen quietly until she is done. Then,

Say This: "I'm glad this incident has clarified some things for you. I'm curious… What do you think your punishment should be? Before you tell me, you should know that what you say won't affect my decision. Like I said, I'm just wondering."

———◆———

Listen quietly until she is done. She is telling you how she views the magnitude of what she did through her adolescent eyes. Then,

Say This: "That's interesting. Well, here's what I decided." Pull out your paper and read off of it so she can confirm your decision was made earlier. Otherwise, she'll suspect you are making it up now, and won't have faith in the process.

———◆———

After giving her a chance to share her input, she is less likely to rail against her punishment. If you give off calm vibrations, she, too, will be calmer.

Nevertheless, be prepared for the possibility of her blowing up. If you know it's coming, meet her emotions with love and respect, but stand your ground.

Say This: "I love you, and I want to give you a chance to tell me what you think, but I really can't focus on your words when you are so emotional. Why don't we talk later?" Then, follow up.

———◆———

If you enforce the limits consistently, she won't put so much energy in stretching the envelope. When she knows what to expect, she will understand when she gets her own way, and when she doesn't.

The little darling may try to negotiate the rules, which is an appropriate (and much calmer) approach. Maintain your constancy by telling her she is welcome to offer alternatives through a discussion, but be firm about the fact she does not contribute to the decision-making. You, as the adult, make the decisions. Then, stick to your guns until you have substantial evidence that she can handle a change in the rules.

> Only one of you gets to act like a teenager at a time, and right now, it's her turn.

Otherwise, her snarky reactions to your inconsistent discipline will push your buttons and bring out the worst in you. Irritation compounded by guilt can propel you into your own mini-volcanic eruption.

But before *you* slam that door, let me remind you that only one of you gets to act like a teenager at a time, and right now, it's her turn. Remember, *you* are the Awesome Mom.

What To Change First

Your history does not have to be your future.

If you have an explosive temper yourself, or if you indulge in or abuse drugs (prescription or otherwise), or overindulge in alcohol, your daughter never knows who to expect when you are together… the Normal You, or the Distorted You. That's scary for a child. She won't be able to confide in either version of you. The Normal You might not be there in an hour, so unburdening her teen torment won't produce any positive results. The Distorted You is completely unreliable and leaves her to assume the role of protecting herself in your home.

Unless, of course, she has decided that if your habits are good enough for you, then they are good enough for her, and she uses alcohol/drugs or smokes as well. Either way, the situation will create trust issues that will haunt her into her adult relationships.

☑ **Do This:** Rescue Your Family

Do: Find a professional who will help you deal with addiction and/or anger. You don't have to go it alone! There is nothing wrong with seeking help from a professional who can teach you better ways to cope. Make them part of your Support Team.

Don't: "Do As I Say, Not As I Do" is not an effective strategy for communicating with your daughter. As the person who mirrors everything you do, don't be surprised if your daughter does as you do, not as you say.

Besides, she knows if it's bad for her, it must be bad for you, too.

If you try to tell her otherwise, she won't believe you. In what way can you justify continuing something detrimental to someone who depends on you? Instead, she will see you valuing a bad habit too much to stop, even though you claim she's the most important thing to you.

Please don't hear this as judgmental. It's just the way it is. Your continuation of a bad habit diminishes her worth. Otherwise, wouldn't you be doing what's right for her sake? So, of course, that messes with her self-concept.

Do: Discuss your substance use with her and tell her you are seeking help. A teenager can't rely on an adult who struggles with self-control, but she can learn to trust a mother who is turning her life around. She takes her cues from you, and, to paraphrase Ben Franklin, she needs you to be healthy, happy, and wise.

Do: Find a counselor for her to help your child deal with what's going on with you. There is a very good chance she feels some burden of guilt for your situation. Why? Because, that's what our children do. (*Mama wouldn't get high if I wasn't stressing her out. Daddy wouldn't have left if I had been quieter. They wouldn't have divorced if I had helped keep the peace.* (That last one was my childhood guilt.)

If you have an addiction issue, come clean with your daughter, so she knows that:

- You have a problem that is not her fault.

- You are getting help so your lives will be better.

- You are learning how to best battle your addiction.

- She needs to talk to a counselor who is trained to help her cope with having an addicted parent.

The best way to deal with your daughter is through open and honest healthy communication. When kids get only half of the story via their own observations, they make up the other half on their own.

That reminds me of a story...

I had a student who I'll call Sandra. She was an A-/B+ student whose grades suddenly plummeted. A meeting was called between Sandra, her parents, and her teachers. She sat there with her hands tightly clasped, eyes downcast in front of the assembled adults. After each teacher shared which assignments were missing, and how she could get caught up, the unanswered question remained. *Why?*

Her math teacher pointed out that the young lady sometimes giggled in the back of the room with her girlfriend, who also happened to have low grades. "Is that why you aren't doing your homework, Sandra? Because she's distracting you?"

The student's eyes widened and she nodded rigorously.

Assuming they had identified the problem, the adults launched into a series of strategies to remedy the situation. "Separate the girls." "Move her seat to the front of the room." Etc.

At first, like the others, I was pleased we had found the cause, but something just didn't feel right to me. Maybe it was the relieved look on her face, or how eagerly she agreed to everything the adults were saying. I had to ask. "Sandra, do you live near that girl? Is she distracting you at home?"

She froze, shot a sidelong look at her father, and slowly shook her head.

He responded with a quizzical expression then sat up straight, clutching his hat. He looked at his wife, whose eyes widened. "Oh, my dear. You know?"

Sandra burst into tears. Her parents leaped to their feet and gathered her into their arms while we teachers looked on, dumbfounded.

It turned out that Sandra's father was seriously ill and usually spent his afternoons resting until her mother came home from work. They had not shared the extent of his illness with Sandra, but she had overheard him tell her mother he hoped he would pass peacefully in his sleep. Unbeknownst to them, Sandra was now holding vigil by his bedside every afternoon, watching him breathe until her mother got home. Then she would slip into her own room. She no longer took care of her own obligations because she wanted to be there to wake him in case he stopped breathing.

Our meeting occurred because the teachers and parents were part of the same Support Team, although, in our eagerness to be of service, we almost missed the truth of the situation. As it was, Sandra was able to receive the counseling she needed and got her grades back on track.

If you want your child to know what's going on instead of her drawing her own conclusions, talk to her. Consistent communication and accepting responsibility for your actions will have a huge positive impact on both of you. You will replace your victim status with an empowered one. In the process, you will model empowering behavior for your daughter, not victimized behavior, or out-of-control behavior.

Let go of that self-blame, and instead, embrace self-responsibility. **Kick that guilt to the curb**.

♦ Make sure there is nothing going on that will make the situation worse. Get help before *you* get worse.

♦ Figure out a way to improve the situation. Tell your daughter what you are doing, and your plan to change things.

♦ Ask your daughter for her forgiveness. She may not be ready to give it yet (and that's okay), but your attempt will register somewhere in the deep recesses of her brain.

♦ Finally, and I've said this before, the hardest part to kicking guilt to the curb is forgiving yourself. But, you have to do it. No one asks for addiction, whether it stems from youthful decisions or the doctor's prescription pad. If you could go back in time and make a different decision, you would. Since you can't, recognize the mistake now, and **forgive yourself!**

☑ **Do This:** Forgiving Yourself

Try to imagine your best friend caught up in a similar type of situation, and it was negatively impacting her. If she asked you for your forgiveness because her problem interfered with your relationship, would you forgive her? You would if you had history together and valued your friendship.

You need to be able to value yourself the way you value your best friend. *Correction*: You need to be able to value yourself *more* than how you value your best friend. If you would want to help her, you should want to help yourself. If you can forgive her, you can forgive yourself. You have to matter *more* to yourself than any best friend because your life matters, and your daughter is depending on you to recognize your value.

Right now, forgive yourself for your mistakes. Yes, do it now.

$$\Longrightarrow\!\!\blacklozenge\!\!\Longleftarrow$$

Say This: "I forgive myself for making that choice. If I could have done better, I would have." Gently pat your chest while you repeat that aloud five times.

$$\Longrightarrow\!\!\blacklozenge\!\!\Longleftarrow$$

You were doing the best you could with what you had at the time. In hindsight, might you have made a different choice? Maybe, but as my Grammy used to say, "That and a couple of dollars will buy you a cup of coffee." (Actually, she used to say, "That and twenty-five cents will buy you a cup of coffee.") You can't worry about the past, but you can make sure you don't repeat your mistakes.

So, stop believing you should have been perfect, and forgive yourself for your human mistakes. It's time to look forward and embrace a happier you, free of that absurd and inappropriate guilt.

Good to Know

How about some stats regarding teen smoking? A study done by Mark Connor, of the School of Psychology at the University of Leeds funded by England's Economic and Social Research Council, found that girls in the 13-14 age group were twice as likely to be smokers as boys. A daughter is more likely to smoke if the people she lives with are smokers (her role models), if she has friends who smoke, or if she's around people who approve of smoking. And, it's not just cigarettes, pipes, cigars, and snuff anymore. Now there are all kinds of alternatives that suck in new users.

♦ Take E-cigarettes and vaping, for example. They're *flavored* for marketing to kids, but they also have nicotine, and therefore can lead to addiction, lung destruction and death.

♦ The CDC's Morbidity and Mortality Weekly Report states that unless there is a sharp drop in youth smoking rates, **5.6 million youngsters currently aged 17 and younger will die** early from smoking-related diseases.

♦ **The Good News:** If you smoke, quitting before the age of 40 reduces the risk of dying from smoking-related disease by about **90%**. So, before Mini-You offers you a cigarette from her pack, find out how to quit. Share your commitment with her. And, then follow through. If she has become a smoker, quit together. You'll be saving your daughter's life… and extending yours.

♦ You don't have to do it alone. Check *Answers at the Back of the Book* for resources to help you.

Your Own Mini-Pep Rally

We all have history. You are the product of that history, the sum total of all the events in your life, some good, and some not so good. These facts will be the same ten years from now, when your daughter is old enough to be out on her own. She will be the sum total of all her experiences, a year from now, or a decade from now. How will her history look to her?

Your history does not define you. It's only what happened to you, but *You* define you. It's time to get about the business of adjusting your life for the better. It's not too late to help yourself, and, as a result, regain your daughter's respect... and restore your own. You are in a position to create the history your daughter needs. All together now...

> *Moms are great.*
> *There's no debate.*
> *We love our daughters*
> *Even when they're late.*

Oh, the power! It's scary—but awesome—at the same time.

How Did You Do?

To reflect how you feel about the outcome, put one of the following emojis next to each task you undertook.

Assigned Task	Results	Assigned Task	Results
Mom and Me		New For You	
Where She Stops and Where I Begin		Surviving the Teen Tantrum	
Enhance Your Awesome Foundation		Define Your Limits	
Life As Mom		Rescue Your Family	
Take a Me-Moment		Forgiving Yourself	

Chapter 3

Science Class: The Teenage Brain, and What To Do With It

The 3 Rs… Reveal. Replace. Resolve.

- **The Curse of The Teenage Brain**
  - Pop Quiz: What Does Your Face Say?
  - Homework: What Do Their Faces Say?
- **When the Teenage Brain Short-Circuits**
  - Homework: The Happy Hormones Experiment
- **Why She Can't Think She's In Charge**
- **The Brain Without Sleep**
  - Homework: Step Back and Come Back Intervention
  - Homework: Cause and Effect
- **Caffeine, The Creepy Addiction**
- **That's Habit Forming**
- **Why New Year's Resolutions Fail**
- **Living Your Life S.M.A.R.T.**
  - Pop Quiz! Setting a Good Example
- **Good Intentions = Life Without Goals**
  - Pop Quiz! Goal or Intention?
- **Maintaining Your Resolve**
- **Your Own Mini-Pep Rally**
- **How Did You Do?**

When it comes to school, Science isn't exactly on everyone's Favorites List, and it certainly was not on mine. Personally, I didn't become a fan until my sophomore year in college. The first day of second semester, my University of Massachusetts physics teacher, Professor Brehm, permanently blinded me with the wonders and magic of science when he walked to the front of the room, and laid down on a bed of nails to teach the first class of Physics 101. I was an instant fan, a bona fide Science Geek from that day forward, before the term was even invented. I channeled my awe of science into my teaching career where I focused on Environmental Science.

The most important thing I learned over thirty years of teaching science is this: Applying Knowledge Is Power. They say write what you know, so I've applied my science knowledge to this book. Science can explain why your daughter does what she does, and why you do what you do. What makes science knowledge so cool is it's the great equalizer. You can't just slide by in science, so you have to use your brain.

> **Applying knowledge is power.**

Speaking of brains, let's talk about yours and hers. Recognizing the differences between an adult brain and a teenage brain will help both of you understand why she acts like a teenager, and why you react to it like a mom. Combine that understanding with improved communication, and stand back as the awesome power of your mother-daughter relationship is unleashed!

Besides, if two heads are better than one, so are two brains.

The Curse of The Teenage Brain

Let's start with that wonderful place where your dazzling daughter creates her own little world… her brain. She is not interested in becoming the teenager you were, even though her brain has the same messy stuff bouncing around inside as yours did. What she wants is to figure out how to be the teenage version of The Awesome Mom you are today, to grow and explore her world as an adult… at least, as how her teenage brain interprets adulthood.

Unfortunately, she keeps coming up against your desire to protect and shelter her, which is born from fear. (*"What if I give her enough latitude to hurt herself?" "What if I'm being overly strict?"*) After all, she does suffer from the same malady you had all those years ago… *The Curse of The Teenage Brain* (cue ominous music).

> "All mothers and daughters want the same things: love, understanding, respect. And, they want them from each other. Mom wants love, respect, and understanding from the child she brought into the world. And, daughter wants the same from the woman who gave her life."
>
> Dr. Charles Sophy

The brain you have now is not the brain you had when you were a teenager, and that teenage brain was not the same as the one you were born with. Science now understands the brain continues to develop and grow until most of us reach about twenty-six years old, give or take a few years. After that, we continue to learn, with all the parts now developed.

Your daughter's brain is growing and evolving like crazy (unless she is doing drugs/alcohol, smoking, or eating a lot of chemical food additives), but unfortunately this maturation is not evenly disbursed over the entire organ. The brain tends to develop from the back of the head toward the forehead. As she progresses from her tween years to her twenties, some areas of the brain (fear, instant gratification) develop much earlier than others (logic, reasoning).

> Some areas of the brain (fear, instant gratification) develop much earlier than others (logic, reasoning).

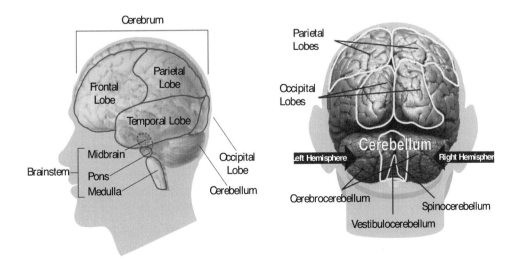

Yes, this is the basis for the characteristic risky behavior exhibited by teens. When she ponders, "Should I or shouldn't I?" the higher risk levels appear more reasonable because her forebrain isn't quite ready to help her out with logic. That's where you, the Awesome Mom comes in, with your fully mature brain.

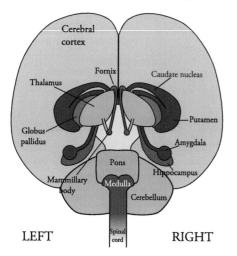

LEFT   RIGHT

The developed adult brain uses the frontal cortex (behind your forehead) for reasoning, logic, planning, and detecting subtlety... all the characteristics you wish your fledgling had. In contrast, teens have already developed their amygdala (lower interior section of the brain), the part of the brain reserved for:

♦ gut reactions
♦ triggering fear
♦ defensive behavior
♦ and, of course, instant gratification.

Sound like anyone you know?

The logic and reasoning thing may not fully ramp up until their mid to late twenties, but those excitement and anxiety triggers are alive and kicking right now.

Ahhhh, now you see why they do what they do (and why you did what you did).

Have you ever noticed how the child actors on the Disney Channel put in such an exaggerated performance? It's all part of the show's intention to be more appealing to kids. Those exaggerated facial expressions make it easier for a younger audience to interpret what the character is feeling. That's the way their limited young brains interpret the emotions being portrayed. Unfortunately, it drives the developed adult brain crazy because all we see is the exaggeration.

Teens do not correctly interpret facial expressions.

One really cool study, done by Ekman and Friesen in 1976, used an MRI on "normal" teenage brains (I mean, seriously, what is normal in teenagers?) and on fully mature adult brains. When shown photos of an adult facial expression, grownups correctly interpreted it as "fear," but teenagers saw "shocked, surprised, angry." *Teens do not correctly interpret facial expressions.*

Suppose your daughter watches your face while you're talking and misconstrues your expression. This could explain why she sometimes inexplicably blows up in the middle of an innocent conversation. She's reading you wrong and is reacting to what she thinks she sees. Meanwhile, you're standing there with your mouth hanging open, saying, "Huh?"

Now imagine your daughter's inability to interpret facial expressions in a classroom with twenty other people with the same inability to interpret facial expressions…. Yes, the perfect kindling to inflame high school drama.

On top of that, teens misinterpret facial expressions 50% of the time! These results mean the middle school, high school and college years are filled with adolescents unintentionally creating drama out of nothing because they misinterpret a look on someone's face.

Pop Quiz: What Does Your Face Say?

Here are some of the photos used in the Ekman and Friesen test. Take the test yourself, and then see how well your daughter recognizes expressions. Share this with her, and then check out the *Answers at the Back of the Book*.

DIRECTIONS: Name the emotion each adult is displaying.

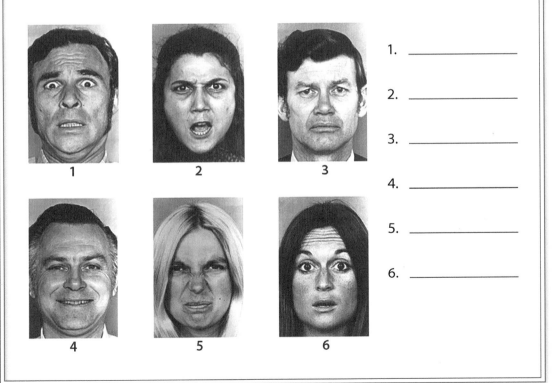

1. _____

2. _____

3. _____

4. _____

5. _____

6. _____

Homework: What Do Their Faces Say?

Without sharing the theory behind it, have your daughter take the same quiz. Knowing the point of the quiz may color her responses. Hey, if any of her friends are around, have them take it, too.

It's especially confusing for your daughter to interpret your expression when you are trying to control your anger and present a calm front. How can you communicate well if your daughter isn't going to get the nuances of your expression? Therefore, you need to make your words very clear by providing extra clues.

- "That makes me angry. We'll discuss this when I calm down."

- "I worry about you. Let's talk so you can explain things to me."

- "I'm concerned about your safety. Let's talk about this in more detail."

If your daughter is experiencing behavioral problems, one of the related issues may be that she misinterprets facial cues from her teachers. I just informed you that your child doesn't recognize expressions well, but her teachers may still need to be reminded of that.

Solution: Share the results of your experiment with your daughter's teachers to raise their awareness and encourage them to provide additional verbal clues. Every good teacher wants your daughter to succeed, and the more information they have, the better equipped they will be to address her circumstances.

> **Good to Know**
>
> In a separate study published in *The American Journal Of Psychiatry*, researchers found kids with bipolar disorder made the same amount of errors interpreting adult expressions as the non-bipolar subjects did. However, they made even more errors interpreting the expressions on kids' faces. Unfortunately, they commonly mistook many youthful expressions for anger. Imagine how confusing school is for these children.

When the Teenage Brain Short-Circuits

When I was in college, I took an animal behavior course. There, I learned about the lowly moth at the bottom of the food chain. The moth has enough brainpower to steer its course, but when being pursued, all bets are off.

A rush of air from an approaching predator triggers teeny hairs on the moth's little backside. As a result, his teeny little brain "short-circuits". The moth completely loses control and its brain causes it to fly erratically, making it nearly impossible for the predator to catch it. That unpredictable behavior created by its brain saves its life.

"Why the heck are you telling me this, Deborah?"

Glad you asked! As you know, the adolescent brain works differently than an adult brain. I believe under certain circumstances, the teen brain short-circuits under pressure, just like the moth brain. This short-circuiting produces random, erratic behavior in both teens and moths. What else would explain the following situation between some of my relatives?

That reminds me of a story…

Taylor was so excited to have her learner's permit for her driver's license. Finally, she would be able to show her parents how responsible she could be. With her mother in the passenger seat, she carefully checked her mirrors as she buckled her seat belt, mentally reciting everything she should do before pulling out of the driveway. As she backed out, her mom's, "Good job" warmed her soul.

Carefully, she maneuvered the vehicle towards the grocery store in town, one hundred percent of her concentration devoted to her task…

I wonder if anyone is noticing me. I must look so mature, she thought to herself as she drove along.

She didn't realize her attention was drifting until an approaching vehicle refocused her. Heart thumping, she tightened her grip on the steering wheel. A sidelong glance at her mother confirmed her little lapse in attention hadn't been noticed. She squared her shoulders. *That's the last time that's going to happen. I'm a young adult, fully capable of driving a car. I got this. Check the mirrors. Hands correctly positioned on the wheel.*

Whoa! That light is turning yellow! Hastily, she applied the brakes, jerking them both forward. Another glance at her mother.

"You're doing fine." Her mom patted her knee. "You might want to think about slowing down before you reach a light in case it changes."

Taylor nodded rigorously and muttered, "Right. Right." *Pay attention, you idiot. If you don't do a good job, she's not going to let you drive by yourself.*

Taylor looked down the road to anticipate the oncoming traffic, determined to put in a perfect performance behind the wheel. *Wait. Where am I? Is that Harry's Hot Dog Stand?*

The sight of young people milling around tables with ice cream and drinks in their hands caused a tsunami of excitement to erupt in Taylor, one that she could barely contain. The instant the light turned green she stomped on the accelerator. The sound of her squealing tires ramped up the thrill of watching heads whip around as she peeled by. This is what life was about, being wild and impetuous, the power of a vehicle at your command—

"TAYLOR!"

Her mother's shriek startled her back to reality. As she stomped on the brake, she noticed her mother's steadying hand on the steering wheel.

> "Pull over," her mom managed through gritted teeth.
>
> The tires crunched in the gravel as the car rolled to a stop. Taylor released the steering wheel as if it was burning her hands, and panted.
>
> "What were you thinking?" cried her mother.
>
> "I… I… I don't know…"

I'm sure Taylor had no idea what she had been thinking while her brain was short-circuiting, especially when confronted with reality crashing in on her fantasy, and the horror of her actions riveting her attention.

Besides, what kind of sane answer could she come up with that would fix the situation? "I was so excited about people watching me drive I forgot you were in the car"?

Nope. I don't think so.

Here are 10 other realistic responses to the query, "What were you thinking?" that you will never hear her say. Why? Because it's too embarrassing to admit to herself, let alone admit to you:

1. How cool will I be if I try that?
2. Is that cute boy (popular crowd, mean girl) watching?
3. This looks good on that popular girl in school, so it will make me more popular if I wear it, too.
4. I don't think I can do the assignment, so I'm not going to try it.
5. *This* will make him notice me.
6. I'm completely lost.
7. It seemed like a good idea at the time.
8. I saw someone do it on YouTube.
9. Being popular is more important than making sense.
10. I don't think I was thinking. My emotions just took over.

Good to Know

All high-school-age drivers are inexperienced behind the wheel. This lack of experience can result in difficulty making the best decision in a split-second crisis. Take the young drivers where my daughter graduated from high school in Connecticut, a rural town with a huge high school of about 2000 students, sporting about five hundred kids per grade. That means in any given year, there are about five hundred juniors getting their brand-new license, plus *another* five hundred seniors who've been driving for almost a whole year. That's approximately *one thousand* inexperienced drivers in one country town. How scary is that? Yeah, there're a lot of fender benders, especially near the school.

☑ Do This: Brain Talk

Talk to her about her brain as if she can handle it. She will feel respected by you, which will increase your trust status in her eyes. Be straight and direct, communicating that you have her back, the way a best friend would talk to her.

> This is about *being like* a BFF, *not being* the BFF. This is *not* a suggestion to try to act hip or cool with her. This is about being close enough to her to make her want to turn to you when she has a problem. If she trusts you, she will share with you, the way she would with her best friend.

But if you don't trust her enough to have a grown conversation, she will feel like you don't get her. If she believes you don't understand who she is, she won't depend on you to have her back when you talk. If that's your situation, you probably get a lot of this type of conversation:

Awesome Mom: You look a little low. How are things going?
Awesome Daughter: Fine.
Awesome Mom: C'mon, you can open up to me. How are things *really* going?
Awesome Daughter (frowning): *Really* fine.

Why should she reveal anything to you if you won't understand? It's not worth her time or energy, and sharing her distress with someone who doesn't get it will just make her feel even more isolated than before… which ups her angst.

Good to Know

In the example, why is the Mom conversing with her Daughter awesome, even though her approach is ineffectual? Because she is reaching out to her daughter and trying to make things work. Awesome Moms never stop trying. They pick up books like this when they want a new strategy.

All daughters are awesome, especially yours. On a planet filled with billions of people, there is no one else in the entire world like her, not even a twin. She is the miracle you've been nurturing for years, the product of your grand experiment in parenting. She is remarkable.

If you want her to trust you with her inner turmoil, you have to find a different approach.

According to Loretta Garziano Breuning, author of **Meet Your Happy Chemicals**, all humans have *mirror neurons*. Think about watching a movie. You feel triumphant when the heroine does, and you cry when she is devastated, just as if you were experiencing it yourself. Yup, that's your mirror neurons at the helm.

Repetition builds our neural pathways, so without effort or intent, you can reinforce pathways that bring you sorrow in the guise of entertainment. In other words, you can train your brain to be unhappy by watching sad movies and listening to sad songs.

These mirror nerve cells are especially powerful in our young because that's the way they learn how to conduct themselves. If your cheery cherub watches a lot of movies about desperately unhappy teens, her rapidly developing brain reinforces pathways of discontent, but way faster than they would develop in an adult because she is physically growing.

> You can train your brain to be unhappy by watching sad movies and listening to sad songs.

I never got into reading the newspaper (except for the comics) despite adult peer pressure telling me I was missing out if I didn't. ("But, you're a *teacher*! How can you be in the classroom without knowing what's going on?") However, back in the '80s, my quirk was validated at a Hartford teacher workshop on *Humor In Education*.

Good to Know

The Bad News: Your daughter's brain won't be done developing until she is past college age.

The Good News: Even though her common sense is not fully baked, it turns out if she knows this, she will make better decisions for herself regardless. Studies show that even though their brains are geared toward immediate satisfaction and risk-taking, a discussion of what their brain does to them can lay the groundwork for good decision-making.

The presenter stated that although he hadn't picked up a newspaper in twenty years, he could guarantee that somewhere in the world:

- there was war starting, ending, or escalating
- some politician had perpetrated a crime
- an atrocity had been committed
- the paparazzi had caught some celebrity being outrageous

None of those things made a difference in his day-to-day existence, and he did not miss the disquiet it lent his life. He chose, instead, to fill his life with positive input and humor.

That suited me just fine.

I'm not suggesting the anxiety generated by one single news broadcast matters. I'm saying if you have the news on all day, those constant alarm reactions are biologically reinforced in your brain, *and in the brains of your kids*. When I was a kid, the news came on at 6:00 p.m. for one hour only. Today's adolescents live in homes where the news is on all day in multiple rooms. They hear the gloom and doom (even if you don't notice them paying attention), they discuss it with their friends, and it contributes to their overall anxiety. They might not be paying attention to the announcer's words, but you better believe they notice your negative reactions to bad news.

Personally, I watch and read content that contains a lot of humor, or about surmounting insurmountable odds, and only media with happy endings. That's what I want my brain to be good at. Plus, I really enjoy boosting my happy brain chemicals.

Pay attention to the shows you and your daughter watch and the music you listen to. Invite her to participate in an experiment where you watch only feel-good movies and listen to only feel-good music (in her genre, of course) and see how you both react at the end of the week.

Homework: The Happy Hormones Experiment

Of course, I've managed to slip an experiment in here for you to try. Every good science experiment needs to have a way to measure its results, so, I made an awesome data chart just for you.

The Happy Hormones Experiment Prep

Preparation: This is going to take some planning because your habit is to choose the same kind of movies and music you've always chosen. Make your selections ahead of time and have them ready to go.

When comparing your mood to the day before, use an Up-Arrow (↑) to indicate it's better, a Down-Arrow (↓) if it's not as positive, and an Equals Sign (=) to show it's the same. If you accidently fall back into your old habits, that's okay. Just start the 14-day experiment period over. Print out two new charts, and resume.

Delving Deeper

Week 1: What's Normal? Record what is typical for the two of you in *The Happy Hormones Experiment Chart*. This baseline data will be used to identify changes at the end of the experiment.

Make two copies of this chart. Give one to your daughter, and keep the other on your nightstand with a pen. On the back, keep a list of TV shows/movies you normally watch, and the songs you usually listen to.

Fill out this chart first thing in the morning before you get up, and again as the last thing before bed. Use Emojis for the comparison columns.

Part 1: The BEFORE Part of the Before & After

Week 1 Date:	Morning Mood When You Wake	Compare Mood to Yesterday	Evening Mood Before Bed	Compare Mood to Yesterday
Monday				
Tuesday				
Wednesday				
Thursday				
Friday				
Saturday				
Sunday				

Week 2: The Positive Effect. Print out two copies of this chart. Give one to your daughter, and keep the other on your nightstand with a pen. For this week, watch only the feel-good comedies and happy-ending movies you planned for. You may only listen to feel-good music (in a favorite genre you both like, of course) with upbeat, positive lyrics. For added impact, conduct this phase for two weeks instead of one.

Fill out this chart first thing in the morning before you get up, and again as the last thing before bed. Use Emojis for the comparison columns.

Do not compare your results yet because you don't want to influence your data collection.

Part 2: The MIDDLE Part of the Before & After

Week 2 Date:	Morning Mood When You Wake	Compare Mood to Yesterday	Evening Mood Before Bed	Compare Mood to Yesterday
Monday				
Tuesday				
Wednesday				
Thursday				
Friday				
Saturday				
Sunday				

Week 3: Life Returns to Normal. Print out this third set of charts, one for you and one for your daughter. Keep them on your nightstands with a pen for easy access. Return to your normal viewing and listening habits, and record your moods for one more week. Fill it out first thing in the morning before you get up, and again as the last thing before bed. Use Emojis for the comparison columns.

Part 3: The AFTER Part of the Before & After

Week 3 Date:	Morning Mood When You Wake	Compare Mood to Yesterday	Evening Mood Before Bed	Compare Mood to Yesterday
Monday				
Tuesday				
Wednesday				
Thursday				
Friday				
Saturday				
Sunday				

Week 4: The Results. Compare your own three charts by yourself while your daughter compares hers. Schedule some time with your daughter to share your results. Then lay out your charts side by side. Compare the differences and similarities of how the experiment affected each of you. Hold a follow up discussion.

🗨 **Say This:** "Which emoji would be the ideal emotion you'd like to feel all week? How easy would it be to design our lives to produce that emotion as the norm? What do you think would be the best way to approach a change like this?"

Although I began by instructing you to pay attention to the media your daughter watches and listens to, what did you learn about how your own entertainment practices influence your mood?

_____

_____

_____

_____

_____

_____

What practices would you like to add to your lives in light of this data?

_____

_____

_____

_____

_____

Why She Can't Think She's In Charge

Your daughter's developing brain is geared toward impulsivity and tidal waves of emotion. In your efforts to make things better for her, you may find yourself in the strange position of not feeling fully in control of your challenging cherub.

How could that be? You were in charge when she was an infant, so what happened?

Over the years, this role confusion may have crept up on you via one too many compromises to keep the "happy" in your Happy Home. You may have inadvertently set upon this path when you propelled that first sweet treat into her mouth to thwart a tantrum.

Then, one day, you realize *you* aren't calling the shots anymore. Her temper is. You find she no longer does what you're telling her to do. Now, *she* informs you when she's coming home, and explodes if you argue with her about her curfew. You feel her disdain when she disrespects you. She's becoming more overbearing by the day, and may even be bullying you. None of that happened overnight. The situation just gradually snuck up on you.

> **Good to Know**
> **The Good News**: You can still regain your authority, and this book will show you how.
> **The Bad News**: If you don't establish your authority, some other authority will.

Once the line of responsibility between parent and child blurs, you've basically turned over your control to her. But, let's be clear. **She cannot be the one in charge**. She may be mature enough to babysit, but she's not developed enough to go up against her amygdala.

> Her teenage brain can't look ahead at the big picture of how to usher herself into adulthood.

You must save her from herself. First of all, her teenage brain can't consistently make logical, well-thought-out decisions; and it certainly can't look ahead at the big picture of how to usher herself into adulthood. Even if you aren't certain how to do all that yet, your brain is capable of recognizing what you need to know, figuring it out and implementing a plan. Developmentally, she can't.

Second of all, she *needs* you to be in charge. If she's in charge, the weight of her upbringing falls on her shoulders. That puts her in a limitless position. Can you imagine your personal world without limits? The sheer number of possibilities would paralyze you, or make you grab at the nearest one, and that's frightening.

Now, picture such a world without limits, combined with a brain without self-control. Do you know what you get?

Yes, it's your standard comic book bad guy (cue *Mwah hah hah hah hah*)… or, your random, run-of-the-mill teenager (cue *shrill, high-pitched giggle*).

> "Understand that if your child is in control, [s]he now sees [her]self as being in charge. But again, that's also very frightening for kids. As much as they enjoy that sense of power, it's very scary to feel like they're controlling their parents. Understand that a teen is never going to say to you, 'I'm scared because you have no control over me. I'm 16 and I'm running the house through intimidation and threatening behavior.' Children, and even teens, want parents to have control and set boundaries around their behavior, but they're not going to admit that."
>
> Janet Lehman

The Brain Without Sleep

If that teenage brain is going to keep developing and maturing, it needs sleep. During the day, the brain is linked to all your senses, receiving constant input from the world, and instantly processing it. According to Jim Horne, a sleep neuroscientist from England's Sleep Research Centre, the more you use your brain during the day, the more it needs to recover, and the more sleep you need.

Without good sleep, everything suffers: schoolwork, sports performances, mood, social interactions, etc. Have you ever tried to hold a conversation with an overtired, cranky teen? It's not a pretty picture. Their ability to interpret facial expressions decreases as rapidly as their patience. Frustration flourishes, exasperation abounds, and the innocent household bystanders sneak out of the room as fast as they can.

You can save the day with the *Step Back and Come Back Intervention*, which helps to de-escalate emotions, and allows you both to leave room without cutting each other off, i.e., *without slamming the emotional door*. It includes a scheduled return to the conversation when everyone feels calmer.

Homework: Step Back and Come Back Intervention

What do you do if you, or your darling girl, are overtired, and things are getting snarky?

Say This: "I love you so much. Is there something I can do to help, or should I come back later?" Or,

Say This: "We need to talk about what happened, but you have enough on your plate tonight. Let's talk about this tomorrow. I love you." Or,

Say This: "I'm tired, so I'm reacting negatively to your words, and I don't want to do that. Let's take a step back because I need to get myself together. Why don't you finish what you have to take care of, and we'll talk after that. I love you."

Don't Say This: "I know you're tired, but..." It diminishes the importance of her conversation and reactions.

Later, at the agreed time, approach her and assess how she is doing. Offer her a nice cool glass of water, or a hot cup of chamomile tea.

Say This: "I feel more relaxed. Can we talk now, or do you have something to finish first..."

Honor her reply. The intervention has already achieved its purpose. Emotions have de-escalated. You've maintained a positive emotional link to her during a time of conflict. You stepped away respectfully, and you have returned as promised. Best of all, your reliability credit goes up.

> **Good to Know**
>
> To optimize the *Step Back and Come Back Intervention*, introduce it to your daughter during a calm moment when it is not needed. That way, when the situation calls for it, she will know what you are talking about when you use it. Who knows? Maybe she'll have the presence of mind to invoke it herself. If she does, it's time for a Happy Dance!

Have you noticed how the snarky factor goes up as the amount of sleep goes down? There's no doubt that we all do better with more sleep, but interestingly enough, the brain doesn't shut down during shuteye. There are as many neurons firing at night as there are during the day. This is especially important for students studying for a test because our brains consolidate and link memories during sleep. This is the basis for remembering, and what we use for recall during a test. Contrary to popular belief, missing sleep the night before an exam can lower your ability to retain information up to 40%. All-nighters are not all they're cracked up to be.

Add a few late nights in there, and you lose the opportunity to refresh and replenish yourself with the sleep your body requires. When the brain isn't getting enough downtime to repair itself, it reacts slowly to stimuli. That may not matter to a test taker who knows the academic material (unless she's finding it difficult to finish on time), but what about how sleep deprivation affects other parts of your lives? Did you know more than half of all road accidents have a sleep deprivation factor contributing to them?

> Sleepiness or alcohol; it doesn't matter. They both create the same issues in drivers.

It turns out that **missing sleep can actually impede your driving performance, just as much as if you were consuming alcohol**. Sleepiness or alcohol; it doesn't matter. They both create the same issues in drivers. Sleepy people don't usually detect a delay in their own reaction time. When you're missing sleep or feeling tired, bicycles and motorcycles will appear and disappear before you even register their presence.

Good to Know

If you absolutely have to drive after you have missed sleep—even if you don't feel tired—keep a **HUGE** distance from the other cars, and stay out of the passing lane. By providing extra distance between you and the next car, you give yourself more time to react, thus increasing your reaction window if something should happen in front of you. What else can you do?

♦ Set your intention to drive more slowly than usual.

♦ Open your windows (the breeze may help keep you alert).

♦ Turn your radio up full blast.

♦ Be *very* careful around pedestrians or cyclists.

♦ Munch on fruit or nuts.

If your daughter is driving, be sure to share this with her. Speaking of daughters driving, remember that earlier story about the mother and daughter driving practice when the girl's teen brain short-circuited in front of her friends? Driving lessons are a great opportunity to open the lines of discussion… just, not when she's driving. Why risk the distraction?

Use yourself as the model. When you are driving, tell your daughter what you are doing so she will adopt those behaviors with her own driving practice. She's watching you anyway. Don't leave her to draw her own conclusions. Direct her understanding by describing your situation and explaining the solution you're choosing.

Say This: "I'm more tired than usual, which is going to affect my driving. People who miss sleep have slower reaction times. But, I don't have a choice. I have to pick up your brother. What I'm going to do is keep this big distance between me and the next car. That will give me plenty of time to react to traffic. I just have to be extra careful around pedestrians and bicyclists. What I want you to do is let me know if any bikes come up beside me, okay?"

What if we add distracted driving to an already sleep-deprived, inexperienced driver? The stats become frightening. Can you imagine your daughter driving the length of a football field with her eyes closed? If she texts while driving, that's basically what she's doing. According to Kiernan Hopkins' article, *25 Shocking Distracted Driving Statistics:*

"The average speed in the US is about 55mph. Taking five seconds to read a text in this time means that the driver travels the length of a football field without looking at the road."

(using information from Icebike.org)

She might as well have her eyes shut.

What they don't say is that if you add an oncoming car on the other end of that football field, also travelling at 55mph, that five seconds is cut in half. In 2.5 seconds of that 5-second glance at her phone, that car from way over there is now at her bumper.

Again, share this information with your daughter when it doesn't matter. Any time is a good time if she's too young for a driver's permit. If she's driving age, hold the conversations when you are driving.

Say This: Every time I get behind the wheel, I think about you being here. Did you know…?"

Homework: Cause and Effect

Engage your daughter in conversations about cause and effect. Make them exploratory and nonjudgmental. Use the example below as a template for engaging in other issues.

Find and read studies on the effects of sleep deprivation and on reflexes and reaction time to share with your teenager. (You can start with my *Bibliography* in the *Answers In the Back of the Book*.)

Pick a time when your darling girl doesn't have a test due (the week or so after report cards go out is usually test-free). Try introducing the conversation by making it about you, not her, and then you can read the studies together with her.

> Try introducing the conversation by making it about you, not her.

☑ Do This: Start the Discussion

Open your magazine (or book, or laptop) to a sleep deprivation study, and go sit in the room where she is. Continue reading for a few minutes. Suddenly say, "I can't believe it! This explains *exactly* why I had difficulty with my _____ test back when I was in high school. You gotta hear this."

Share the article with her and ask what she thinks.

Say This: "I went to sleep at _____ last night, and _____ the night before. I think that's why I feel so draggy today. What time do you think you fell asleep last night? How did you feel this morning?" (Notice the question does not ask what time she went to bed. That would lead to a conversation about rules, not about cause and effect.)

Continue to ask her open-ended questions related to you: "When I get behind on my sleep, do you see any differences in me?"

After she discusses her take on the situation, ask, "How about when you get behind on your sleep? Do you see any differences in yourself?"

Laugh, and ask, "When *you* are missing sleep, do you see any differences in *me*? Who do you think is actually experiencing the differences?"

Tell her about how it was for you when you were in school: "You should've seen my best friend when she stayed up late studying. She was ready to take my head off if I walked too close to her… How does [your daughter's best friend] treat you when she misses sleep? You should show her this article. I'll email it to you."

Excuse yourself and go back to the other room, leaving her in the wake of an informative but pleasant, nonconfrontational interaction.

Caffeine, The Creepy Addiction

The topic of missing sleep brings me to caffeine, the creepy addiction. Why do I call it that? Because by secretly slipping it into foods you consume, they create your need to have more, basically trapping you into becoming a permanent customer. That's the same reason why Coca-Cola used to lace its products with cocaine, that is, until they were prevented from doing so in the early 1900s when cocaine was banned in the USA.

Nowadays, caffeine is the drug of choice for the processed food industry. Did you know that gobs of caffeine are added to something as innocent and delightful as chocolate? You can find it listed in the ingredients under its other names, like *Spices* or, my favorite misnomer, *Natural Flavorings*, both of which are code for "we aren't going to tell you what's in here."

> You can find it listed in the ingredients under its other names, like *Spices or Natural Flavorings*, both of which are code for "we aren't going to tell you what's in here."

Everyone knows energy drinks and sodas are loaded with caffeine, but now, according to Honor Whiteman's 2015 article in *Medical News Today*, so are things like jellybeans, waffles, chewing gum, and syrup. That's crazy (in my humble opinion). Do you see how these kinds of "food" could affect you and your children?

That reminds me of a story…

Suppose you understand the negative effects of caffeine on the body and brain, so you conscientiously limit yourself to 1 cup of coffee in the morning. But, you also have waffles and syrup, you chew some gum on the way to work so you won't have coffee breath, and you grab a handful of jellybeans from the candy dish at the reception desk. An hour later, you're sitting at your desk wondering why you feel anxious and tense inside. It's because you've unknowingly plied yourself with way more than one coffee cup's worth of caffeine (not to mention all that sugar).

Later on, your energy crashes, so you grab another handful of jellybeans before you go home to a night of fitful, restless sleep. The next morning, you drag yourself to the kitchen and decide to have waffles again because you felt so energized after breakfast yesterday… and history repeats itself.

Now apply that same scenario to your daughter sitting across the breakfast table from you. After her breakfast of caffeinated waffles and syrup, she spies the pack of gum you left on the counter and snags it, shoving a piece in her mouth. By the time she gets to school, it has lost its flavor, so she trades it for another. The pack is gone by the time she gets to lunch. Then she has a diet soda she brought from home because she's trying to lose weight, but it leaves her craving something sweet.

If these events become routine, and her classes are not on a rotating schedule, every day she experiences the jitters and anxiety in one particular subject, and her energy crashes during another. She's determined to go to bed early tonight so she won't feel tired at the end of the school day. The only time she really feels good is after breakfast, so she takes to snacking on waffles and syrup after school. Many nights she feels the jitters while doing her homework. She gets to bed at a reasonable hour, but lies there, feeling anxious because she can't fall asleep right away, wondering what is wrong with her.

The next morning you both wake up irritable and growling. You end up squabbling over who ate the last piece of gum before you head out for the day.

How does caffeine contribute to the classic moody teenage girl? Let me count the ways. Caffeine creates an unnatural energized happy feeling, similar to the one her body is supposed to create with its serotonin production. Unfortunately, when she chemically creates an artificial mood, her body quits that job. Why bother when that latte will do it for her?

But, when she misses that expected dose of caffeine, and her body is out of practice for producing serotonin, lack of caffeine makes her feel emotionally low… cue the mood swing.

> **Teenage Brain + Normal Hormonal Swings + Extra Emotional Lows + Sagging Energy = One Very Moody Teenager**

Wow! That's quite a combination.

How can anyone expect your daughter to engage in meaningful conversation when she feels like that? I'd get out of the way if I were you.

Now that you're armed with knowledge, you can be more diligent about selecting the foods that you bring into the house. Remember, you are her role model. The proper nutrition will positively impact both of you.

☑ Do This: My Caffeine Symptoms

On the following list of *Caffeine Withdrawal Symptoms*, circle the ones you experience in general. Put a star next to any symptoms your daughter has. If you try to reduce your caffeine intake, you might find these are the ways your bodies will react, since these symptoms are already warning you about a problem that needs tending to.

Caffeine Withdrawal Symptoms

massive headaches	muscle pain	nausea
fatigue	stiffness	vomiting
irritability	cramping	anxiety
lethargy	insomnia	brain fog
constipation	flu-like symptoms	dizziness
depression	lack of concentration	heart rhythm irregularities

As I mentioned before, changes should start with small steps. Trying to quit caffeine can create some serious side effects as your body detoxes. Wean yourself off slowly, otherwise you may experience something off of that last list.

☑ Do This: Weaning Yourself Off Caffeine

If you aren't a serious coffee, tea, hot chocolate, or soda drinker, *DON'T START!* (Your white teeth will thank you in a few years.)

If everyone avoids you or your daughter until you've had that first cup, and you would like to stop on your own, try these baby steps:

♦ Gradually substitute true decaf for your caffeinated drinks. Start by subbing in just 1/8 of a cup of decaf to your drinks. Increase the amount a little at a time, until you're drinking all decaf.

♦ Reduce the sugar you put into your hot drinks gradually. DO NOT substitute another sweetener. The goal is to help you reduce your sweet tooth, not make you gain weight. (Yes, sugar alternatives have been linked to the obesity epidemic.)

♦ Drink a lot of water to stay hydrated, and to flush the toxins out of your systems. (I know that one's a challenge. Kids don't drink at school to avoid the school bathrooms.)

♦ Avoid processed foods and their myriad of mysterious ingredients. Fresh produce is less likely to be caffeine-infused, and can be found along the perimeter of the store (where you can also find fresh sources of protein, like fish and chicken).

♦ Model food label awareness if you have to buy any processed foods. If you want her to read the labels, you have to read them in front of her.

―――――◆―――――

If you're going to quit cold turkey, may I suggest the Friday of a three-day weekend so you can see if you can handle the symptoms by Tuesday? Don't schedule anything over that weekend, and send the kids to Grandma's. If your daughter is going to kick her caffeine addiction, do it over summer vacation or winter break so her studies don't suffer.

That's Habit-Forming

Again, let me repeat, you are the sum total of all your experiences. So are your habits. Everything you are today is the result of millions of decisions made over time. Everything you do right, and everything you do wrong, contributes to your present-day habits.

Your undesirable habits are the results of dozens of small incremental changes over the years. Your wish to change them has probably been motivated by some negative impact on your life (cancer, diabetes, high blood pressure, heart disease, a daughter experimenting with alcohol, etc.). The way I see it, you have two choices:

♦ You can keep doing the same thing and hope the negative impact doesn't worsen. (Good luck with that.)

♦ Or, you can make a change in your life that will reduce or eliminate the negative impact.

I vote for the second choice. If you want tomorrow to be different than today, you have to do something differently *today*. How about making today Day 1 for creating a new habit?

A habit is an ordinary tendency that is especially hard to give up. Although this applies to good habits, I'll bet your thoughts just turned to some bad habit you want to get rid of. That's natural, since our society emphasizes things like forming New Year's Resolutions, which usually fail. Half the time you drown in ads for products that break habits, and spend the other half trying to ignore advertisements promoting the habits you want to break.

> If you want tomorrow to be different than today, you have to do something differently *today*.

All habits, the good and the bad, make up your daily routine. From my experience, the best way to affect change is to replace an undesirable habit with a beneficial one. It sounds easy enough, especially if you feel motivated to change. Be patient and self-forgiving. A habit is a behavior that doesn't disappear in a week. It takes time, but you can do it with the right approach.

Example: Do you have to post reminders so you will remember to brush your teeth every day?

No.

And, why not?

Because it's a habit.

When you were younger, your mom trained you every day until you brushed your teeth on your own. Now, it's so much of a habit, you just automatically do it as part of your routine, without thinking. In turn, you trained your daughter to brush her teeth every day. Now she does it habitually, without thinking.

Imagine being able to take that kind of daily training, and apply it to other positive elements in your life.

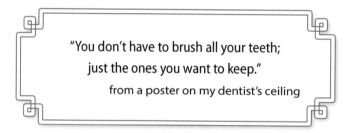

"You don't have to brush all your teeth;
just the ones you want to keep."

from a poster on my dentist's ceiling

You don't have to imagine it. You actually can do it, and I'm going to show you how.

First, let's break down the elements that helped make teeth brushing part of your life so you can apply them to other positive habits.

♦   Brushing your teeth is simple to learn because it's an uncomplicated process.

♦   It is also simple to do. It took a little while for your little hand to coordinate that big brush in your mouth while looking at a backwards reflection in the mirror, but correcting mistakes was part of the lesson.

♦   It doesn't take much time. You merely have to allocate a few minutes twice a day (in the morning and before bed).

♦   You had a reminder system in place, a.k.a., your mom.

♦   The financial rewards outweigh the cost of the habit. Just compare the cost of toothpaste and floss to the cost of dental work.

♦   The health benefits are enormous. Your mouth is the main entrance to your body. Keeping it clean is the first line of defense for your immune system.

If you want your new desired habit to have the same "stick-to-it-ness" as teeth brushing, follow the same strategy.

- ◆ Keep it simple; make it an uncomplicated process.

- ◆ Allow for a learning curve as your new habit integrates into your life; correcting mistakes is part of the process.

- ◆ Create a reminder system. I'm a big fan of sticky notes on the bathroom mirror and on the fridge, two places I visit frequently.

- ◆ Allocate a few minutes twice a day to focus on your new habit. Before you fall asleep, visualize your routine, including the new habit.

- ◆ Figure out what the old habit is costing you each year. Include medical bills. The financial rewards outweigh the cost of negative habits. Make a plan for the money you save. That will make it all the more exciting to replace the old undesirable habit with this new one.

The health benefits are enormous. Deciding to create a new habit, following through with it, and achieving your goal will empower you. All those happy chemicals will replace the negative chemicals from the bad habit *and* promote good health.

Any Awesome Mom can improve her life for a day or two, but what I'm talking about here is **changing your lifestyle**, not changing something for a few days and then lapsing back into your old habits.

> Deciding to create a new habit, following through with it, and achieving your goal will empower you.

Changing your lifestyle is a big deal. It does not mean planting your fists on your hips, staring nobly at the sunrise, and declaring for all to hear, "I will do this from now on!" That lasts about as long as the sunrise. Then, the kids get up, and you're back to business as usual, good intentions all but forgotten.

As delightful as it would be if all the things you'd like to change in your life could become part of your automatic routine, you can't just "free-will" an undesirable habit away. You have to replace it with something else to fill the void. The sensational news is *any* lifestyle change (a.k.a., new habit) can become automatic.

That reminds me of a story...

When I was a teen, they used to say it takes seven days to form a habit. "Hey," said my undeveloped teenage brain, "I can get rid of my messy room habit in a week!" I figured I could do anything for seven days, and so it began.

I sorted and put away my clean clothes and made sure all my dirty clothes were in the hamper. I organized my bookshelves and uncluttered my desk. In a single day, I was able to produce a clean room that made my mama proud. If the truth be told, the decluttering and reorganizing were great fun. So, how hard could it be to keep my room pristine for just seven short days, especially if that was my intention?

But, I was thwarted by an evil Clutter Curse someone must've cast upon my clean room. Somewhere midweek, coats began to drape themselves over the furniture. Books stacked themselves on my nightstand. The hamper surrounded itself with a moat of dirty clothes. I was back to doing homework on the floor due to the disappearance of the top of my desk.

By the time the week concluded, I had forgotten my intention to keep my room clean. No new habit formed. Remembering it a few days later only made me despair about my ability to control my lifestyle habits.

Would you believe there was a silver lining to not being able to stick to a new habit? Yes, unfortunately, my room remained unorganized, but I was also never able to maintain any of those fad diets me and my friends experimented with during our youth. Carb loading. No carbs. Low fat. No fat. All protein. No protein. We tried them all and forgot them all, which was great since fad diets aren't even quick fixes, and none of them were healthy for our bodies anyway.

About six decades ago, the *7-Days-To-Form-A-Habit* myth was replaced with the equally erroneous *21-Days-To-Form-A-Habit* myth. This mistake stemmed from an incorrect interpretation of Dr. Maxwell Maltz's 1950s research on amputees, which showed it took an amputee about three weeks to stop sensing a phantom limb. For some reason, his research was inappropriately extrapolated and applied to the length of time it takes to form a habit. Some noted self-help gurus picked up on the idea, and then eventually everyone ran with it.

By 2009, the study by Phillippa Lally at the Cancer Research UK Health Behaviour

Research Centre showed it actually takes months to form a new habit. If you've ever tried to create a new habit in less than a month, and failed, this probably feels more accurate to you.

People who cling to the hope of developing a new habit in a short amount of time are doomed to failure. Those who acknowledge the time needed, and embrace the journey, can achieve success.

Yes, my friend, it's a marathon, not a sprint.

If you currently believe your previous failed attempts are proof that any future attempts will also fail, **Stop Right There**. Your earlier efforts to change your lifestyle were doomed from the beginning because you expected results in a mere 7 or 21 days. So, now that you know the truth, you can reorient your efforts and try again… this time with realistic goals.

Let's just say that forming a new habit takes as long as it needs to. The objective is to obtain that seamless, everyday behavior. It might take a couple of months for the new habit to take root, but by this time next year, you can have a desired behavior integrated effortlessly into your life. **This time, you *can* succeed**.

But wait! There's more great news from Lally's study: Messing up occasionally *does not* stop the new habit from becoming a reality. Do you know what that means? Your failed attempts at changing a habit still count towards changing your lifestyle. I can personally verify this.

> It actually takes months to form a new habit.

> Messing up occasionally *does not* stop the new habit from becoming a reality.

That reminds me of a story…

Since plastic and paper grocery bags are both bad for the environment, I really wanted to try reusable bags for grocery shopping. However, my desire to help the ecosystem was difficult to convert into a habit because I went shopping only a couple of times a month, making it hard to develop a consistent habit. I always ended up in the checkout line without my bags.

Finally, I hit upon a solution. Any time I forgot to bring my bags, I made myself purchase a reusable bag. Eventually, I replaced the habit of accepting paper or plastic, with the new, although inadequate, habit of purchasing a new reusable bag, which was not my goal.

My collection of reusable bags grew rapidly. I left them in every vehicle, and by every exit from my house. Still, I forgot to bring them into the store.

After a while, I got tired of purchasing reusable bags, so I replaced that habit with another. Instead of buying one more unused reusable bag, I made myself leave my over-flowing shopping cart in the checkout line and run back to the car where a dozen or so bags relaxed in the back seat. (In hindsight, on days when my shopping was light, I suppose I could have simply loaded my purchases back into the cart, wheeled them to my car, and bagged them there.)

One miraculous day, I remembered to grab the bags and brought them into the store with me. Why that day? I have no idea. There was nothing special going on. I simply remembered to do it because thinking about it had become a habit.

I was so thrilled, I called my husband to tell him about my Big Bag Breakthrough. For some odd reason, he didn't share the same excitement. Weird, right?

The whole process took about eleven months, but Ms. Lally was correct. Forgetting hundreds of times did not stop the habit from forming. Nowadays, the bags make it into the grocery store about 95% of the time.

The habit is so much a part of what I do that now I bring them into other stores, like pharmacies and hardware stores, about 70% of the time. I still have to improve the frequency for clothing stores. Currently, reusable bags make it into the mall with me only about 20% of the time, but I have high hopes for the future. I probably just need to go to the mall more often.

Since I started on this quest, I estimate I've kept thousands of single-use bags from the landfills all by myself. Yes, I'm very proud of my small contribution toward protecting our planet. Do I sound a tad empowered? You bet, I am!

That's what happens we build desired habits simply by repeating intentions until they're actions. It means reorienting our thinking, our approach, and even our philosophy, to convert desires into action. It means altering the setting to support the development of our new habit.

 We build desired habits simply by repeating intentions until they're actions.

When a new behavior finally becomes a habit, you have essentially changed your lifestyle. The automatic by-product is your own empowerment because *you* took control, and through your determination, made a lifestyle change.

If I can do it, you most certainly can do it because we are both Awesome Moms!

Why New Year's Resolutions Fail

People have been vowing to do better since people were invented. Take the traditional New Year's Eve Resolutions. Every year, when January 1st rolls around, many of us vow *this* year will be different. We declare we are going to eat better, exercise more, drink less coffee, skip the booze calories, improve relationships, stop smoking, work harder, etc. I'm sure this has *never* happened to *you*, but for 80% of the other people, by February 1st, most of those good intentions have flown out the window.

Why? If you read the previous section on forming habits, you know why. One of the biggest contributors to our lack of change is the unrealistic time frame we set for our accomplishment. January comes and goes, but the resolution hasn't become a reality, so we become defeated. Our resolution falls into the gutter of good intentions, and we are left feeling like failures, inadvertently supporting the *mistaken notion* we don't have the ability to change.

Where do resolution-makers go wrong? There are plenty of reasons, all of which you can avoid if you know what they are. Do any of these sound like you?

- ◆ We privately set warm and fuzzy, but unmeasurable, intentions, instead of specific, measurable goals for which we are accountable, *and* which have a realistic time frame of several months. (Notice, I said "we." Yeah, I've been through all of these.)

- ◆ We set our goals in our heads, and they stay there. We don't say them or write them down. We just think them, which makes them intangible, and makes us unaccountable if we fail.

- ◆ Dr. Avya Sharma of the Canadian Obesity Network says people fail because we set resolutions with unrealistic goals and expectations. We idealistically bite off more than we can chew, and our initial goals are a bit unrealistic.

♦ We aren't ready to change our lifestyle to accommodate a new habit, so it never was going to be more than an inspiring idea.

♦ Sometimes, well-meaning (and sometimes, not so well-meaning) people sabotage our efforts. We fall back on old habits, and our New Year's Resolution becomes a faint, guilty memory (and by now, you know that holding on to New Guilt is a no-no).

♦ Misunderstanding the relationship between cause and effect can incapacitate us. We think if we decrease our debt, or get along better with people, or morph our bodies, then our entire life will suddenly change for the better. Without immediate obvious gains, we get discouraged and mentally wander off, eventually losing all small advances we made.

♦ Our attempt to change direction midstream is simply overwhelmed by the preexisting current.

Forewarned is forearmed. It's time to get S.M.A.R.T.

Living Your Life S.M.A.R.T.

I first heard the term *S.M.A.R.T. Goals* at a Staff Development meeting when I was a teacher. The first known use of the term was by George T. Doran, in 1981 in **Management Review**, a business publication, but one of my schools applied it to teacher lesson plans. I immediately brought the concept of clear, measurable goals right into my classroom, and created science lessons around S.M.A.R.T. Goals. I used them as examples so I could teach my students how to apply this powerful tool for themselves.

To make sure your goals are the S.M.A.R.T. kind, each one should be:

♦ **S**pecific (who, what, when, where, how)

♦ **M**easurable (quantifiable, detectable)

♦ **A**ccountable (someone else knows what you are doing)

♦ **R**eminder driven (a way to keep it in the forefront)

♦ **T**ime-frame targeted (deadline-based, time limited)

Pop Quiz! Setting a Good Example

Compare the New Year's Resolution with the S.M.A.R.T. Goal in the example below. Which one has a better chance at success?

Example 1:

   New Year's Resolution: I'm going to use this book to find a way to keep my daughter from slamming her door.

   General Components: I'm going to use this book to find a way (How) to keep my daughter (Who) from slamming her door (What).

Example 2:

   S.M.A.R.T. Goal: I'm going to initiate a conversation with my daughter in the car on Tuesdays while I drive her to practice, which will amount to four conversations a month. I'll start by sharing my S.M.A.R.T. Goal, and then discuss how she feels when she slams the door. I'll put a sticky note on my steering wheel so I'll remember.

   Specific Components: I'm going to initiate a conversation (What) with my daughter (Who) in the car (Where) on Tuesdays (When) while I drive her to practice (Time-frame), which will amount to four conversations a month (Measurable). I'll start by sharing my S.M.A.R.T. Goal (Accountable), and then discuss how she feels when she slams the door (How). I'll put a sticky note on my steering wheel so I'll remember (Reminders).

   And the winner is: _____

   Awesome Moms set doable S.M.A.R.T. Goals and define their desired outcomes.

Answer: Example 2: S.M.A.R.T. Goal

One Realistic, S.M.A.R.T. Resolution

Design a simple S.M.A.R.T. Goal right now. **Choose** a habit easy to integrate into your current lifestyle. Figure out the **cost** benefit. Calculate **how long** you think it will take, and then **double that time** to make it more realistic. **List any materials** you will need to pull this off (sticky notes, anyone?). **Pick someone** to be your Accountability Partner and tell her/him what you are going to achieve by the end of the year. **Schedule** a monthly meet-up over the next four months to get together with your Accountability Partner to share your progress.

Goal (Be **Specific**):	
How will you **Measure** success:	
Accountability Buddy (who are you going to tell?):	
Reminders (where to post reminders):	
Time-frame Completion Date:	
Benefits:	
Materials Needed:	
Progress Check Dates:	

You don't need to wait for New Year's Day to decide to make changes.

Sharing my goals with someone takes them from fantasy into reality. Find someone and start today! For example, I'm proud to say that, although I am a certified Personal Trainer, I hire another trainer to workout with me because I need a reliable Accountability Buddy. Otherwise, life interferes with my best intentions.

You don't need to wait for New Year's Day to decide to make changes. To me, January 1st seems like such an arbitrary date if you have kids and/or if you're a teacher. It's the middle of winter, the middle of winter break, and sometimes it's the middle of the week. Okay, yes, it's the beginning of our calendar and fiscal year, but how does that fit organically into the flow of your life? It doesn't, unless maybe if you pay quarterly taxes.

Why not make your New Year's Resolutions for your lifestyle changes coincide with a true beginning already built into your lifestyle? If your job is seasonal, set your goals when the new season starts. It's the perfect time to make lifestyle vows.

Or, being a parent, every August/September summer vacation ends and the new school year begins. When your kids, and sometimes you, return to getting formally educated, everything switches up at home. Piggyback on that wave of momentum signaling the start of the school year!

Another perfect time? May/June, when school ends, and the new summer begins. Summer jobs, family trips, reading lists, summer leagues, and vacations all represent organic new beginnings. Use your new summer lifestyle, a perfect time for the resolutions, as a springboard for reinventing yourself.

Other good times to make resolutions are:

- When daylight savings time changes
- The equinoxes
- The solstices
- Your birthday
- Your anniversary

- With a new job, or a promotion, or graduation
- The beginning of a new sports season
- After a job evaluation
- _____
  (fill in the blank)

Doesn't it make sense? Your life is already scheduled to change, and you are going to have to form new habits/routines for the shift anyway. It's the ideal time to create S.M.A.R.T. Goals! As long as the day already brings significant changes to your life, it's a good day to start a S.M.A.R.T. Goal.

> **Good to Know**
>
> Am I telling you to avoid New Year's Resolutions on January 1st? Nah. Go for it! By the time it rolls around, you'll have finished this chapter and will know exactly how to stack the odds in your favor.

Good Intentions = Life Without Goals

The new school year represents a fresh start. Regardless of how the previous year went, everyone begins the school year anew… new teachers, new classes, new classmates, new subjects—a chance to leave the past behind and embrace a new start.

Whether they admit it or not, kids emotionally anticipate the new beginning. They all want things to be better this year than last year. They want to fit in better, get better grades, etc. Although their emotions may declare, "This year will be different," they are in fact only stating a vague intention. To be sure, intentions can set you on the path to success, but they are only the precursors to setting goals, not actual goals.

If the school administration requires their teachers to submit concrete written goals and objectives to increase their chances of success, wouldn't that practice benefit our students as well? What a difference S.M.A.R.T. Goals made for me, and for my students. They felt much more empowered and successful using S.M.A.R.T. Goals, and as an added bonus, they could more readily keep track of deadlines.

Pop Quiz! Goal or Intention?

Here are a few common statements I've heard over the years from moms and daughters.

1. **"I hope this school year feels better than last year."**
   This statement is an example of:

   a.   an intention
   b.   a goal
   c.   none of the above

2. **"I just want things to be better between me and my daughter."**
   This statement is an example of:

   a.   an intention
   b.   a goal
   c.   none of the above

3. **"Wouldn't it be nice if I had more friends."**
   This statement is an example of:

   a.   an intention
   b.   a goal
   c.   none of the above

4. **"I hope I don't fight with my mom as much."**
   This statement is an example of:

   a.   an intention
   b.   a goal
   c.   none of the above

The answer to #1 is (c) none of the above. The answer to #2 is (c) none of the above.
The answer to #3 is (c) none of the above. The answer to #4 is (c) none of the above.

All of these statements are merely wishes. Intentions or goals are not part of this framework. You might as well throw your wish and your coin into a fountain if you are expecting success this way (unless, you are wishing you could throw your coin into a fountain; in that case, your wish will come true.).

> If you want to improve your year, or better your relationship with your daughter, or increase your friendships, or decrease your conflicts, then you must move beyond wishes, desires, and intentions. Set S.M.A.R.T. Goals, and then create the environment that will help you stick to them.

I'll be the first to tell you that putting all this detail into your goal setting is a royal pain, especially to someone like me who wants to jump in and get started right away. It's simply not conducive to the way I like to approach things.

While I (inappropriately) may not care for the delay due to preparation, I'm much more calm when I follow the S.M.A.R.T. Goals path, versus pursuing the Build The Plane While Flying It path.

Good to Know

When I wanted to paint our bedroom, my husband, who has been building homes for decades, insisted I tape up the doors, windows, and molding. It took forever! But, he was so right. Once I started painting… *zip, zip, zip!* I was done in no time, and clean up was a breeze. All I had to do was wait for the paint to dry, and then peel off the tape. Yeah, I may not be a big fan of the preparation, but I sure do love being able to execute a project quickly because of it!

If you want to create a new lifestyle habit, begin by examining the behavior you would like to alter. It's important to understand whether you are dealing with a core issue, or whether it's a symptomatic expression of another problem. If it's the latter, you might want to consider addressing the original problem as your first goal.

For example, I used to get migraines following a stressful (holiday) interaction with my family. I tried to address the migraines themselves with relaxation techniques and trigger-food avoidance, but it wasn't until I recognized them as a symptom of my stress that I could implement real change. After a therapist helped me look at family dynamics over the holidays, not only did the migraines stop, but I felt less anxious overall when dealing with relatives. Today, I anticipate my buttons being pushed, and can counter in a healthy way. Isn't that what we all want?

Once you identify the pressure that stresses you out, you can find a behavior to substitute for your old reactions, set and execute a S.M.A.R.T. Goal, and *Ta Da!* A new habit replaces an old habit, and your lifestyle improves. That's a wonderful way to model how to handle your pressures for your observant daughter.

Maintaining Your Resolve

You've probably figured out by now that, like everything else I've discussed in this book, achieving your S.M.A.R.T. Goals is a marathon, not a sprint. This is about permanently changing your life from this point forward by creating new habits… which, by definition, will become integrated into, and redefine, your lifestyle. But until you reach that point, how do you keep from sliding back into the old habits?

Here's how:

Keep at it. That's all. Just keep trying.

What doesn't work is attempting to stop an undesirable habit by *trying to not do it*. You spend too much time

Good to Know

The more you repeat a thought, word, or deed (that's a nod to all you former Girl Scouts out there), the more you change your thinking by rewiring your brain. According to brain scientists, Antonio Damasio and Joseph LeDoux, and psychotherapist Stephen Hayes, the use of MRIs has shown *habitual behavior is created by thought patterns*, which create your neural pathways and memories. When you're faced with a choice or decision, they become the go-to basis for your behavior.

thinking about *not* thinking about it, which employs (and therefore reinforces) the already established neural pathways you want to minimize. You are basically reinforcing your unwanted behavior.

Real change stems from creating new neural pathways from new thinking. You *can* teach yourself a new habit. After all, you're an Awesome Mom.

☑ Do This: Obsessing Reinforces

Basically, thinking about avoiding something just strengthens it. For example, if there is cake in the house, and you are trying not to eat it, if you're like me, you obsess about it instead. Over the course of an hour, you might:

♦ walk by it (✓), and tell yourself not to give in to eating it (✓)

- feel proud for not giving in to cake consumption (✓)
- look at it many, many times while preparing dinner (✓✓✓✓✓✓) and tell yourself to not eat it each time (✓✓✓✓✓✓)
- crave something sweet (✓) and try to ignore it (✓)
- wonder if anyone else has eaten the cake (✓), and go check to see (✓)
- feel proud for once again not giving in to cake consumption (✓)
- get something to munch on during a commercial (✓), and heroically don't get cake (✓)
- pass it on the way to the bathroom (✓), and remind yourself "no cake" (✓)
- strengthen your resolve by repeating "I won't eat the cake" 25 times (25 ✓s)
- think about taking just a spoonful (✓), and decide not to (✓)
- think about just tasting the frosting (✓), and decide not to (✓)

Go back and count up the number of checks (✓): _____

Your brain registers "cake" every time you obsess about not having it. You probably want some right now after reading this, a desire triggered by seeing the word over and over again. That's what happens when you concentrate your focus on "no cake."

Imagine a teenage brain obsessing about a boy. I'm just saying…

⸺◈⸺

Don't allow yourself to be the victim of an obsession created by reinforcing denial. Take charge! Instead of constantly denying yourself the cake sitting in the kitchen (which, personally, makes me feel resentful), throw the cake out (it's not good for *anyone* in your household anyway). Remove it from sight and availability. Then awesomely substitute a new healthy behavior for the obsessing behavior.

☑ **Do This:** Substitute Better for Bad

Set up a comedy movie night with your daughter and teach her how to pop your own popcorn. That will create new neural pathways in both your brains (a healthy mother/daughter activity) to substitute for old habits (grabbing something sweet and retiring to your separate rooms). You will be free from obsessing over a bad behavior or habit, *and* growing positive neural connections in the process.

—————◆◆◆—————

Bonus: If you dare, tell your daughter why you threw out the cake, and explain that your objective is to substitute a better behavior. Leading by example will help her model her positive behavior after your positive example (after she gets over not having any cake).

So, go ahead and make those plans for improvement and growth. Whether they be New Year's Resolutions, New Summer's Resolutions, or New School Year's Resolutions, if you want them to work, make them S.M.A.R.T.!

Your Own Mini-Pep Rally

You obviously are the brains of this *Science Class*. When you lead by example, your daughter benefits, even though her brain is still half-baked. By planning out your journey together, not only will you both grow, but you also will be able to measure that awesome growth. You don't have to be blinded by science to make it work for you.

So, get up and cheer. Or, better yet, sing this to the tune of Thomas Dolby's *She Blinded Me With Science* :

(Daughter's Name)'s got the rhythm.
Mom's got the motion.
And when we get together,
We cause a commotion!

How Did You Do?

To reflect how you feel about the outcome, put one of the following emojis next to each task you undertook.

Assigned Task	Results	Assigned Task	Results
What Does Your Face Say?		My Caffeine Symptoms	
What Do Their Faces Say?		Weaning Yourself Off Caffeine	
Brain Talk		Setting A Good Example	
The Happy Hormones Experiment		One Realistic, S.M.A.R.T. Resolution	
Step Back and Come Back Intervention		Goal or Intention?	
Cause and Effect		Obsessing Reinforces	
Start the Discussion		Substitute Better for Bad	

Chapter 4

Math Class: Super Solutions To Teenage Tirades

The 3 Rs… Reconsider. Regroup. Restore.

- ◆ **Math to the Rescue**
- ◆ **Commonalities Abound**
- ◆ **The Valuable Venn Diagram**
- ◆ **Clothes and the Vibrant Venn Diagram**
- ◆ **40 Versatile Venn Diagram Applications**
- ◆ **Zero Common Ground?**
- ◆ **Factoring In the Fun**
- ◆ **Your Own Mini-Pep Rally**
- ◆ **How Did You Do?**

Do you remember when you were young, the other kids whining about complex math equations?

"Why do we have to learn this?"

"We won't use it when we grow up."

No one questioned whether or not it was important to read, but math… well, that was another story. As it turns out, math is one of the most useful communication tools we have. That's right—communication tool—and every Awesome Mom should be armed with it!

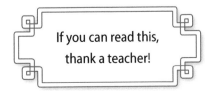

If you can read this, thank a teacher!

Math to the Rescue

I, myself didn't much appreciate math as a teen because I had no idea how it applied to my life. Math was only a means to an end for my report card grade. I saw my parents read books and newspapers all the time, but as far as I could tell, the only time they actually did math was once a month on Bill Day (cue ominous music), when they would sit down together to pay the bills. Even then, I didn't witness much math. I always made sure to be out of the house when they were paying bills, because apparently math made my parents... cranky.

However, there was one thing I did like about math—the concept of balancing equations—the idea that one combination of variables could achieve balance with another completely different set of variables, like:

$$2 + 6 = 8$$
$$4 + 4 = 2 + 6$$
$$8 = 7 + 1$$
$$1 + 7 = 6 + 2$$

> According to Collins Dictionary, "an equation is a situation in which two or more parts have to be considered together so that the whole situation can be understood or explained. An equation is solved by figuring out which variables make the equation true."

Think about this definition in terms of mathematical relationships. If any of the variables are unknown, or missing from the equation, you have a problem to solve in your relationship. Identifying the missing variable(s) always leads to the solution, and thereby achieves balance.

Is that an awesome metaphor for life, or what? Let us delve deeper, shall we?

When your balanced equation ($2 + 6 = 8$) has new variables introduced, the equation becomes unbalanced.

$$\text{from: } 2 + 6 = 8$$
$$\text{to: } 4 + 2 + 6 = 8 + \ldots?$$

Additional variables are required to restore balance, and they, too, become part of the equation.

$$4 + 2 + 6 = 8 + \mathbf{3} + \mathbf{1}$$

The same is true for emotional relationships. For example, here is your basic equation for happiness:

Happy Mother + Happy Daughter + Love = Happy Relationship + Love

The three variables in this equation are:

♦ Happy Mother

♦ Happy Daughter

♦ Happy Relationship

Do not mistake *Love* for a variable, although some people treat it like it's a variable. *Love* is the constant, and it is unconditional.

Can you name the variable that eventually shows up in every household and throws the equation out of whack?_____

Did you say *Puberty*?

Ding Ding Ding Ding! You're right!

Happy Mother + Happy Daughter + Love + Puberty = Rocky Relationship + Love

Yup, definite lack of balance there. There's nothing like a hefty dose of puberty to throw off a balanced relationship. But, don't worry. With a little work, you can regain the balance in your happy home like this.

Happy Mother + Happy Daughter + Love + Conversation + Maturity =
Happy Relationship + Love + Puberty

Whether you realize it or not, you picked up this book because you are trying to achieve or maintain balance in the relationship with your daughter. It's a simple equation. If you're happy, and your daughter is happy, then your home is happy.

Happy Mom + Happy Teen + Love = Happy Home + Love

You can see from the next relationship that if the mother frequently gives in to the daughter, thus losing her power, the lack of balance will make the mom unhappy, and ruin a Happy Home:

$$\text{Turbulent Teen} - \text{Happy Mom} + \text{Love} = \text{Rocky Home} + \text{Love}$$

Honestly, can any teen be happy if her mom isn't happy? How wonderful can your life be if your daughter isn't happy?

$$\text{Grim Mom} - \text{Happy Teen} + \text{Love} = \text{Rocky Home} + \text{Love}$$

Your relationship must contain all the variables and constants needed to attain and maintain balance.

$$\text{Love} + \text{Respect} + \text{Defined Limits} + \text{Clear Communication} = \text{Happy Home} + \text{Love}$$

And this equation…

$$\text{Respect} + \text{Consistency} + \text{Love} = \text{Happy Mom} + \text{Happy Teen} + \text{Love}$$

Notice that although *Love* is a constant in all balanced equations, *Happiness* is a variable. Unfortunately, temporary balance can be achieved without *Happiness*, but it never lasts. Regardless, no balance exists without *Love*.

☑ Do This: Identifying My Variables

Make your own equation that represents your relationship as it *currently* exists:

_____ = _____

Rewrite your equation to represent how you want your relationship to be one year from now.

_____ = _____

> **Good to Know**
>
> As a nod to all my former middle school math teachers, I concede we do need math to conduct our lives—for budgeting, paying off credit cards, understanding the tables and graphs scattered through the news media, doing taxes, reading food labels, calculating calorie intake, taking measurements for new carpeting, and of course, creating a positive, interactive relationship with your daughter.

Commonalities Abound

Does it ever feel like *everything* you say or do creates a verbal tussle with your daughter? Let's take a moment to revise your perspective. Be grateful for these red flags. They alert you to missing variables in your relationship, which need to be identified in order to solve your problem.

In order to maintain balance in the equation of your relationship, don't forget the givens, the reasons why your relationship is designed to succeed, no matter what state it's in right now.

10 Givens for Balancing the Equation

1. You both want to be close.
2. You both want a loving, long-lasting, healthy relationship.
3. You both want to be respected, valued, and admired.
4. You both want to give love and receive love.
5. You both want to be heard.
6. You both want to be able to express yourselves without being judged.
7. You both have to deal with relationships/pressures outside the home.
8. You are both females in a male-dominated culture.
9. You are both pressed for time.
10. You both would love your relationship problems to magically get better.

☑ **Do This:** The Unknown Shared Variables

Make a more specific list of the variables you and your precious teenager already share. Hey, why don't you ask her for some input as a way to start another conversation?

	10 Other Variables I Have In Common With My Awesome Daughter
1	
2	
3	
4	
5	
6	
7	
8	
9	
10	

Do you and your glorious girl have everything in common? Of course not, and that's one source of conflict. But, what if I told you there is a quick mathematical way to take stock of the things you want, versus the things she wants, and quickly sort them out to find the things you agree on? What do you think would happen to your relationship if you were able to easily identify, and therefore focus on these commonalities?

Have I got a math trick for you! One that worked miracles for my charming cherub and me, and can do the same for you and yours.

The Valuable Venn Diagram

When my high school math teacher taught us about logic and Venn Diagrams, my teenage brain thought, "Yeah, yeah. I'm never going to use this." I was so wrong! The valuable **Venn Diagram** can actually be used to identify the things you have in common with your growling offspring. More importantly, you can use those items to rebuild trust and understanding.

Welcome to the venerable Venn Diagram, that gloriously, fabulously perfect illustration of Common Ground. It's a graphic used to clarify differences and similarities. Math uses them. Science uses them. And now, Awesome Moms can use them.

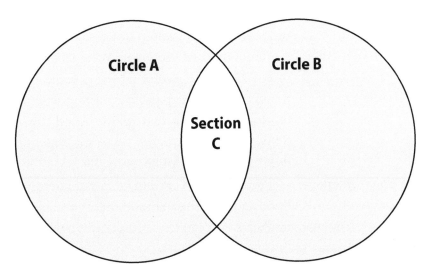

Circle A represents *your* choices. **Circle B** represents *your daughter's* choices. Your Circle A selections make her roll her eyes and throw her hands up in frustration. Her Circle B items make your teeth grind and causes occasional panic.

> Section C is where conflict goes to die, and relationships are skirmish-free.

But the intersection of those two circles at **Section C**, that overlapping of your two worlds, *that*, my friend, is where the magic happens.

Section C consists of the choices you both love. It is the realm of Win-Win, void of conflict and competition. Section C is where conflict goes to die, and relationships are skirmish-free. I can't begin to tell you how many times Section C saved my daughter and myself from temper tantrums… on both our parts. (Hey, don't judge. I'm an Awesome Mom, not a perfect mom).

Section C is your friend.

I *love* Section C.

Clothes And The Vibrant Venn Diagram

> My five-year-old wanted ensembles that exposed her little round tummy. My mind fast-forwarded ten years, and I knew I was in trouble.

I first realized I was going to need some kind of clothes-shopping strategy when my five-year-old began arguing over every outfit. She wanted ensembles that exposed her little round tummy. My mind fast-forwarded ten years, and I knew I was in trouble.

Section C of the viable Venn Diagram came to my rescue. One day I was using the graphic in my classroom to teach comparing and contrasting leaves. Suddenly, it hit me. I could use that undervalued Venn Diagram to diffuse petty arguments when my Awesome Daughter didn't buy into my philosophy.

From that point, whenever I set foot in a mall with my daughter in tow, I was armed with Section C of the virtuous Venn Diagram. The verbal disagreements and emotional tussles that had previously characterized shopping for tween outfits instantly transformed into a fun and pleasurable experience for both of us.

Before we'd leave for the store, I'd orient us by making a circle with each hand, and holding them up so the circles overlapped. *Voila!* Instant Venn Diagram visual.

"This," I'd say, waving around my right hand, "is what I love on you. This…" The left hand would shake under her nose, "is what you love on you."

Overlapping the two circles, I would peer at my daughter through the oval my fingers created, that superb Section C. "This is what we're going to buy. You're not going to argue with me, and I'm not going to argue with you, because everything in here will be something we both love."

It always worked, because we followed three guidelines.

1. She had to try on everything I suggested.
2. I had to permit her to try on anything she wanted to.
3. There was no arguing allowed because:
    a. We were both entitled to our opinions.
    b. Arguing wasted time for both of us.

If my agitated adolescent started fussing about a garment I was nixing, I'd just hold up my hands, let my fingers form that magnificent Section C and say, "Venn Diagram, sweetie, Venn Diagram. Remember, you're going to love everything you bring home."

She'd calm right down. It worked every time we shopped. We'd returned home with our bundles, individually satisfied we had gotten our own way. Besides, whatever it was she had been pining for was forgotten by the time she hung her purchases up in her closet.

Not all teenage girls fly off the handle, or blow things out of proportion. But if you happen to be living with a human roller coaster, it can be very difficult to find a resolution for:

♦   What she should be allowed to wear
♦   How much makeup is appropriate
♦   Hemlines and necklines
♦   Food and beverage intake
♦   Movies, music, and books
♦   Dating, parties, and socializing

> "
> Trying to argue with an angry teenager is like trying to teach a pig to sing. For all your effort, the pig never learns to sing, and you just end up annoying the pig.
> "

Trying to argue with an angry teenager is like trying to teach a pig to sing. For all your effort, the pig never learns to sing, and you just end up annoying the pig.

Use the versatile Venn Diagram whenever you have a decision to make together, or when you have differing opinions, or when you want to teach her about compromise. Draw the two circles, designating one for you and one for her, and brainstorm. As the ideas spill forth from your lips, put the ones you both enjoy into the scrumptious Section C. Separate the ones she's not keen on and the ones that curdle your cream into their designated A and B spheres. Then zoom in on that sassy Section C, and let it work its magic.

This is a venerable Venn Diagram I did with my daughter on our favorite movies. We began by preparing our own separate lists:

My List	**My Daughter's List**
1. Galaxy Quest	1. Crazy, Stupid Love
2. When Harry Met Sally	2. My Cousin Vinny
3. Mrs. Winterbourne	3. Rent
4. Transformers	4. Notting Hill
5. Thor	5. When Harry Met Sally
6. The Avengers	6. The Wedding Date
7. Ironman	7. Dear White People
8. Penelope	8. Mama Mia
9. Star Trek: Voyage Home	9. Moulin Rouge
10. Star Trek	10. About Time

When we sorted out our lists via a Venn Diagram, it looked like this:

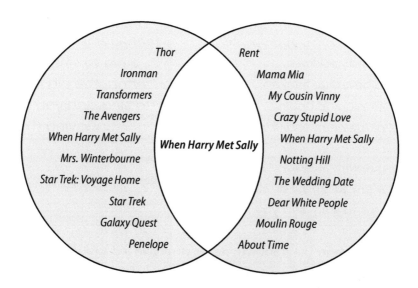

As we shared our lists, I realized there were movies on hers that I loved, and she wanted to claim some of the ones on my list. We modified the versatile Venn Diagram by adding those movies into Section C, and it ended up looking like this:

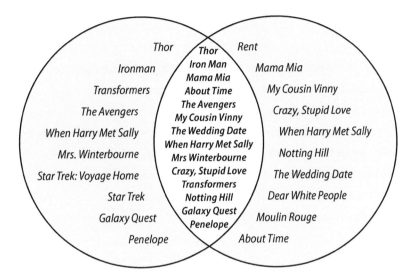

See how easy it is to generate amiable conversation from a simple math tool?

I recommend you try a couple for practice before you need them. It will grease the wheels of compromise while giving you a **Mom & Me Moment** to share. Visit my website (**http://AwesomeMomTribe.com/Venn-Diagram/**) to find a virtual Venn Diagram template you can download for free.

You are both going to love the **Great and Powerful Venn Diagram**!

40 Versatile Venn Diagram Applications

Are you ready to have some fun? There are unlimited uses for the valiant Venn Diagram. Here are 40 just off the top of my head. Try to come up with at least 10 or more options each. That will really give you something to talk about.

Individually, make a list of your top 10+ items while your daughter makes a list of her top 10+ items. When you and your daughter each have a list, insert them into a validating Venn Diagram. Section A and Section B are for your differences in taste, philosophy, and opinion, the things that make you individuals. The ones on both your lists obviously go into Section C, but feel free to add any others you think of as you go along.

☑ **Do This:** 10 Ways to Build Strong Relationship

Pick one of the following ideas to try, or select your own.

1. The 10 things do you like about your relationship right now
2. Ideal personality traits in a best friend (or significant other)
3. Best physical features (do yours first, and then do hers separately)
4. What makes a good mother/daughter relationship?
5. Top best ways to stop an argument
6. Favorite relatives/friends (contact one of them, or send a funny card)
7. Alternatives to Dating (where she can interact with boys within a group)
8. Most embarrassing moments
9. Favorite memories of all time
10. Characteristics of a best friend

☑ **Do This:** 10 Entertaining Ideas

Create a viable Venn Diagram. Try one of these concepts, unless you have a better idea:

1. Fun female activities you can do together (manicure, tai chi, etc.)
2. All-time best movies (then watch the Section C movies together)
3. Day trips to go on this week, month, or year
4. Impressive heroines—fiction and nonfiction
5. Best-looking male celebrities
6. Where would you like to go/do on your next vacation?
7. Possible makeover ideas (including the less obvious: rooms, people, relationships)
8. Best sports or teams
9. All-time best TV series
10. Favorite outfits for a high school dance/cocktail party with associates

☑ **Do This:** 10 Cool Ways to Pursue Good Health

Create a vivacious Venn Diagram with one of these choices, or ask your dazzling daughter for a suggestion:

1. Best-looking school/work outfits (have a fashion show just for you two)
2. Physical activities you can do together (go do them)
3. Things to remove from your cupboards/desks/closets
4. Ways to conserve water and other resources
5. Best places to go for a walk
6. Ways to turn your house into a spa-for-the-day
7. Workshops you would like to take
8. Hobbies/sports you would like to learn
9. Hazardous Chemicals you can remove from your home
10. Things you would like to grow in a garden

———◆———

☑ **Do This:** 10 Funtastic Food Ideas

You've got the idea, but here are some more suggestions. Create a venturous Venn Diagram with one of these:

1. Most delicious desserts (then prepare one together)
2. Favorite dinner/lunch/breakfast dishes
3. Yummiest side dishes for menu planning
4. People to invite to a BBQ
5. Things to remove from your fridge/pantry
6. Healthiest snacks
7. Ethnic cuisines to experiment with
8. Best/favorite restaurants
9. Things you can do with a blender, pressure cooker, etc.
10. Ways to simplify meal preparation

———◆———

Now that you see what your awesome self and your awesome daughter have in common, pick something in Section C, and *GO DO IT!* Once you find the things you both like, accentuate them. Create new memories and new mirror neurons. Feel that old closeness again.

And again.

And again.

Zero Common Ground?

Once you identify your common ground with the versatile Venn Diagram, the process usually blossoms into other unexpected things you both share. In my example, my charming cherub and I picked a movie from Section C and watched it together. Afterward, we ended up digging out the old home movies and watched footage of me as an Awesome Mommy when she was a Terrific Toddler. You never know where the conversation will lead. It starts the ball rolling, enabling you to find other commonalities. And, *Ta Da!* You have a new happy memory to cherish, and another positive variable to add to your equation.

"But, Deborah, what if me and my daughter completed a Venn Diagram, and there was nothing in Section C?"

Lack of Section C items comes under the heading of *Valuable Learning Experience*. It can be turned into a *powerful* Teachable Moment if you take the opportunity to reach out to your daughter.

Say This: "It's okay that there is nothing in Section C. That just means we need to learn more about each other. I'm curious about your list. Pick one for me to try. Make it something you think I'll like, and if that's not possible, make it something you think I will be alright with."

⟫━◆━⟪

Accept her selection without judgment and try it with an open mind. Make sure you find a couple of redeeming points if her choice doesn't suit you. Explain to her why you prefer something else (your age differences, your childhood, etc.). Remind her that a big difference in your backgrounds is that you were raised by your parents, along with their personality quirks, but she's being raised by you, with your personality quirks.

Ask her if she would share one of the items in your circle after you've experienced one of hers, and watch the connection between you grow.

Say This: "Well, this just taught me a lot about you. Thank you for sharing. Let's do a different Venn Diagram." Then select a topic that insures there will be overlap between you, like food.

Factoring In the Fun

Creating a vigorous Venn Diagram isn't enough. You must apply it to an activity you can experience together. I'm sharing 10 of my favorite activities here, but I have to tell you, there are so many opportunities out there, it was difficult to limit myself to a mere 10.

☑ Do This: 10 Super-Duper Section C Applications

Using the valuable Venn Diagram and its stupendous Section C can enhance your lives. Here are 10 random activities that popped into my head while I was making those 40 Versatile Venn Diagram Applications:

1. Revamp your home together. Go to the library (field trip!) and look through Interior Design magazines and books for ideas that won't cost anything. Rearrange the furniture. Declutter by removing 10 items each for donations. Move wall hangings around. Organize the garage and/or attic. Design the landscape, or create a vegetable garden.

2. Find books you both like and read them together. Share the books you enjoyed at her age. Discuss plot lines and author styles. Read a book aloud, with each of you playing one of the characters.

3. Volunteer together: Habitat for Humanity, storm cleanup, Soup Kitchens, reading to the elderly at the Senior Center, collect blankets and food for the homeless shelters, conduct a food drive for the local pantry.

4. Take a field trip to trek the public spaces: parks, museums, outdoor exhibits,

libraries, art galleries, amusement parks, zipline parks, roller-skating rinks, historical tours, craft fairs.

5. Explore non-franchised ethnic cuisine: vegan, Ethiopian, Greek, Mongolian hot pot, traditional Mexican, Polish, Portuguese, British High Tea, Jamaican, French, Thai, Vietnamese, Japanese, Korean BBQ, Mediterranean, etc.

6. Make a playlist of the songs you both love. Have it play as background music when you hang out together. Make a playlist for the songs:
    - from when she was in middle school
    - from last year
    - that were your favorites when you were her age
    - from every year for the last five years

7. Cook together. Prepare dinner together. Create an elaborate dessert together. Buy fruits you've never tasted before. Try recipes from a different country. Sample different cuisines. Experiment with different cookware and utensils.

8. Waltz down Memory Lane by creating family photo albums (digital or physical), scrapbooking, making a family tree, investigating the family tree, testing your DNA for your origins.

9. Join a community organization together: community theater, civic orchestra, church choir, women's sports league, YWCA.

10. Do sports together. There are plenty out there for nonathletes.
    - walk, skip, jump, run, dance
    - golf, mini golf, Frisbee Golf
    - swim, snorkel, scuba, row, paddle
    - basketball, soccer, lacrosse, volleyball
    - zip-line adventure park, weight training
    - roller-skating, ice-skating, snowshoeing, skiing
    - tennis, badminton, Ping-Pong, handball, racquetball, squash

Okay, that might be a little more than 10 ideas, but it's hard to stop once you start. The point is to find things you both like to do or want to try, the things you have in common.

The more you target and repeat your fun times, the faster her trust in you will grow. The more your daughter trusts you, the more she will confide in you. The more she confides in you, the better you will understand her. The more you understand her, the less strained your relationship will be. And finally, the less strained your relationship is, the more she will listen when you communicate with her. It's a sure sign you're building your trust with her again when she is willing to listen to you.

> **Good to Know**
>
> One more time…
> Find Common Activities So You Can
> → Increase Trust
> → Have Better Conversations
> → Expand Your Understanding
> → Decrease Relationship Strain
> → Improve Listening
> → Create a Closer Relationship

Trust brings a lot to the table. Her trust in you means your daughter believes:

- You've got her back.
- You really listen to her.
- It's safe to talk to you.
- You will be there when she needs you.
- You believe in her.
- She has your support.
- You see how she is maturing.
- You believe that she's trustworthy.
- You understand her.
- She does not have to navigate the teen years alone.

I suggest you focus on what you have in common *every* chance you get. Keep it in the forefront of her mind. Let her know how precious she is to you. In the process, add more positive memories to your growing pile.

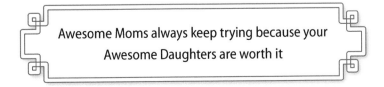

Awesome Moms always keep trying because your Awesome Daughters are worth it

Your Own Mini-Pep Rally

Math concepts are conveyed in logical sequences, but life and relationships tend to be a little bit more… messy. Math is organized, which is a relief to many. It's about equations and balance, but so are our messy lives. Your ultimate goal is to combine the relationship you're building with your daughter with your improved communication patterns so you can achieve balance within your life together. Happily, the awesome skills in this chapter will serve you for many years to come.

Go get your daughter and see if she'll yell this with you:

This Awesome Mom,
Tried and true,
Has an Awesome Daughter.
How 'bout you?

How Did You Do?

To reflect how you feel about the outcome, put one of the following emojis next to each task you undertook.

😁😃🙂😄🙂😐😮😑😑😖😫😲🙁😠😤

Assigned Task	Results	Assigned Task	Results
Identifying My Variables		10 Cool Ways to Pursue Good Health	
The Unknown Shared Variables		10 Funtastic Food Ideas	
10 Ways to Build Strong Relationships		10 Super-Duper Section C Applications	
10 Entertaining Ideas			

Chapter 5

Social Studies: The Most Important Female in Her Life—You

The 3 R's… Reconnect. Realign. Reinforce.

- ◆ **What You See Is What You Get**
  - ◆ Pop Quiz! Awesome Mom's Learning Style Quiz
  - ◆ Pop Quiz! How Well Do I Know My Awesome Daughter's Learning Style?
  - ◆ Homework: Learning Style Inventory For Awesome Daughters
- ◆ **Applying Your New Knowledge to Life**
- ◆ **Strategies for Strengthening Learning Styles**
  - ◆ Homework: Now That We Know…
- ◆ **7 Mistakes That Diminish Parental Power**
  - ◆ Cutting Parental Power Through Lack of Limits
  - ◆ Reducing Parental Power Via Prolonged Arguments
  - ◆ Weakening Parental Power By Being Your Child's Best Friend
  - ◆ Shrinking Parental Power With Power Struggles
  - ◆ Decreasing Parental Power By Losing Your Temper
  - ◆ Impeding Parental Power Through Conversation Landmines
  - ◆ Sabotaging Parental Power With Non-Conversation Landmines
- ◆ **Your Own Mini-Pep Rally**
- ◆ **How Did You Do?**

Now that you've been bitten by the S.M.A.R.T. Goals bug, and you have the valuable Venn Diagram at your fingertips, all that's left to do is to share your insights with your cherub and get her on board. Does that idea make you hesitate, or possibly cringe? I'm sure it does if your daughter tends to get upset when you least expect it. If her reactions surprise you, it's because you are not on the same page. What better place to examine your social interactions than in *Social Studies Class*?

Social Studies is the study of *social* relationships and the functioning of society. People with different approaches to life have different responses to situations. The problem is the human tendency to look at the world through our own point of view, instead of considering how it appears to other people. We are most compatible with people who have similar personalities, although we are attracted to people who are different from us. There is no problem living with personalities different from your own *if* you understand how to interact with them.

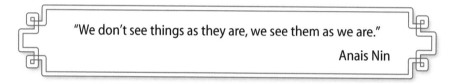

"We don't see things as they are, we see them as we are."

Anais Nin

The first step is to identify your personality characteristics and the impact they have on other people. That knowledge will help you understand how they influence the way you see and interact with your world, and how you form and maintain relationships.

Emotional booby traps can be avoided if you know where they are.

The next step is to identify the personality characteristics of your daughter. Your personality differences will make it obvious why you do not get along… and why you do. It will describe who she is and how she functions in relationships. You will also recognize areas that create a wall between you, and strain your mother/daughter bond. Emotional booby traps can be avoided if you know where they are.

What You See Is What You Get

Do you learn better by reading? By listening? By doing? Do you prefer to have someone demonstrate how to do something, or would you rather try it yourself? Do these preferences enhance or interfere with your relationship with your daughter? If you begin by examining yourself, and then your daughter, you can reveal why those buttons she pushes exist. There is no mystery here. You simply have to understand the reactions you are seeing in her.

May I suggest a personality test? They are easy to do, and most of them are surprisingly accurate. There are dozens of personality tests online, but I happen to have one right here. As a teacher, my old standby is the Learning Styles Inventory (LSI) used in the school systems where I taught. Your particular Learning Style:

- affects everything, both inside the school arena, and out

- is how you take in information

- steers your interpersonal relationships

- colors your belief system

- can be the determining factor of your self-perception, depending on the Learning Styles of the important people in your life

Over the years the LSI has been modified and refined—some versions include a dozen different styles—but I prefer this basic, three-style inventory for the sake of simplicity and ease of application.

Find out what's your strongest Learning Style by taking *The Learning Style Inventory* on the following pages, and answering the questions at the end. Use them to gain clarity about your daughter and yourself, how you each perceive the world, and how you react to each other.

The following quizzes were adapted from *The Learning Style Inventory* used by the Georgia Department of Education.

Pop Quiz! Awesome Mom's Learning Style Quiz

DIRECTIONS: Circle the letter of the choice that best describes you *today*.

1. If I have to learn how to do something, I learn best when:

    a.   I watch someone show me how.

    b.   I hear someone tell me how.

    c.   I try to do it myself.

2. When I read, I often find that:

    a.   I visualize what I am reading in my mind's eye.

    b.   I read aloud or hear those words inside my head.

    c.   I fidget and try to "feel" the content.

3. When asked to give directions:

    a.   I see the actual places in my mind as I say them, or I prefer to draw them.

    b.   I have no difficulty in giving them verbally.

    c.   I have to point or move my body as I go through them.

4. If I am unsure about how to spell a word:

    a.   I write it in order to see how it looks.

    b.   I spell it aloud in order to hear if it sounds right.

    c.   I write it in order to see if it feels right.

5. When I write:

    a.   I am concerned with how neat and well spaced my letters and words appear.

    b.   I often say the letters and words to myself.

    c.   I push hard on my pen or pencil and can feel the flow of the words.

6. If I have to remember a list of items, I remember it best if:

    a. I write them down.
    b. I say them over and over to myself.
    c. I use my fingers to name each item.

7. I prefer teachers who:

    a. use a board or overhead projector while they lecture.
    b. talk with lots of expression.
    c. provide hands-on activities.

8. When trying to concentrate, I have a hard time when:

    a. there is a lot of clutter or movement in the room.
    b. there is a lot of noise in the room.
    c. I have to sit still for any length of time.

9. When solving a problem:

    a. I write or draw diagrams to see it.
    b. I talk myself through it.
    c. I use my entire body or move objects to help me think.

10. When given written instructions on how to build something:

    a. I read them silently and try to visualize how the parts will fit together.
    b. I read them aloud and talk to myself as I put the parts together.
    c. I try to put the parts together first and read directions if I have a problem.

11. To keep occupied while waiting:

    a. I look around, stare, or read.
    b. I talk or listen to others.
    c. I walk around, manipulate things with my hands, or move/bounce my feet as I sit.

12. If I had to verbally describe something to another person:

   a.   I would be brief because I don't like to talk for a long time.
   b.   I would go into great detail.
   c.   I would gesture and move around while talking.

13. If someone was verbally describing something to another person:

   a.   I would try to visualize what I'm hearing.
   b.   I would enjoy listening, but would want to interrupt with my thoughts.
   c.   I would become bored if the description is too long or detailed.

14. When trying to remember people:

   a.   I remember faces but forget names.
   b.   I remember names but forget faces.
   c.   I remember the situation where I met the person rather than the person's name or face.

SCORING DIRECTIONS: Add up the number of responses for each letter and enter the totals below. The area with the highest number of responses is your go-to mode of learning. If your numbers are all close, you can function well in all areas.

Number of A's _____ = My Visual Learner Side

Number of B's _____ = My Auditory Learner Side

Number of C's _____ = My Kinesthetic Learner Side

My Learning Style Summary

My go-to Learning Style:	
My secondary Learning Style:	
I learn really well when:	
I'm going to start strengthening:	

Armed with this understanding about yourself, how does your Learning Style influence relationships when interacting with other adults—in your personal life, your employment life, and social life?

_____

_____

_____

_____

_____

_____

_____

_____

_____

_____

_____

   How well do you know your daughter? Now that you've taken the *Awesome Mom's Learning Styles Quiz* for yourself, pretend you are your daughter and take this quiz.

Pop Quiz! How Well Do I Know My Awesome Daughter's Learning Style?

DIRECTIONS: Circle the letter of the choice that best describes how your daughter will respond to the questions today.

1. If she has to learn how to do something, she learns best when:
   a. she watches someone show her how.
   b. she hears someone tell her how.
   c. she tries to do it herself.

2. When she reads, she often finds that:
   a. she visualizes what she is reading in her mind's eye.
   b. she reads aloud or hears those words inside her head.
   c. she fidgets and tries to "feel" the content.

3. When asked to give directions:
   a. she sees the actual places in her mind as she says them, or she prefers to draw them.
   b. she has no difficulty in giving them verbally.
   c. she has to point or move her body as she goes through them.

4. If she is unsure about how to spell a word:
   a. she writes it in order to see how it looks.
   b. she spells it aloud in order to hear if it sounds right.
   c. she writes it in order to see if it feels right.

5. When my daughter writes:
   a. she is concerned with how neat and well spaced her letters and words appear.
   b. she often says the letters and words to herself.
   c. she pushes hard on her pen or pencil and can feel the flow of the words.

6. If she has to remember a list of items, she remembers it best if:

    a. she writes them down.
    b. she says them over and over to herself.
    c. she uses her fingers to name each item.

7. She prefers teachers who:

    a. use a board or overhead projector while they lecture.
    b. talk with lots of expression.
    c. provide hands-on activities.

8. When trying to concentrate, she has a hard time when:

    a. there is a lot of clutter or movement in the room.
    b. there is a lot of noise in the room.
    c. she has to sit still for any length of time.

9. When solving a problem:

    a. she writes or draw diagrams to see it.
    b. she talks herself through it.
    c. she uses her entire body or moves objects to help her think.

10. When given written instructions on how to build something:

    a. she reads them silently and tries to visualize how the parts will fit together.
    b. she reads them aloud and talks to herself as she puts the parts together.
    c. she tries to put the parts together first and reads directions if she has a problem.

11. To keep occupied while waiting:

    a. she looks around, stares, or reads.
    b. she talks or listens to others.
    c. she walks around, manipulates things with her hands, or moves/bounces her feet as she sits.

12. If she had to verbally describe something to another person:
    a.   she would be brief because she doesn't like to talk for a long time.
    b.   she would go into great detail.
    c.   she would gesture and move around while talking.

13. If someone was verbally describing something to another person:
    a.   she would try to visualize what she's hearing.
    b.   she would enjoy listening, but would want to interrupt with her thoughts.
    c.   she would become bored if the description is too long or detailed.

14. When trying to remember people:
    a.   she remembers faces but forgets names.
    b.   she remembers names but forgets faces.
    c.   she remembers the situation where she met the person rather than the person's name or face.

SCORING DIRECTIONS: Add up the number of responses for each letter and enter the totals below. The area with the highest number of responses is what **you believe** is your daughter's go-to mode of learning. (If the numbers are fairly close, it indicates she can function well in all areas.)

Number of A's _____ = Her Visual Learner Side

Number of B's _____ = Her Auditory Learner Side

Number of C's _____ = Her Kinesthetic Learner Side

Summary of What I Perceive My Daughter's Learning Style To Be

I believe her go-to Learning Style is:	
I believe her secondary Learning Style is:	
I believe she learns really well when:	
I believe she could start strengthening:	

Which of these results make sense to you, and which ones surprised you?

_____

_____

_____

_____

_____

_____

_____

_____

_____

"People only see what they are prepared to see."
Ralph Waldo Emerson

No matter how well you know your daughter, this quiz is only speculation. The next step is to have her take the quiz herself so you can verify your beliefs, or clear up any misconceptions.

Homework: Learning Style Inventory For Awesome Daughters

Before sharing your results, have your daughter take *The Learning Styles Inventory* two times, the first as herself, and the second time pretending to be you. You can find a free printable version for her on my website: **https://AwesomeMomTribe.com/Learning-Style-Inventory/** where you can also find additional resources, books, webinars and info on live events.

Comparing your results is an awesome opportunity for a discussion about your differences and similarities, how they have impacted your relationship to this point, and why disparities don't have to interfere with your relationship anymore.

> *"Many of the truths we cling to depend greatly on our point of view."*
> Obi-Wan Kenobi

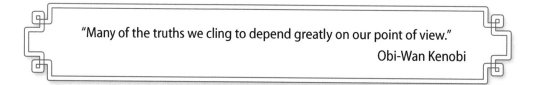

Applying Your New Knowledge to Life

Before you compare your results to your daughter's results, I'd like to point out that this process has already started you both thinking in terms of putting yourself into each other's shoes. That's the path to clarity and understanding, which benefits every relationship.

Let's take a closer look, shall we?

☑ Do This: Are We Compatible?

Find out if your Learning Style is compatible with your daughter's. Write the results of the LSI you took for you, and the LSI she took for her.

My Learning Style:	
My Daughter's Learning Style:	

Do you and your daughter have the same Learning Style? *Congratulations*! You are blessed with a relationship where she reacts the way you expect, and you react the way she expects. You also sport the same weaknesses, but now that you know what they are, you can address them together.

However, if the LSI verifies you and your increasingly volatile daughter differ, you may have just uncovered a fixable source of friction in your home, one that can be eliminated with a little understanding and compassion.

☑ Do This: Reality Check

Now would be a great time to reaffirm your love. Remind her that since you both currently understand what's going on between you, you can work together on your issues as a team, bonded by love. Remind her: Different isn't bad. It's just different.

Your child's Learning Style reflects how she best takes in and processes information, but it affects much more than the mere school realm. As it is with everyone, her Learning Style:

♦ steers her interpersonal relationships

♦ colors her belief system

♦ can be the determining factor in her self-perception

If the important adults in her life (parents, teachers, coaches, etc.) have a Learning Style similar to hers, or if they know to use methods conducive to her "mismatched" style, your child has been flourishing. But, if her history includes criticism about the way she learns and processes, she could privately doubt her own intelligence and ability. You would never know.

Children who fall back on a single dominant Learning Style may feel inadequate when that style doesn't serve them, especially if influential people react negatively to their dissimilarities.

By identifying her strengths and weaknesses, you can help her learn to develop her weaker areas. At the same time, you can build her confidence by emphasizing her stronger areas where her talent lies.

Although her damaged self-esteem may cloud the inherent silver lining, there definitely is one: *By identifying her strengths and weaknesses, you can help her learn to develop her weaker areas. At the same time, you can build her confidence by emphasizing her stronger areas where her talent lies.*

Different isn't bad. It's just different.

How Well Do We Know Each Other?

It's time to look at those second inventories you both took when you pretended to be each other.

My daughter's Actual Learning Style:	My Actual Learning Style:
What I thought my daughter's Learning Style was:	What my daughter thought my Learning Style was:

Important Message To Mothers And Daughters

Don't waste your time being offended if she got you wrong in the quiz. We all view the world through a filter based on who we are. This exercise serves to remove that filter and lets you see each other in the natural light. Moving forward, before you assume how she is going to react or respond or feel or think, and instead of basing it on what makes sense to you, adjust your perception to consider what makes sense to her. Then verify it by asking her if you are right.

How did you and your daughter do when trying to describe each other? Did your results surprise you? You're not alone. At my Mother-Daughter Weekend Retreats for moms and their teenage daughters, they complete a variety of exercises, some similar to the LSI. It's not surprising that the mothers and daughters who shared personality traits typically experience minimal difficulties in their relationship. It also comes as no surprise that things get a bit more challenging when the two females have different personality types.

However, would you have expected these revelations?

♦   Using the tool, the mothers correctly assessed their daughters' personality type and tendencies, even though the results sometimes surprised them.

♦   If the mother and the daughter both had the same traits as each other, they had no problem correctly identifying characteristics in each other.

♦   However, if the mother's and daughter's personalities differed:

   ♦   the mothers could still figure out their daughters.

   ♦   the teenage daughters could *not* figure out their mothers. Not only did the children identify the mom's trait *incorrectly*, but they ended up characterizing the adult's personality as being *the same as their own*.

Good to Know

Do you get the full impact of those findings? Tween/teens process everything through their undeveloped brain. Daughters interpret/misinterpret their mom's actions and reactions through the narrow lens of, "That's what I would do/feel, so that's what she is doing/feeling." When a mom reacts in a manner outside of the daughter's expectations, it damages her perception of her mothers' ability to support her—and thereby decreases her trust in her mom.

What more evidence do you need that the teenage brain provides her with skewed information? (Just remember this when she asks for permission to go to a party. It will make "No" easier for you to say.)

As you begin to recognize how the perception differences between you and your daughter have contributed to your miscommunications, and produced the adolescent angst that *always* (emotional word bomb) seems to be present, it would be a HUGE mistake for you to blame yourself or feel guilty. *You were doing the best you could at the time.*

> If you can change your perception,
> you can change your emotion.
> Edward de Bono

Good to Know

When we purchased a dictation program, I was ready to jump in and use it immediately. While my husband read the directions, I played around with it, poking buttons and clicking links. What we figured out was that when the program produced a word other than the one we dictated, we had to tell it the correct word so it could learn to recognize our voices and our personal speech nuances. The next time the question arose, the program asked for verification. The more we used it, the more it verified, and the more it learned.

You see where I'm going here with this metaphor, right? When your words invoke a prickly response from your daughter, you can learn more about her by asking what caused her reaction. Her answer may clue you in to an approach better suited to her personality. The more you verify, the more opportunities arise to ask questions, and the more you learn about her.

Right now, your current best is being redefined because you are developing new perspectives. I can't stress this enough: It's inappropriate to compare yourself to others, even though the school system (with their rankings and report cards) and the media (with their advertisements and models) have trained you that way since before you were a teenager.

Instead, look at where you've been, and how far you've come, as if you were moving along a continuous path, which you are. We are all on a developmental continuum.

Forget about criticizing how fast you progress. *All* progress, whether baby steps or huge strides, is true progress.

When you are ready to progress faster, you will. Meanwhile, embrace the journey of your self-development, the same journey we are all on, including your tightlipped teen.

"

All progress, whether baby steps or huge strides, is true progress.

„

Share this book with her as evidence that, even though *your* brain has fully developed, you are a Lifelong Learner; and even though she may not know it yet, so is she. Remind her there are amazing, wonderful new opportunities out there, no matter what your age.

Strategies for Strengthening Learning Styles

Have you noticed that different teachers all have different ways of teaching? My individual Teaching Style reflects my personal Learning Style. I teach the way learning makes the most sense to *me*. Students with similar Learning Styles automatically do well in my class because my approach makes sense for the way they learn. The students who differ also do well because I work to insure I include multiple styles of teaching. That way, everyone (including me) learns to find success outside of their comfort zone.

Back in the day, if you ended up with a teacher whose Teaching Style matched your Learning Style, you probably sailed through the class. Unfortunately, pairing a student who receives information one way with a teacher who presents material another way creates a scenario where the student struggles. If the way your student learns is not the way the teacher teaches, it can be more of a challenge.

Suppose your daughter does poorly in a class taught by a teacher whose style is drastically different from hers. Her struggles mess with her self-esteem and her belief in her abilities. When she doesn't feel good about herself, doubt starts eating away at her… so she puts off doing the homework she can't understand… which makes her feel worse… and then she gets in trouble for not having her homework done… and then she feels badly about that… and….

You get the idea.

> Many kids hide their failures from you. They can't bear the idea of seeing disappointment in their parents' eyes.

Many kids take it a step further and hide their failures from you. On top of how badly they feel about themselves, they can't bear the idea of seeing disappointment in their parents' eyes. They want to postpone your finding out about their "secret flaw" for as long as possible. They convince themselves that if you discover what their teenage brain already knows—that they're stupid—then you'll be disillusioned with them… or worse, love them less.

All that unnecessary mess just because she and the teacher have different Learning Styles. It's so sad when a simple conversation can alleviate her youthful misconceptions and the pain they cause.

Don't worry if your daughter and her teacher are a mismatch. The next few pages contain 10 strategies for each of the three Learning Styles to help bridge the gaps impeding with your daughter's success.

Share the techniques that apply to your daughter with her teacher. If you don't feel comfortable doing that, share these ideas with her Guidance Counselor, and ask her/him to talk to her teacher. As unique as your daughter is, there are probably other kids in her class experiencing similar issues. Speaking up will help them, too.

Hey, all good teachers want to figure out the best way for their students to learn.

Your daughter is all set if her mentors (teachers, coaches, etc.) have a similar Learning Style, or if they are schooled in working with different Learning Styles. However, if that's not her situation, here are 30 strategies (adapted from *Learning to Study Through Critical Thinking* by J.A. Beatrice) that can support your daughter at school, or you at work. Don't be concerned if any of the terms are unfamiliar. You can find plenty of information, definitions, and examples on the Internet.

And, the best part? You absolutely can use them to find ways to improve the communication between the two of you.

10 Learning Style Study Strategies for the VISUAL LEARNER

1. Organize work and living space to avoid distractions.

2. Sit in the front of the classroom so you see fewer students; sit away from doors or windows where action takes place; sit away from wall maps or bulletin boards.

3. Use neatly organized or typed material.

4. Allow enough time for planning and recording thoughts when doing problem-solving tasks.

5. Use visual association, visual imagery, written repetition, flash cards, and clustering strategies for improved memory.

6. Participate actively in class or group activities. It helps you remember facts and concepts.

7. Use notepads, sticky notes, to-do lists, and other forms of reminders.

8. Practice turning visual cues back into words as you prepare for exams.

9.   Use organizational outlining for recording notes—underlining, highlighting in different colors, symbols, flowcharts, graphs, or pictures in your notes.

10. Before answering essay questions, develop written or picture outlines of your responses.

10 Learning Style Study Strategies for the AUDITORY LEARNER

1.   Work in quiet areas to reduce distractions, avoiding areas with conversation, music, and television. Sit away from doors or windows where noises may enter the classroom.

2.   Rehearse information aloud so you can hear yourself. Using old exams, first speak your answers and then practice writing your answers.

3.   Discuss topics with other students and teachers. Ask others to hear your understanding of the material for feedback.

4.   Use mnemonic devices, rhymes, jingles, and auditory repetition through tape recording to improve memory. (There are great biology videos on YouTube that use popular songs to explain the systems of the body.)

5.   Examine illustrations in textbooks and convert them into verbal descriptions. Describe them to a Study Buddy.

6.   Use tape recorders to record classes and for reading materials. Use audiobooks when you can. Read your written notes aloud.

7.   Read the directions for tests or assignments aloud, or have someone read them to you, especially if the directions are long and complicated.

8.   Use time managers. Turn written appointment reminders into verbal cues. Put a reminder on your phone or calendar to review details.

9.   Do verbal brainstorming and record it or videotape it so you can listen to it later.

10. Leave spaces in your lecture notes for later recall and clarification (like an extra-wide margin on one side). Expand your notes by talking with others and collecting notes from the textbook.

Learning Style Study Strategies for the KINESTHETIC LEARNER

1. Teach the material to someone else. Keep verbal conversation short and to the point.

2. Actively participate in discussions at school or in study groups.

3. Physical manipulation, imagery, and "hands-on" activities improve your motivation, interest, and memory, so use them.

4. Organize information into the steps you need to physically complete a task.

5. Try to take courses that have laboratories, field trips, and teachers who give real-life examples.

6. Use practice, playacting, and modeling to prepare for tests. Physically move around when solving problems.

7. Don't start a task without instructions. Read or summarize directions, especially if they are long and complicated. Break them into chunks and do them a section at a time.

8. Using audio reading materials, listen while you read.

9. Ask your teacher if you can be allowed to do physical movement and have periodic breaks during tests, while reading, or while composing written assignments. Just don't distract anyone else.

10. Role-play the exam situation. Practice sitting and writing for the same length of time as the exam is going to be. Write out practice answers, paragraphs, or essays.

With a little ingenuity, incompatibilities between Teaching Styles and Learning Styles can be resolved.

But wait! There's more!

Don't be surprised if you found a few ideas for yourself from the list of strategies. Some of those strategies might be just what you need to relate better to your world, and to your daughter. Your relationship is your daughter's most important female bond, and she needs you to figure this out.

Let's move this Learning Styles concept out of the classroom, where it's traditionally used, and bring it into your home. The way we look at the world is filtered by our Learning Style, as is the way we form connections with other people, how we interact with people, and how we receive information from people.

Your relationship is your daughter's most important female bond.

If you and your daughter have different Learning Styles, then the expectations you have for each other may be incorrect. You are basing your predictions of her reactions on what makes sense to *you,* and the way *you* react… and she is doing the same, but from *her* younger perspective.

When *her* action or reaction is unexpected, you as the parent begin to wonder whether or not you know her as well as you think you do. It makes you suspicious and interferes with your trust.

When *your* actions or reactions are unexpected to your daughter, they alarm her because she can't tell why you are upset, or what's going on. Based on her understanding of the world, what you say and do may feel unreasonable to her. When it's not working, it unnerves her and can lead to the crumbling of trust… all because you simply have different Learning Styles.

Homework: Now That We Know…

No relationship is perfect when it involves two or more people, so don't expect yours to be. And, don't be afraid to look at the conflicts so you can talk through them. Ask your daughter to come up with 5-10 memories where you clashed because of your different styles. Separately, you do the same. Come together and share them.

Ooh! Ooh! Put them into a versatile ***Venn Diagram***! It will be a real eye-opener to see which incidents stand out in her mind, and which ones impacted you more.

Select a mutual incident from ***Section C***. Together, find a couple of strategies from the ***Strategies for Strengthening Learning Styles*** section and create a couple of alternatives you could have used during the incident. Make a commitment to employ one of the strategies this week. Being proactive will empower both of you and fortify your relationship.

Do: Be enlightened by her list. She is sharing incidences that impacted her, irrespective of how they impacted you. There is no offense intended.

Don't: Past events are colored memories at best. Don't contradict (I didn't say/do that!) what she shares. It's her memory of how she was impacted.

7 Mistakes That Diminish Parental Power

Have you ever witnessed a parent yelling at their kids in public? My personal favorite is, "If you do that again, I'm going to make you wait in the car!" C'mon, ma'am. Everyone knows you're not going to abandon your shopping cart to drag your growling girl outside. And, she knows it, too, because she doesn't stop her objectionable behavior. *I* know it because I already heard you say it five times.

Who is in control of the situation between you and your kids? What if, over the years, the power in your household has actually shifted? There's an easy way to tell. How often do you feel like hollering at your youngsters?

> Losing your temper is the number one most obvious sign you're struggling for power.

Losing your temper is the number one most obvious sign you're struggling for power. If you still had the power, you would be in control and feeling calm. Once you lose your power, you will also lose your ability to guide your daughter. When you can't enforce household rules, you can't insure her safety.

Your daughter needs you to be in control because without you, she won't have anyone to guide her through her own angst. Without a strong role model to respect and follow, she'll feel isolated and uncertain, even when you're in the same room.

Despite your best intentions, there are too many external and internal pressures impacting your relationship for everything to run smoothly all the time:

- ◆ hormonal swings
- ◆ how consumed foods affect mood
- ◆ how consumed ideas affect outlook
- ◆ illness, tragedy
- ◆ critical or mean people

When your daughter loses faith in your ability to understand her, she also loses trust in you and your ability to advise her or guide her. As her trust is whittled away, she feels anxious at having to negotiate the world alone.

This lack of trust underlies every noisy exhalation and every slammed door. They are expressions of her fear that you can't help her, and that she is on her own.

Let's face it, even with the best-laid plans in place, there are always going to be struggles, clashes, and problems. But you *can* help her. Establishing procedures and policies, *and then sticking to them*, will help you regain your power, and rebuild her trust.

> Establishing procedures and policies, *and then sticking to them*, will help you regain your power, and rebuild her trust.

A natural fluctuating balance exists between parents and children. As time goes by, children mature… and parents mature. The children are supposed to learn to take control of their own lives (i.e., the growing-up process), little by little. Meanwhile, the parents have to figure out how to dispense that control in doses their children can handle.

This would be a great time to investigate things that undermine this very important process. Would you like some help recognizing areas that compromise your position while the power struggles are still minor? Here are six typical behavioral patterns that can reduce your parental control. And, of course, I also provide solutions to help you get back on track.

1. Cutting Parental Power Through Lack of Limits

Some families want to encourage their kids to share in the family decision-making. True, it's a great way to help them learn how to be independent and deal with larger issues. However, if not handled correctly, the children may come to believe they have an equal say in *everything* that the parents have a say in. The authority lines become blurred, and the kids develop an inappropriate sense of entitlement.

Problems also arise if your role is not clear to *you*, and if you are inconsistent in your communications to your daughter. She will feel uncomfortable if your parameters keep changing.

Wouldn't you?

If you do decide to let your daughter chime in, **these four areas should be off-limits, and should not ever be up for debate:**

- **her safety**
- **her health**
- **her performance at school**
- **anything that prepares her for life as an adult**

These are the areas that require a view of the big picture; something the teenage Immediate-Satisfaction Brain is not capable of handling responsibly, especially if there's a more appealing agenda calling her.

☑ Do This: Reclaim Your Rightful Role

You must clarify two types of limits for yourself:

1. the discussion roles of the parent (you), and the child (your daughter)

2. which topics your child is allowed to debate (what to wear to school, dying her hair, decorating her room, etc.) and which ones are not up for discussion, (curfews, allocating chores, putting homework first, etc.)

Let the kids know that while they may have a limited voice in what is discussed, *they do not make the decisions.* Decision-making is the job of the person in charge, the parent, i.e., *You.* Remind her that making these decisions is your job as her mom, and as the ranking grown-up in the room.

———◆———

For topics you deem negotiable, you can use the venerable *Venn Diagram* to exchange ideas. I actually used a Venn Diagram regarding eating at buffets. Our initial conflict stemmed from my daughter being dazzled by the array of choices (aren't we all?) and aggravated by the limits I wanted to impose. We used a Venn Diagram to select the foods she could eat, and because *Section C* only contained foods she liked, she did not fuss when I told her these *Buffet Rules*:

- You have to eat everything you put on your plate before you can get more, which means take small amounts in case it tasted differently than expected.

- You can return to the buffet as many times as you like, provided you eat what you took the last time.

- Every plateful you bring from the buffet has to be 50% green (veggies and salad), including the dessert round.

These rules, which pertain to healthy choices, served to teach her moderation in the face of unlimited offerings. They also kept her calorie count down and her fiber intake up, despite the varied concoctions of fat, salt, and sugar. And, of course I benefited as well because I had to model the behavior I wanted her to adopt, which provided me with the same benefits.

2. Reducing Parental Power Via Prolonged Arguments

Your daughter will want to discuss/debate/argue about any decision that doesn't suit her desires. If you change your mind the fourth time she brings it up, you are teaching her to bring it up four times so she can get her way. If you hold out until her fifth attempt, then five tries becomes her personal sweet spot.

☑ Do This: Hold the Line

Remind her before the decision is made—even before the discussion starts—that any follow-up discussion won't be held until 24 hours later. That will give everyone time to calm down and rethink their positions. However, it does *not* mean the decision will be changed. She is merely allowed to resume the conversation the next day. Reiterate that she does not participate in the actual decision-making.

Don't worry. She'll get used to this policy after you learn to enforce it.

⟫◆⟪

Suppose, for example, you've told her she can't attend an unsupervised party. Her anger escalates as she argues, but you stand firm.

Say This: "Like I told you before this discussion began, we can revisit this tomorrow if you still want to discuss *future* parties, but I've made my decision about this one."

That reminds me of a story...

My daughter's middle school was small, so the dances were held for 5th-8th grade. Anyone who's been around kids knows a 10-year-old and a 14-year-old should not be together in a setting where there is slow dancing. When I asked if there would be parental chaperones, the administration said no, because they didn't want the students to feel inhibited.

Really?

I was actually perfectly fine with my budding femme fatale feeling inhibited around those older boys, so I nixed the dance. Over the next week, my previously sane daughter:

- blew up at me
- tried to get Daddy on her side
- sat down to have a "grown-up" discussion with me
- obtained phone numbers of her friend's parents who had already given their daughters permission to go
- sat down for a "grown-up" discussion with Daddy
- sat Daddy and me down for a group discussion
- blew up at us both
- wrote us notes about how we were ruining her life
- broke into tears at dinner while arguing about the dance

You have to admire her perseverance. She was very resolute.

But, we stood firm. I kept telling her the decision was already made, but she was welcome to discuss it. Anytime she lost her temper, I halted the discussion, but invited her back when she cooled off.

Throughout it all, I remained cool, calm, and collected, because I had a plan.

I'm just kidding. It took all my patience to not blow up at her the twentieth time she brought it up. Behind closed doors, my husband and I wondered whether we were being overly cautious. Actually, he wondered. I worried. By the time the dance came, I was worn out, but we hadn't given in.

Came the Monday following the dance and the juicy gossip about what she had missed. After school, she told me stories about the embarrassing things the older boys had done to the younger kids, and, for a brief moment, she was glad she had not been there. For a much, much longer moment, I was glad I hadn't wavered.

I continued to stick to my guns, despite the wailing and debates, until she reached eighth grade. That year, since she would be among the oldest in the crowd, I told her she'd be allowed to attend the dances. Her response?

"Nah. I don't like what goes on there. They let the boys grind up on the girls."

My response? "Oh, okay. Whatever you decide."

My internal reaction? *Score one for the Awesome Mom team! Score another one for the Awesome Daughter team!* Call me old-fashioned, but I still don't believe 10 to 14-year-olds have any business grinding their bodies together to the Top Forty Hits in a dimly lit gym.

The bonus benefit is that because I held the line about preteen/tween dances, it came as no surprise when I drew a line regarding other issues as my tenacious teen got older. As time went by, her attempts to engage me in a verbal marathon all but disappeared.

Call me old-fashioned but I don't believe 10 to 14-year-olds have any business grinding their bodies together to the Top Forty Hits in a dimly lit gym.

3. Weakening Parental Power By Being Your Child's Best Friend

Note: Before you react negatively to this topic, don't confuse having a great relationship with your daughter with being her BFF (Best Friend Forever).

Some moms mistakenly buy into the impossible myth that being their daughter's Bestie or BFF during the teen years will foster communication and trust. True BFFs are supposed to be on equal ground, but the power imbalance between an adult woman and a female child prevents that from actually happening.

- You are responsible for her welfare and well-being; she is not supposed to be responsible for yours.

- You are her protector; she is not supposed to be your protector.

- You have a fully developed brain; she doesn't.

- You are not the same age so you don't experience issues the same way.

- You are not peers with similar experiences. You are decades older.

BFF Moms and their daughters have fun together just like BFF adolescents would, *as long as the daughter gets her way*. The BFF Mom doesn't want to do anything to jeopardize their relationship, so to avoid confrontations, she doesn't enforce deadlines or limits. Then she makes excuses for her daughter's negative behavior.

Adult roles and child roles get confused when discipline decisions are based on not upsetting the child. Bribing, cajoling, distracting, and caving in serve to keep momentary peace only. The small child who never hears, "No," also never learns how to handle "No" in a graceful and emotionally strong way. Instead, she is taught that in order to receive the reward, she must initiate and/or escalate her tantrum. It may be wearying for her, but in the long run, it pays off.

> Stand your ground until she wears out. Be loving, kind, and firm, but *do not give in*. You put that rule into place for a reason, and all the tantrums in the world will not change that reason.

When her daughter's inability to cope with disappointment produces rude behavior, the BFF Mom blames outside factors (She's just overtired. Her friends are letting her down. She gets cranky when she hasn't eaten.), and thereby teaches her dictator daughter to do the same. Unfortunately, the girl never gets to experience the power brought by taking responsibility for her actions, something that would serve her well as an adult.

Being your kid's best friend means you are robbing her of the opportunity to form and navigate a significant relationship with friends her own age. Figuring out life with an equally clueless teenage girlfriend provides a unique set of experiences that she will miss if her mother has inserted herself into that role.

☑ Do This: Be the Adult/Mother/Protector

Being a mother comes with great responsibility that a child simply cannot comprehend. But, guess what? I'm not saying you can't ever be *Besties*, because you can… when your daughter is married and has kids of her own. Until then, she won't fully understand your world.

For right now, you have to protect and nurture her. A protector cannot be the best friend. It must always be clear that you are the adult, and you make the decisions. Treat your daughter with love, respect, and care, but as her mother, *not* as her best friend.

Most of all, you have to be brave. When you say, "No," because your adored adolescent wants to cross a forbidden line, be prepared to weather the storm. It can't last forever. Stand your ground until she wears out. Be loving, kind, and firm, but *do not give in*. You put that rule into place for a reason, and all of the tantrums in the world won't change that reason.

As the adult/mother/protector, you can listen respectfully to what she has to say, and when she's done venting, you can give advice that reinforces the limits you have set.

Then, you have chocolate… or hang out, or go have some fun. After all, just because you're not BFFs doesn't mean you can't have fun together or share your innermost thoughts and feelings. You can still get mani's-and-pedi's together. You can still discuss boys together. You can still grow together. Just don't give up your power. Your daughter needs you to stay empowered.

Good to Know

The difference between being her *BFF* and being her *Awesome Mom*:

Being her BFF: You hold her hair back while she barfs from drinking too much alcohol at a party. (Although, a teen BFF would probably be too grossed out.)

Being her Awesome Mom: You might do the same thing, but it's followed by a lecture and consequences.

She doesn't need you to be her BFF. More than anything else, she needs you to be her Awesome Mom.

4. Shrinking Parental Power With Power Struggles

Power struggles never work. If you are fighting with each other, there will be casualties, either you, or her.

Every argument between moms and their daughters constitutes a power struggle. How you navigate arguments is key, because power struggles never work. If you are fighting with each other, there will be casualties, either you, or her.

This point is so important that we're revisiting it. If your current mode of arguing produces a winner and a loser, it will also produce a wall between you and your daughter. There are only two possible outcomes from a power struggle between you and your daughter, and both are negative.

1. **She wins**… which means she takes away your power. Who wants that? It will not make her feel truly empowered; trust me on this one. It will ultimately serve to make her feel confused and lost, and resentful that you are no longer in charge. Mostly it makes her even angrier with you because you let her force you into a weaker position instead of remaining a resilient role model. *She needs you to have your power.* Taking it away removes the safeguards between her and the world. That's frightening for a child who is not ready to live on her own.

    So, what's the outward portrayal of inner fear? Anger. Loud, tearful, door-slamming, name-calling anger. Everything feels permanent to girls, so expect her explosion to be nuclear if it's fueled by her fear that she's burned her bridge to you. That emotional eruption is a clear demonstration of panic. Girls don't understand that anger blows over, and that relationships survive moments of pain. Girls hold grudges, and believe everyone else does, too. When she wins a power struggle with a fight, she can't judge the damage she's created, and it's very scary for her.

2. **You win**… which means you've beaten down your childish cherub. When a daughter loses a fight with her mother, the adult has emotionally coerced her and taken her sense of power… and her trust. The child never feels valued in a relationship when she loses her power.

Nobody wants that. We want to raise empowered young women who won't be coerced into decisions by outsiders. We want our girls to use their power for good, to move through life with confidence. When you beat her in a Power Struggle, she loses that. You may have won the battle, but war still wages.

Power Struggles need to be diffused, not won. Ultimately nobody benefits when producing a winner and/or a loser because it deteriorates the quality of your relationship. Instead, an Awesome Mom helps her wondrous warrior join their team, where together they build the tools and skills to do battle in the world, and not war against each other.

Power struggles need to be diffused, not won.

There are no winners or losers between a mother and daughter when you are on the same team. Instead of focusing on winning your dispute, convey the importance of making your family unit stronger; or zero in on how improving communication will ultimately increase trust between you two.

☑ Do This: Team Up To Win

Let's change the approach. Instead of perceiving Power Struggles as being between parent and child, realize the opposing force is not your child. The Power Struggle is actually between your parent-child bond, versus the never-ending hurdles fabricated by the world. The true opposition?

- ◆ *The Inevitables*—those unavoidable, looming situations (extending curfew, crushes, necklines, going out with friends, etc.)

- ◆ *The Possibles*—those situations typical of teenage life that may or may not happen to your Adventurous Angel (sleepovers, dating, dances, etc.)

Awesome Moms and Awesome Daughters belong on the same team, one that allows them to face what life brings—together.

—◆◆◆—

Present this concept to your daughter. If you frame it right, she'll enjoy the "Us against Them" approach. Still, the occasion may arise when when she gets upset about not getting her way,

💬 **Say This:** "This is not the way I want us to behave with each other. How about you? I love you, no matter what. We are on the same team. Let's find a better way to communicate."

———◆———

When kids argue with parents, what's at stake for them is not merely the debated topic. It's much more. They want the parent to acknowledge their growing maturity, their admirable capability, and their human value.

When you are at an impasse about a limit you have set, like bedtime,

☑ **Do This: Research is Your Friend**

Instead of allowing the conversation to deteriorate to, "Because I said so!" invite your teen to show you research that supports her point of view. Arrange to have the discussion on the weekend so you, too, will have time to find information that supports your side.

Remind your child that, as the parent, the decision is ultimately yours, but you are open to learning more. Also, state that you will come to a decision by the following weekend, after you've had time to consider new facts. That will give you some breathing room.

In the ensuing discussion, both of you share your information, and talk about what it reveals. Make sure you listen and consider what she brings to the table. Tell your young researcher, regardless what decision you reach, how impressed you are with how she handled the process.

———◆———

Good to Know

This research method gives your touchy teen what she craves: respect, value, admiration, and empowerment. She will better understand you and your view, but more importantly, she will feel like you understand her. If you use this routine repeatedly, she will come to expect it, and will broach contentious subjects in a less antagonistic way.

This is also a great platform for demonstrating the importance of vetting sources of information for authenticity, especially in this world of fake news. (That last bit is from the teacher in me.)

5.   Decreasing Parental Power By Losing Your Temper

Losing your temper is like having a neon sign above you blinking, "I've Lost Control. I've Lost Control." Your daughter is fully aware of this. How? Because less than a decade ago she was flinging herself, kicking and screaming, into a rack of women's clothing. Okay, maybe that was my toddler's tantrum, but if your darling diva has ever had a *pre*-preschool tantrum or two, she recognizes the emotion that goes with losing her temper.

☑ **Do This:** Nip It In The Bud

The trick here is to pick a fallback strategy to employ *before* her temper ignites your own. Interrupt the interaction the minute you detect the slightest bit of heat in the discussion, or when she stonewalls you. You could try something like the old ***Step Back and Come Back Intervention***, or firmly raising your voice (not yelling or screaming) *before* you feel upset.

There is a difference between yelling with a loss of temper, and employing your raised voice as an audible exclamation point. The latter can be used as a calculated move to focus her attention while you still have your control intact. That's completely different from flying off the handle in anger and losing your power.

⊰─◆─⊱

Remember how the teachers who couldn't control their class would yell a lot? And how eventually it all became ineffectual background noise? They had lost their power.

If you lose your temper repeatedly, it becomes background noise for your daughter. You understand that kind of background noise if you have ever been in a store, listening to a child say, "Mom. Mom. Mom. Mom. Mom. Mom. Mom. Mom," and for some reason, Mom doesn't notice her at all (although it irritates *me* to no end). Her child's voice has become background noise for her. I don't pass judgment, though. Usually, that's a symptom of a worn down mom who needs some support.

If yelling has become background noise in your relationship, employing an alternative, like the good ol' ***Step Back and Come Back Intervention***, will surprise her into paying attention. That doesn't mean you can't raise your voice for emphasis to get your daughter's attention, especially if you still have your control intact. A well-placed holler can help make your point and may prevent an issue from spiraling out of control. But, beware. An ill-placed bellow can also inflame the discussion, especially if you are prone to losing your temper… and your power.

That reminds me of a story…

I never lost my temper with my students, but I had no qualms about *pretending* to lose my temper. Sometimes I used a strategically placed yell to wield control over unusual circumstances… like the first time "Fight! Fight!" gleefully echoed in the hallway, prompting a dozen butts to shoot out of their collective seats.

I mustered all my strength and shouted, *"Sit Down!"* as loudly as I could.

Shocked by my "outburst," they literally froze in their tracks, mouths open and eyes wide with astonishment. I wish I could have taken a picture. It was all I could do to maintain my frown when every fiber of my being wanted to belly laugh. If I had been a teacher who yelled all the time, my yell would not have impacted my students the way it did.

6. Impeding Parental Power Through Conversation Landmines

Despite your best intentions to hold a calm, neutral, nonjudgmental discussion with your daughter, there may be hidden landmines embedded in the landscape of your conversation. These are habitual words used so routinely, the speaker doesn't hear them. However, the listener does, and they push her buttons.

☑ Do This: Tracking Landmines Before They Explode

Certain words betray the exasperation/frustration/lack of coping, even when the speaker is striving for impartiality. Identifying verbal landmines is the first step to neutralizing their effect.

Beware of innocent trigger words that can produce an adverse emotion, not because of what's going on currently, but because the word has been used negatively at a time when the conversation was heated. Watch out for words like:

- always
- constantly
- never
- no one/nobody
- don't ever
- still
- everyone/everybody
- every time

Let's not forget the irritating single-word responses (Sure. Right. Yeah. Okay.). Are they merely habit, or are they attempts to block or end the conversation? Just like military landmines indicate unrest in the area, these conversation landmines indicate emotional angst. Your verbal landmines may push her buttons, triggering responses that take you completely by surprise. If you notice when you use them, you can head off emotional explosions.

———◆◆◈———

Identifying your daughter's landmines can help you identify why sometimes you react to what she says, and sometimes you don't. If you notice when they are occurring, you can keep your buttons from being pushed, and head off your own emotional reactions.

Verbal landmines can also be a key to understanding your child. When she says *always* or *never*, that's code for "I'm aggravated" or "I feel powerless." When she feels that way, your discussion is at risk.

> **Good to Know**
>
> Word bombs in her conversation:
> ◆ "You *always* say that!"
> ◆ "You *never* let me do what the other kids are doing."
>
> Word bombs in your conversation:
> ◆ "You're *always* late!"
> ◆ "You *never* clean your room!"

Once we understand the negative power of these conversation bombs, we can diffuse them if they escape our lips, or when we hear them.

☑ Do This: Diffusing Landmines

Explain the concept of Conversation Landmines to your acerbic adolescent. Challenge her to a contest to see who can count the most landmines used over the course of one evening, but don't pay attention to who says what. You can keep track by dropping coins into a single jar, *but don't keep score as to who drops more word bombs*. You want to be on the same team, not opposing each other. If you are feeling brave, extend it over a weekend.

Warning: Don't let aggravation build. Stop this exercise if anyone feels picked on.

What other landmines are typically scattered through your speech? Think about it. Ask your daughter. I expect she'll be able to come up with a few more. I find it quite enlightening to have my triggers pointed out by my daughter.

Okay, so truthfully it's really irritating, but it's still enlightening.

After you get an idea of how often the verbal landmines crop up when you two talk, tell her you would like to get out of the habit of using landmine words. Suggest pausing the conversation long enough to identify the underlying emotion associated with the use of the landmine. It will make your communication more direct and clear.

———◆———

 Say This: "When you say [insert word bomb], I feel [insert your reaction]. How were you feeling when you said that? I don't think you meant for the conversation to turn negative. Let's try that again."

And, acknowledge any word bomb you dropped that your daughter points out.

 Say This: "When I said [insert word bomb], I was feeling [insert your reaction]. How did that make you react inside? That wasn't my intention. I'd like to try that again."

———◆———

7. Sabotaging Parental Power With Non-Conversation Landmines

Unfortunately, we also have to deal with the silent but deadly conversation landmine: Incongruent Body Language. Verbal messages can be obscured by contradictory behavior. Your expression may convey one thing, but your words say another. *Boom!* Hidden Landmine.

In the 1990s, the pioneering work of social scientist Dr. Albert Mehrabian in nonverbal communication (body language) revealed that when someone is talking about her feelings and attitudes, the actual words have only a 7% effect on the listener. The largest communication impact, about 55%, comes from facial expressions, and another 38% impact comes from the tone of voice.

> Your tone of voice and face rivet her attention, not your message.

Yes, 93% of your communication is *not* your words. Your message, strategy, argument, clarification—whatever it is— is shrouded by the emotions you convey. When you and your daughter are discussing your relationship, your facial expressions dominate the conversation, followed closely by your tone of voice. That's why she doesn't hear a word you say when you are angry and yelling. Your tone of voice and face rivet her attention, not your message.

That's also why your daughter's communication to you gets lost during *her* tirades.

On top of that, if you'll recall the work by Ekman and Friesen from the **Science Class** chapter, teenagers only have about a 50% chance of correctly interpreting your expression anyway. That just further complicates things.

Imagine yourself trying to convey confidence that your new strategy is going to help the two of you move forward. However, while you tell her about it, your arms are tightly clasped over your chest, or you are nervously lighting a cigarette, or you're reaching for a drink. Do you see how all of these actions silently undermine your message?

☑ Do This: Prepare!

If it helps, write your message out ahead of time. In case you get rattled, you can always read off the paper. Tell her why you wrote it down, that you want to insure you don't leave out anything important. Rehearse what you are going to say. Imagine what would be her typical responses, and prepare for them.

That reminds me of a story…

When I was a new teacher, I was asked to do a presentation at a faculty meeting. I was sooo nervous. Speaking in front of kids was easy, but adults? Although I practiced in front of a mirror, I couldn't generate the sensation of standing before my peers. I knew I'd be nervous, despite my preparation, and I didn't know how to hide it. So, I didn't.

When I got up there, the first thing I said was, "It turns out I'm comfortable getting up in front of students, but this is the first time I've spoken to adults. Instead of trying to hide my nervousness, I'm just going to tell you I'm nervous, and get on with it."

My audience laughed and applauded, and like magic, I had my power back.

Don't hide your anxiety. If you feel nervous initiating a discussion with an emotional teen, talk about it as part of your discussion. Make sure she understands you are reclaiming your role as the adult in this relationship, and then get on with it. Explain you are willing to weather the storm in order to keep her safe, healthy, and productive because you love her.

As you use these methods, they will come easier over time. Each conversation serves as more practice for the new habits you are trying to form. For her, repetition will lead to predictability. In turn, that will make her feel more secure about where she stands with you, and where the boundaries are to the envelope she's been pushing.

Note: She will understand your determination *over time*, not over one conversation.

I made sure my daughter learned early on she wasn't going to get her way through anger. I *never* allowed her emotional eruptions to change my mind, even if I considered her request to be reasonable. If the truth be told, I was just being plain obstinate, a snarky reaction to her outburst—which turned out to be a very effective response. Over time, she figured out her chances of winning me over increased exponentially if the discussion didn't deteriorate.

> When your precious girl stands before you, wearing her anger like it's her superpower, you don't have to react in kind.

You, too, can train your daughter to talk instead of yell. Personally, when someone yells at me, I tend to mentally withdraw to a safe distance. I hear my daughter's words much better without her emotional blasts. She knows this and tries to control her temper.

Knowing what you know now, both of you can adjust how you interact… that means you need to share this with her before your next argument. When your precious girl stands before you, wearing her anger like it's her superpower, you don't have to react in kind. Try to see past the message her body language is blasting at you, and instead, focus on the content of her words.

Say This: "I think you are trying to say _____, but your anger/attitude is distracting me from hearing you. Let's step away for 10 minutes to calm down and try again. I really want to understand what you mean."

Yup, *Step Back and Come Back* comes to the rescue again.

Your Own Mini-Pep Rally

By analyzing your relationship, and studying how you socialize and interact with your daughter, you can anticipate and head off problems between the two of you, creating an environment of trust and respect. Have faith. Time, patience, and consistency will keep your awesome relationship running smoothly. You can do it!

Now, march down to your daughter's room, fling open the door, and give a cheer!

I won't give up.
I won't be whipped.
I'll stay focused
On this relationship!

How Did You Do?

To reflect how you feel about the outcome, put one of the following emojis next to each task you undertook.

Assigned Task	Results	Assigned Task	Results
Awesome Mom's Learning Style Quiz		Hold the Line	
How Well Do I Know My Awesome Daughter's Learning Style?		Be the Adult/Mother/Protector	
Learning Style Inventory For Awesome Daughters		Team Up To Win	
Are We Compatible?		Research is Your Friend	
Reality Check		Nip It In The Bud	
How Well Do We Know Each Other?		Tracking Landmines Before They Explode	
Now That We Know		Diffusing Landmines	
Reclaim Your Rightful Role		Prepare!	

Chapter 6

Health Class: Sex, Drugs, Rock & Roll, And...

The 3 R's... Reexamine. Rectify. Reclaim.

- **The Example You Set**
- **Semester 1: Sex, Drugs, and Rock & Roll**
  - **SEX**, Drugs, and Rock & Roll
  - Sex, **DRUGS**, and Rock & Roll
    - ◇ Homework: Assessing Your White Stuff
  - Sex, Drugs, and **ROCK & ROLL**
- **Semester 2: Models, Media, and Belly Roll**
  - **MODELS**, Media, and Belly Roll
  - Models, **MEDIA**, and Belly Roll: The Media's Influence On You
  - Models, **MEDIA**, and Belly Rolls: The Media's Influence On Her
  - Models, Media, and **BELLY ROLLS**
  - 7 Ways to Tame the Obesity Beast
    - ◇ Homework: Nutrition by the Numbers
- **Your Own Mini-Pep Rally**
- **How Did You Do?**

The Collins Dictionary Of Medicine defines "health education" as being concerned with:

- ◆ personal hygiene

- ◆ cleanliness

- ◆ exercise of body and mind

- ◆ good menu

- ◆ care of the skin and hair

- ◆ avoiding health hazards such as

    - ◆ smoking

    - ◆ excessive drinking

    - ◆ and the abuse of drugs

If you are not living your life within compliance of this definition, you are sending the message to your daughter that something on the list is not important for her. Remember, she models herself after you, so her future is affected by your present-day choices.

I've encountered former healthy-looking students now walking around with so much extra weight, I can hardly recognize them. They are living lives that mimic their parents, eating unhealthy foods and not engaging in physical activity. According to the 2009 Almanac of Chronic Disease, almost 80% of our workforce is afflicted by a chronic disease.

Only 20 out of 100 of my precious students will be healthy? That's heartbreaking in the face of their youth, their energy, and their belief in the great things in store for them.

As a teacher, that frightening statistic is a forewarning of how my students will be spending their adult lives… chronically sick. **Only 20 out of 100 of my precious students will be healthy?** That's heartbreaking in the face of their youth, their energy, and their belief in the great things in store for them.

Thanks to my husband, our daughter grew up in an active household. Today, even though the demands of work and life make it more challenging for her to stay active, she is always uncomfortable if she goes too long without movement in her life, and returns to it as soon as she can.

I, on the other hand, was not raised in an active household. However, when my daughter was a toddler, and I was in my early thirties, I realized the way I was raised had sentenced me to watch from the sidelines instead of participating in family activities. Right then and there, I made the conscious decision to get moving, and to make it a permanent lifestyle change. That's right. I made activity part of my everyday life, so my daughter grew up with an awesome strong female role model.

Do I stick to my movement commitment religiously? Nope, but I try. Even though I became a certified Personal Trainer, to this day I have to hire a trainer to keep me accountable for my workouts. I can spend months working out with her, with no additional exercise (an unfortunately common scenario when I'm working on a book). But that's my compromise until my schedule opens back up. Then I resume the habit of regular, daily activity.

The point is, regardless of how you were raised, you can change your stars. With a concerted effort, you can model the behavior you want in your daughter's life, like incorporating healthy activity into day-to-day living, or healthy eating, or anything you think is important! You just need to begin moving, and then do it whenever you can until it becomes a habit. If you don't, then she won't... and you will be sentencing her to join the 80% chronically ill workforce. Your darling girl deserves better than that.

> Regardless of how you were raised, you can change your stars.

In the *History Class* chapter, you took an objective look at your younger self, and how your past decisions still impact your mother-daughter relationship today. It's time to look at where you are now health-wise, and how the current-day-you influences your daughter. This *Health Class* goes for two semesters. *Semester 1* covers the classic *Sex, Drugs, and Rock & Roll*, and then we'll finish up with *Semester 2* and the less familiar, *Models, Media, and Belly Roll*.

The Example You Set

Your glorious girl wants to experience life as you presently live it, and her teenage brain makes her want it *NOW*. She wants your high heels, your makeup, your perfume, your confidence, your maturity. She wants it all.

That's right. She wants to be *you*!

You are the living, breathing model your daughter has been shadowing since she

> " What you say and do matters. *Always.* "

could sit up. Are you living a life that sets the right example? If you are a *Sex, Drugs, and Rock & Roll* kind of gal, or a *Models, Media, and Belly Roll* kind of gal, remember: She wants to be like you. If you live it, she wants to try it for herself.

What you say and do matters. *Always.* The "Do As I Say, Not As I Do" philosophy simply does not work. Such ambiguous sentiment teaches her you don't actually believe in the "Do As I Say" part. The contradiction only serves to make you appear weak and unreliable. Losing your power that way is not the position you are striving for, especially if you want her to respect your decisions and follow the rules in your home.

When you don't live the example you want her to follow, you teach her to reach for the same alternatives you reach for. There has never been a small child (including you) who said, "I want to be an alcoholic when I grow up," nor a middle-schooler who said, "I want to be a binge eater when I'm an adult." And, you'll never find a high-schooler who'll say, "Mom, I want to be overworked and stressed 24/7 when I'm your age." If any of these types of toxic shifts have crept into your lifestyle, *everyone* knows these were not your original intentions.

The person you are now is the sum total of your experiences. You are a product of the

> " The situation in which you find yourself today is the result of outside influences on your decisions, and *it is not your fault.* "

environment in which you were raised, and all the decisions made by the people raising you, whether good decisions or stupid ones. You imitated the examples modeled for you as a child, believed the barrage of commercials targeting you all your life, and tried to fit in with your peers, who were victims of their own circumstances.

Let me be perfectly clear. It's important to realize you had no control over those conditions. The situation in which you find yourself today is the result of outside influences on your decisions, and *it is not your fault.*

But, now you are aware, and it's impossible to return to being unaware. This is the point where you have to look at how your lifestyle affects your family. It's time to answer the hard questions…

- How are you going to live out the rest of your life?

- How do you want your daughter to live out hers?

- Are you going to be an active grandma, or a bed-ridden one?

- Are you going to choose to make changes to your lifestyle, or are you going to allow outside influences dictate your life… and your daughter's future?

If you want your beloved daughter to be healthy and make her own sound decisions, you have to walk the walk, and talk the talk. That probably includes making a few changes for the better.

As a mother and a teacher who had to juggle 90+ kids every school day, if there was one thing I learned over the years, it's that I need energy to power through my day. And, so do you, Awesome Mom. So do you.

If you want to be able to get up every morning, greeting the day with positive energy, you must tighten up your lifestyle and embrace some kind of regular physical activity. After all, you're not done, not yet. You are in the middle of your own journey. You've still got several more decades to go.

I'm a proud LL— that's a Lifelong Learner. My journey will never be completed because there is always something more to discover. It's part of my Awesome Philosophy to keep moving, improving, and exploring this incredible opportunity called *life*.

> There is always something more to discover. It's part of my Awesome Philosophy to keep moving, improving, and exploring this incredible opportunity called *life*.

That reminds me of a story…

I was lucky enough to be in an accident with a drunk driver when I was nineteen. Yup, I said lucky. This odd twist of fate turned out to be a real game-changer for me.

At first, I was confined to a bed with a cast on each leg, but I eventually graduated to a wheelchair. When I finally recovered enough to try crutches, rehab was added to my care.

During the first three days in rehab, I came to the conclusion that my inability to stand meant the doctors had missed something, and that I was, in fact, going to remain in my wheelchair forever. As is typical of a teenage brain, I didn't confide my fears to anyone. Therefore, no one explained that my wiggling toes indicated I was only experiencing weakness from atrophied muscles, which was to be expected after losing about 50 pounds after the accident. (Fully clothed, me, and the fifteen pounds of casts I was wearing, didn't even add up to 100 pounds.) My body simply didn't remember what I needed to do to stand up.

But, at the end of that third day— that wonderful, miraculous third day— a football player, who had been observing my efforts from an ice bath, said, "Why don't you stand her up and let her sit down. Maybe she can figure it out backwards."

Brilliant! A sturdy young man hoisted me onto my one walking cast, and that was all it took. *I could stand!* I wasn't going to spend the rest of my years in a wheelchair.

Suddenly, the grass was greener! The sun was brighter! The sky was bluer! I had my life back!

And I've been rejoicing ever since.

Your history doesn't define you. *You* choose how *you* define you.

I choose to fill my life with love, laughter, and positive-minded people. You can choose to follow a similar path (but I'd skip the car accident part). It would be awesome if you chose to begin today. C'mon! Let's get this party started!

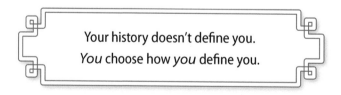

Your history doesn't define you.
You choose how *you* define you.

Semester 1: Sex, Drugs, and Rock & Roll

The party anthem of my youth was "Sex, Drugs, and Rock & Roll!" Did you ever wonder how that translates into the modern world? You might be surprised.

SEX, Drugs, and Rock & Roll

Most high schoolers (and probably you, too) believe *all* the teenagers around them are having sex, which simply isn't true. Actually, it's not even close, which I've been saying since the 80s.

That's right. It's not even close.

In a survey done by the Kaiser Family Foundation and *Seventeen Magazine*, only about a third of the boys left their virginity behind in high school. That means a whopping ⅔ of high-school boys graduate as virgins, not the 99% myth everyone perpetuates.

An even smaller percentage of girls have sex before they graduate. But, before you get all crazy about the 20 girls out of 100 who did it—and ignore the **80 percent who didn't**—out of those who had sex, 24% said it was unwanted, and 7% said it was involuntary. That means only 14 out of 100 high school girls constitute the "Everyone" in the *Everyone Has Sex In High School Myth*.

A more recent survey conducted by the Center for Disease Control (CDC) revealed females (that would be you and your daughter) were twice as likely to believe that 80% of their peers were sexually active, when it simply was not true. That's unfortunate because **almost 2/3 of the girls who had sex were influenced by believing most of their peers were having sex, when in actuality only about a third were**; and of that third, the majority of them wished they had waited until they were older. That's a far cry from the widely held myth that sex before graduation is common.

> That's a far cry from the widely held myth that sex before graudation is common.

How did I already know this? Because over the course of my teaching career, I conducted my own anonymous surveys in my classroom. It was a great tool for teaching data collection and graphing, and if I could debunk a few myths along the way, then so be it.

I was fortunate to work in several different schools over my three decades of teaching—inner city and rural, low and high socio-economic settings, New England and the Deep South—and with a variety of nationalities, cultures, and ethnicities. Regardless of the setting, in each school my anonymous surveys yielded the same results:

♦ Only a *small* percentage of the kids were having sex.

♦ **Almost all of them believed *everyone* else was having sex.**

The way I collected my data was I polled my classes at the beginning of the school year. They filled out a type of answer sheet used for standardized tests, which has a series of circles you color in, similar to a lottery ticket. These "bubble sheets" had no names on them, so the kids knew there was no way I could trace their answers back to them.

No matter where I taught over the course of three decades, the results were basically the same:

♦ Only about 3-5% of sophomores were sexually active.

♦ None of them believed the results, claiming the others were lying.

Every year we debated the validity of the results, although it made absolutely no sense to lie since I couldn't connect people with responses. Nevertheless, every year I ended up conducting the survey a second time, with my students promising to tell the truth. The second set of results?

♦ Only about 3-5% of sophomores were sexually active.

♦ None of them believed the results, claiming the others were lying.

When I polled older students, as you would expect, the numbers for those who were sexually active were higher, but even then:

♦ Only about 9-11% of seniors were sexually active.

♦ None of them believed the results, claiming the others were lying.

There's a really good chance you are reading this and thinking, *"Well, those were Deborah's schools. My daughter's school is different."* But, remember the other surveys conducted by the Kaiser Family Foundation, *Seventeen Magazine*, and the CDC? They all came to similar conclusions.

Honestly, I was so tired of people telling me the student polls I conducted produced results specific only to my school, although I'd often wondered why, over the years, my numbers were consistently lower than the CDC's. I don't know specifically how they qualified their participants, but one thing I did, which the CDC could not possibly do, was I polled *everybody* I taught—a variety of student populations in nearly a dozen different schools in three different states. With all that diversity, the results couldn't be specific to just my classes.

So, what does all that data tell you? That the media hype, the movies, the TV shows, the magazines, the books, the stories the kids tell to fit in, the stories adults tell to sound hip—all of it contributes to an unshakable MYTH that teenagers are going at it like rabbits. That myth contributes directly to the pressure your daughter navigates with every popularity-laced interaction at school.

> All of it contributes to an unshakable MYTH that teenagers are going at it like rabbits.

☑ Do This: Share the Stats

Share these statistics with your daughter. She won't believe you, but she might hear you. The conversation will make her question her assumptions and the things her friends tell her. That alone will put her ahead of the game.

Say This: "I just read this crazy statistic about teenagers. You have to see this!" Then, show her the previous section.

After you read it together, ask her, "How do you think this compares to the kids in your school? What percentage of the kids in your grade are having sex?" Listen quietly. Don't judge.

When she says something akin to, "Well, *my* school is different. Everyone is having sex," don't argue with her (and don't get sucked into believing her opinion). Try looking through last year's yearbook with her. Have her count up the number of kids in her grade she knows have had sex (not rumored). If she doesn't want you to know who they are, just have her share the number. Divide that number by the number of students in her grade to get the percentage of sexually active teens.

Similarly, you can calculate the percentage of girls in her grade, or the high school population, who have had sex. Most likely, you won't get accurate figures, but it will help her sort out prevalent fiction and rumors from fact.

Sex, DRUGS, and Rock & Roll

Pills address symptoms, but not the causes of the problems. Unfortunately, people turn to OTCs (Over The Counter drugs), like, Ibuprofen and Acetaminophen to manage their pain relief, without considering the consequences. These two pharmaceuticals are mistakenly considered safe because you can buy them in any store. In reality, they actually tax your kidneys and liver, and repetitive use can lead to permanent damage, or death.

> Ibuprofen and Acetaminophen actually tax your kidneys and liver, and repetitive use can lead to permanent damage, or death.

The alternative favorites of doctors are opioids. Today the opioid addiction in middle class America is through the roof. According to the US Department of Health and Human Services, in 2016, "2.1 million people misused prescription opioids for the first time." Where do you think these people, who put their trust in their doctors, are today? Where are they going to be a year from now?

Think about it. Otherwise, you may find yourself in a hellish situation, like the one experienced by my friend's son and his wife. They lost custody of their two small children through a series of events exacerbated by a doctor's prescription pad. The father owned a small construction company, and the mother was a nurse-turned-stay-at-home-mom. They were educated middle-class parents devoted to their children.

Everything changed when an accident at work injured his back and opioids were prescribed. Without them, the pain was debilitating. The prescription ran out and he turned to other substances for help managing the pain.

Their problems multiplied when his wife fell and broke her arm and wrist. She, too, was prescribed opioids for the pain. Like her husband, she also became addicted. When they could no longer afford her medication, they turned to cheaper drugs to help her deal with the pain. Within the year, they were both slaves to heroin, an inexpensive, easily obtained narcotic, still trying to manage their pain. Their children were removed from the home.

This was not the life they had expected for themselves.

Before this happens to someone you know, here are several *Alternatives For Dealing With Pain*:

Alternatives For Dealing With Pain:

Acupuncture	Meditation
Biofeedback	Music therapy
Chiropractic manipulation	Reiki Healing
Cranial sacral therapy	Relaxation therapy
Emotional therapy	Stress reduction techniques
Guided imagery	Supplements and vitamins
Hypnosis	Therapeutic Touch
Massage	Yoga

I recommend seeking professional help and alternatives for any and all physical addictions, not just opioids. Try every alternative until you find the one that works for your body. The problem is when a person loses hope, they also lose the motivation to keep seeking help. If that's your situation, expand your Support Team and get help!

Consider your child observing a substance-dependent parent:

♦ At what age do you want her to begin smoking cigarettes?

♦ Does alcohol look sophisticated and cool to her?

♦ Does she see you pop prescribed pills? Or diet pills?

Did you know that daughters are almost four times as likely to be dependent on nicotine when their mothers are dependent on nicotine? I certainly wasn't surprised by these results from Columbia University Medical Center's and the New York State Psychiatric Institute's 2015 study. The question is, which of the above do you want your child to use this week? Or, next month? Before she graduates? Or, while she lives away from you in college, or in the armed forces, or in a home of her own?

In her attempt to make sense of her life, if your teenager doesn't feel she can depend on you for help with her pressures, she may turn to chemical aids, especially if she sees you turning to them. Pay attention! Drastic changes are easy to spot, but it's the gradual changes that sneak up on you. Be on the watch for:

- ◆ decreased interest in activities, more absences from school, or an increase in isolation

- ◆ frequent irritability, hostility, or anger

- ◆ self-injury, such as cutting or scratching with a sharp object, or extreme eating/dieting

- ◆ problems with relationships, or increased insecurity

- ◆ bloodshot eyes, confusion, secretive behavior, unusual borrowing or spending of money

- ◆ sudden dramatic changes in behavior, sleeping habits, or eating habits

You can't afford not to pay attention. Her future depends on it! It's not too late to help your daughter if she's using an unhealthy substance. Look for additional resources in the **Answers at the Back of the Book**.

Speaking of addictive substances, don't forget your consumption of white stuff… sugar, all artificial sweeteners, stevia, flour, bread, crackers, cookies, muffins, cake, pie, waffles, potatoes, salt, lard, rice, flour tortillas, marshmallows, candy, bagels, etc. Everything listed here gives you a boost of energy, and then you crash, which makes you crave more, which gives you a boost of energy, and then you crash, which makes you crave more, which gives you a boost of energy, and then you crash, which makes you crave more, which gives you a boost of energy, and then you crash, which makes you crave more, which…

Okay. You get the idea. It's an addiction.

How much white stuff does your daughter consume in a day? If she eats a school lunch, it's a lot. Consider this: the Federal Government lists pizza as a veggie because it has two tablespoons of pizza sauce on it.

Seriously? They are equating two tablespoons of pizza sauce to a serving of broccoli?

C'mon, people. A tomato is a veggie (okay, scientifically it's a fruit because it comes from a flower, but you get my drift). Pizza sauce is not.

You also have to consider the "undisclosed" ingredients in pre-packaged lunch foods, like ketchup, which are supposed to be allergen-free (although it's loaded with sugar). But, if you read a packet of ketchup (I told you I was a Science Geek), the ingredients include "natural flavors" and "spices," which is code for "we are not telling you what's in here." How can you be sure they are allergen-free if you don't know what's in them?

The bottom line is you can't rely on school lunches to provide healthy, balanced meals until the appealing unhealthy food choices are eliminated. Getting rid of the white stuff is not an option. It's a lifesaver, and one of the biggest gifts any school, and any Awesome Mom, can give your daughter.

According to the CDC, in 2014, over 29,100,000 people had diabetes. That's 9.3% of the US population! That same year, 7.2 million adults had hospital discharges with diabetes, which included the following:

- 1.5 million for major cardio vascular diseases (ischemic heart disease or stroke)

- 108,000 for a lower-extremity amputation

- 168,000 for diabetic ketoacidosis (blood becomes acidic), which can be deadly in children

Just one year later in 2015, out of the 1.5 million **new** cases of diabetes, 23,200 of them were *children*. I have two questions for you.

1. What do you think is happening to those adults today?
2. What do you think is happening to those children today?

This is a preventable epidemic!

Homework: Assessing Your White Stuff

Together with your daughter, make a list of the white stuff you and she typically consume. Next to each item, write something you can substitute for it. Challenge your daughter to see how many substitutions you can come up with in three minutes. Then, combine your lists, and go grocery shopping.
Field Trip!

Example 1: Glass of milk → glass of water and a handful of almonds (for the calcium and protein)
Example 2: Power bar or candy bar → sweet potatoes (for the fiber and vitamins B and C)

Sex, Drugs, and ROCK & ROLL

When I was younger, where I came from the *Rock & Roll* part of ***Sex, Drugs, and Rock & Roll*** referred to partying. When it comes to teenagers and parties, my advice is a big, fat ***NO!*** Granted, this is not a popular point of view, but honestly, when does putting a bunch of hormonal teenagers together in an unsupervised setting, with their undeveloped frontal lobes, turn into a good idea, even if by some fluke, alcohol and drugs are not part of the mix? Off the top of my head, I can't think of anything that would turn that into a sane option. Can you?

Let's look at the message you're conveying if you let her go to a party. You don't want your daughter to drink, but you know there will be alcohol there. You don't want her to do drugs, but chances are drugs will there. You don't want her to have sex, but there will be high, horny guys there.

> When does putting a bunch of hormonal teenagers together in an unsupervised setting, with their undeveloped frontal lobes, turn into a good idea, even if by some fluke, alcohol and drugs are not part of the mix?

I remember watching the classic, *Footloose*, where a small town is permanently changed when they lose a carload of teenagers in a car accident. I remember thinking how lucky they were that it was only one car accident. In the small rural town where I grew up, we lost young lives almost every year due to car crashes, a statistic that hadn't changed by the time I returned there to teach twenty years later. And, it still hasn't changed. I just read three obituaries in the paper, newly graduated hopefuls who will never get to reach their potential because they partied and drove.

What are you going to say to her? "You can go to the party, but even if you are the only one to do so, say no to the drugs, alcohol, and hooking up. Oh, and by the way, have a good time hanging out with a bunch of high, inebriated, horny guys. I'm sure you'll enjoy good solid conversations upon which a meaningful relationship can be built."

Why place her in a situation where she will be offered contraband, and will probably be ridiculed if she says no? That's enormous pressure on her, and she has enough to deal with in her life already. If she's worried that her crush will hook up with someone else if she doesn't go, *you* have to worry he'll hook up with *her* if she does go.

"But, Mom, the parents will be there."

Trust me. The presence of parent chaperones does not mean they will be chaperoning.

That reminds me of a story…

When my daughter was in high school, the parents of a teammate held a birthday party for their daughter who was turning 18. At the time, the drinking age was 21. They only invited the members of her team, and while ordinarily I would have allowed my daughter to go to a team party because the parents (one of whom was a teacher) would be home, we had another obligation that night.

As it turns out, allowing her to go would have been a big mistake. The *parents* served liquor to the girls, after they confiscated everyone's car keys so no one would be driving drunk.

I guess they were trying to be the Cool Parents.

One of the girls posted pictures from the party on social media. The other parents found out and were outraged. One thing led to another, and those same supposedly Cool Parents were arrested. The mother's elementary teaching certification was revoked, and she lost her job.

It turns out serving alcohol to minors wasn't cool after all. Moral of the story: Not all chaperones actually chaperone.

Semester 2: Models, Media, and Belly Roll

My training for teaching Environmental Science exposed me to how much the media affects our everyday decisions. Knowledge changed me. I decided to no longer stand helplessly by and allow commercials and advertisements to influence my self-approval and waistline… and by default, affect my daughter as she modeled my behavior. *Applying knowledge is power.*

> *Applying knowledge is power.*

MODELS, Media, and Belly Roll

Youth is on-the-job preparation for adulthood. Our children model themselves after their parents before even reaching school age. They take their on-the-job training very seriously, whether they know it or not. I remember my pre-school nephew strolling across the lawn with his daddy, one hand in his pocket, the other swiping at the grass with a stick… an exact replica of the larger version accompanying him, doing the same thing with a bigger stick. At the time I thought, "How cute!" but now I think, "That's the perfect example of modeling."

> Tween girls are so eager to emulate their mothers, the most important female in their lives. You did it. Your mother did it. Your daughter does it.

Similarly, tween girls are so eager to emulate their mothers, the most important female in their lives. You did it. Your mother did it. Your daughter does it.

Think about how you modeled your mother. As a child, did you sneak into your mother's room to explore the wonders it held? Did you try on her jewelry? Play with her mascara? Totter around on her heels? That's modeling at its finest.

Modeling good behavior is easy when you're feeling good, but what if things aren't completely rosy in your world? What do you do after your daughter has just emotionally pushed your last button? How you habitually respond is important because that's the behavior she imitates.

Whether a mom raises her voice in frustration, or clams up in anger, she is not solving a problem. She's reacting to a situation… and teaching her daughter a go-to mechanism, which will not help her in relationships. Are you training her to reason things out? Not if you are yelling, and certainly not if you are giving her the silent treatment. You are teaching her how to react, not how to cope. Here is a great way to model a planned response, instead of an emotional reaction.

☑ Do This: Count To 10

On those days when her undeveloped teenage brain somehow concludes it's a good idea to poke Momma Bear again, believe it or not, counting to ten really does help reset emotions. Losing your temper is the equivalent to losing your power, but pausing to count is a prime example of you reclaiming your power. That's you taking control of the situation.

1. Find a neutral time to describe your plan to count to ten, and explain the benefits.

2. Should the situation arise that requires it, be sure to count aloud so she can hear you. It will interrupt the emotional back-and-forth escalating between the two of you.

3. Follow this practice with *Three Mindful Breaths* practice described earlier.

4. If you're not calmed when you finish, count to ten again.

Lovingly remind her of the following:

♦ She is an *equally valued* member of this family and is invited to contribute her thoughts and opinions for your consideration.

♦ *As the adult in charge, you* will be making the decisions, and she will have to adjust to them.

♦ When she blows up, her emotions cloud her message; if she wants you to hear and understand her, she must speak calmly. Otherwise, her body language is too distracting.

If the conversation becomes too heated, invoke the *Step Back and Come Back* protocol. Inform her that you are going to wait 24 hours before you continue. That will give you both time to consider each other's side.

Emphasize that you love her, even when she yells at you, and even when you get upset with her.

The next day Awesome Moms will prompt their Awesome Daughters to continue the conversation with the previous guidelines *if she still wants to*. Take your cue from her. If the angry adolescent verbally goes on the attack, remind her again that if she wants you to hear and understand her, she must talk calmly. Then follow the same steps.

———◆———

Hopefully, she'll be ready to follow your example and resume the discussion, although don't be surprised if finishing the argument isn't important to her anymore. Whichever way the conversation turns out, she will be modeling her future behavior based on your present patterns.

> **The way your daughter feels about her beauty starts with the way you feel about your beauty.**

Behavior isn't the only thing our darling daughters imitate. Believe it or not, their self-perception is strongly influenced by *our* self-perception. We don't notice them watching us criticize ourselves in the mirror, but that's how they learn how to look at themselves. The way your daughter feels about herself, and her beauty, starts with the way you feel about yourself, and your own beauty. Do you see how important it is for you to let your awesomeness shine through?

If you don't believe me, check out the Dove Legacy Project, which asked mothers how they felt about their bodies. The women listed the things they hated, the characteristics they liked, and why.

In a separate room, their young daughters were given the same questionnaire about their own little bodies. The nearly identical answers produced by their daughters shocked the mothers. For example, if a mother confessed that she didn't like her arms, separately her little girl also wrote that she didn't like her own arms. If the adult shared that she liked her smile, the child appreciated her own smile, too.

When they were brought together, their mums chose a positive characteristic that had been written on both of their lists, and asked their child, "Why do you like this?" The

Good To Know

If you want to see a great example of the effects of modeling, watch the YouTube sensation, *Talking Twin Babies*. Their gestures and pre-verbal conversation are obviously imitations of their parents' interactions, even though these babies are too young to understand the content of the adult discussions (or their own).

mothers were stunned to hear their daughters' answers paraphrased their own previously shared reasons.

You can watch the entire 3-minute video by looking up Dove Legacy | A Girl's Beauty Confidence Starts With You, or you can access it via this URL: **https://www.youtube.com/watch?v=Pqknd1ohhT4.**

That reminds me of a story…

When my Italian girlfriend, Marie, married African American Jake, they understood their ethnically blended children could encounter issues, but felt prepared to deal with them. One day Marie showed me a picture of her daughter. In it, 5-year-old Teresa was laughing with a flock of little girls from daycare—a blond girl, a redheaded girl, a black girl, a girl from Taiwan, and another from Ecuador. Somehow Teresa had managed to create a tribe for herself whose members did not resemble each other—a reflection of how her family members didn't resemble each other.

I found it adorable. "The bunch of them look like a Gap commercial."

Marie waved the photo under my nose. "You know what Teresa said when she saw this? 'I wish I looked like them'."

"What?" I held the picture closer to see what she was talking about. To me the girls were as different as different could be, with their distinctive ethnic features, diverse skin shades, and rainbow spectrum of hair colors.

Marie tapped the picture. "They all have straight hair."

Oh.

At only 5 years old, Teresa yearned to be like the others… with hair that also happened to be like her mother's.

Fast-forward almost a decade when Marie shared this story with me:

On a hot August day, she and her now middle school daughter, Teresa, were sitting in the car outside the imposing new school, getting ready to locate her classrooms and locker.

"Mom." Teresa's voice was shaky as she leaned forward to peer at the wall looming above them. "I don't think I can do this."

"Well, I think you can. What exactly is worrying you?"

> "What if there isn't anyone here who looks like me?"
>
> Marie tugged on one of her daughter's soft curls and laughed as she raked her own straight hair with her fingers. "Honey, no one looks like you at home, and you do just fine. They're going to love you, just like we do."
>
> Teresa grinned and put her hand on the door handle. "I wish my hair was straight like yours," she said for the thousandth time.
>
> Marie grinned back. "I wish my hair was curly like yours," she replied for the thousandth time.

Marie never did convince her daughter how lovely her curls were. It didn't help that Jake's sisters not only straightened their own hair, but also straighten Teresa's curls whenever they had the chance. It didn't matter that Marie's sisters adored the curls. There were still two basic obstacles to Teresa appreciating her own hair:

♦   Teresa's hair didn't match her automatic standard of beauty—her mom's hair.

♦   Marie consistently demonstrated her personal dissatisfaction with her hair, so Teresa imitated her example by being discontented with her own hair.

The grass is always greener on the other side, right?

How humbling to be responsible for our daughters, who hang on our every word and deed. Since you want the best for your developing darling, why not positively reframe your self-perception? It's better for you, and, it's better for her. Start here.

☑ Do This: The Best of You

Make a list of your *best* characteristics, starting with your head, and working your way down your entire body. Be strict with yourself. Force yourself to minimally identify the one best feature of each section of your body. If there is more than one, write them all.

Post the list where you will see it every day so you will remember to read it to yourself. Add your other good points when you think of them. Emphasize the positive aspects of yourself daily for 2 months, even if you feel awkward doing it.

Occasionally mention something that you like about yourself in front of your daughter. This simple task can have a hugely positive impact on both of your lives… if you let it.

You represent your daughter's first model of a beautiful woman. She spent her infancy staring up at your face and into your eyes. Of course she's going to see the beauty there. You are the yardstick by which she measures herself.

However, if your daughter resembles her handsome dad, or is adopted, or is the product of an ethnically blended family, she won't see how incredible she already is because she won't resemble you the way she thinks she should. Consider taking extra steps to help her foster a healthy self-image.

Good to Know

Back in the eighties, I was waiting in a doctor's office (which is the only place I ever have the time to read a magazine), when I came across an article by a cosmetic surgeon. She wrote about the oddity of *attractive* women wanting to alter their faces. The high frequency of requests for straightening straight noses and raising high cheekbones bemused the surgeon. Why did pretty women perceive themselves as looking flawed?

To satisfy her curiosity, she started informally polling her patients, and discovered these already-lovely women resembled their fathers. An entire adolescence of being told they looked like a man was not easily reconciled with their concept of what was feminine and attractive. Well-meaning relatives who pinch a preschooler's cheeks and say, "Oooh, you look just like your daddy!" don't understand that it matters to her when she is compared to a male figure.

Blue-eyed blonde Clara told me about her brown-eyed, brunette 5-year-old getting angry when a woman from their church snagged her by the chin and cooed, "You have your daddy's eyes." The child wrenched her face away, planted her fists on her hips, and declared, "I *don't* have my daddy's eyes. These are *my* eyes! I don't look like a *boy*."

Concerned with her daughter's response, Clara came to me for advice. Here is the condensed version:

Do: Tell your daughter about her positive characteristics that remind you of his positive attributes, but for each of those similarities, share two characteristics that you and she have in common.

Do: Emphasize the similar things people like about you so she will perceive how likeable she is.

Do: Share the features people find attractive about you that she has inherited (bubbly personality, kindness, high energy, always smiling, healthy hair, clear eyes, long lashes, generosity, intelligence, etc.)

With the properly targeted input, that awesome girl you are raising will grow to understand and appreciate her self-worth.

If your daughter's father is absent from her life, a stepfather, uncle, or grandfather can become her role model, and make her feel cherished and valued. If her father is absent, *and* you don't have any male backup, you have to take on this responsibility yourself. Don't leave this hole in her self-worth unattended.

If the father is absent by choice, don't be surprised if she has internalized it as her fault, or decided it was due to some *secret flaw* she has that she tries to keep hidden. (Papa would have stayed if she had been more attractive, or smarter, or kinder, or faster.)

Children live in fear of their secret flaw being discovered. When she feels like it might be exposed, watch out! That explosion that came out of nowhere after your outfit suggestion may have struck too close to the secret flaw she hides from you.

> If you have a contentious relationship with your daughter's father, don't bad-mouth him, no matter how much he deserves it.

It can be difficult to get her to reveal her secret flaw to you where you can address it directly. Kids who feel they are undeserving of praise try to hide that they are *frauds*, and she may not even recognize that's what's going on.

Besides, if she feels she has successfully hidden what she thinks is her flaw from you all these years (after all, you stayed), how can she risk you finding out now? How will she handle that inevitable look of disappointment crossing your face? What if you want to leave, too? What if you want to leave, but you don't, because you feel responsible? She'd be sentencing you to years of living with her and her awful *imagined* flaw.

When it comes to her absent father, it's important not to leave her to draw her own conclusions. She will silently imagine lots of secret flaws in herself to explain their relationship, or lack thereof. Have the discussion, and then have it again.

Don't: If you have a contentious relationship with your daughter's father, don't bad-mouth him, no matter how much he deserves it.

His blood flows through your daughter's veins. She will silently believe she has inherited all his negative characteristics. Additionally, from her point of view, if you aren't feeling loving toward him, for all she knows you might not feel loving toward her at some point. Insecurity rears its ugly head, and stomps on your reliability. It's better to focus on his positive attributes for her sake.

If his situation is negative, remain consistently neutral while providing assurance his actions in no way reflect on her. Let her understand that if he could've done better with his current lot in life, he would have.

- If he was abusive, help her understand she doesn't share his inability to cope because she's still growing and developing; plus, she has you to help her polish her coping skills so she can learn to handle anger.

- If he's an addict, explain that his good qualities, which she shares, sadly have been overridden by his addiction. She doesn't have to worry about that happening to her because she is aware, and therefore stronger.

- If he's a deadbeat dad, remind her that a person's character is based on their actions, not their intentions. It's okay to admit that he is a very selfish person, but you didn't realize it when you got together. And, while his intentions may have been good at one point, share how much you pity him for stupidly missing her childhood, and how her big, generous heart is like yours, not his.

Whatever his situation is, remind her that he turned out the way he is because he was raised by her grandparents. She has a huge advantage because she's being raised by you, her Awesome Mom.

You get the idea. Help frame how she views him so it won't damage her. With the properly targeted input, your magnificent daughter will grow to understand and appreciate her self-worth and awesomeness. Without it, she will make it all up in her juvenile head, and it won't be pretty.

Models, **MEDIA**, and Belly Roll: The Media's Influence on You

Wouldn't it be great if the models in the magazines idealized the same body type as yours, and wore their hair like yours, and promoted good health and kindness? Imagine it. Your self-concept would be supported, and you would yearn for things that were in your best interest. How awesome would it be if commercials only advertised products that were good for Awesome Moms, like fresh produce, non-GMO foods, chemical-free packaged process foods, exercise, relaxation techniques, etc.? Healthy food options would be imprinted on your mind and you'd reach for them first, right after you finished playing tennis with your daughter.

Hey, no harm in dreaming, right?

Today's advertisements are designed to create discontent for what we already have and longing for something new. They are very good at what they do, targeting our concepts of self, status, and accomplishment. The media supports the **Supermom Myth**, and we buy into it because the people around us buy into it. The **Supermom Myth** lends credence to the **Plenty Of Time Myth,** and suddenly we are trying to balance a jam-packed life.

If you would like to learn more about how advertising targets you, check out the 20-minute video called **Story of Stuff** (**http://StoryOfStuff.org/movies/story-of-stuff/**). I used to show it to my science classes to empower them, because as you know, *applying knowledge is power.*

> Is your life designed to make a better life for your daughter than you had, but doesn't include her in it because she stays with a sitter?

The only way you can hope to escape the damaging influence of the current media messages is to not watch, read, or listen to it—Do you have any blinders you can wear?— but even then, everyone around you talks about it. So, your best defense is a strong offense.

Without self-blame or guilt, consider the example your lifestyle sets. Do you work late nights? Are you spread too thin with all your obligations on the weekend? Is your life designed to make a better life for your daughter than you had, but doesn't include her in it because she stays with a sitter? Have the media examples convinced you this is a good idea? (Cue "Cats In The Cradle" by Harry Chapin.)

Rebooting this predicament can be as difficult as fighting an addiction.

- ◆ Your job traps you financially.
- ◆ Your family duties lock you in emotionally.
- ◆ The **Plenty of Time Myth** keeps you adding more to your crowded plate.
- ◆ The **Supermom Myth** permanently plants you on the Keeping-Up-With-The-Other-Moms Treadmill.

When the pressure feels overwhelming, what gives way?

Your self-care.

What sense does that make? How can you take care of everything else if you don't take care of you? Still, the media sucks you in to thinking you have to do it all.

Why can't we get sucked into believing a media myth that says the *Awesome Mom Comes First*?

My grandmother used to say, "If you ain't got your health, Lady, you ain't got nothin'!" The media even jumps on that bandwagon, with advertisements that make you crave quick fixes for losing weight, for changing your figure, for improving your looks, etc. The other day, I saw an ad actually claiming to help you lose weight without dieting or exercise. Their solution?

Surgery.

Seriously? Instead of telling you to create a lifestyle change for yourself (which would also be a good model for your daughter), their ad, which you see over and over again, frames unnecessary surgery as a good idea. And, the more you see the ad, the more reasonable it sounds.

But, what happens a year after surgery if you've been living your same lifestyle that created your problem in the first place? You'll be right back where you started. And, where will your daughter be a year from now, still following the same habits?

Consider this healthy solution instead: Make small changes to your lifestyle. Create accountability by talking to your daughter about what you are going to change, and why.

💬 **Say This:** "Because I don't want you to have this issue when you are my age, I'm going to make the same change in your life, too. I hope you will support me in this, because I plan on supporting you. I love you too much not to."

As each change becomes a habit, you add another small change. By the time the year is up, you will feel the effects of intentional positive changes in your life and feel empowered by your progress. Your daughter's evolution will warm your heart, as will any improvement in her self-worth, not to mention her higher regard for you.

Note: Any sudden changes you make will alarm your daughter unless you introduce the idea ahead of time. Try a conversation about calming the stress in your life. Discuss the health benefits of setting a limit to your obligations. See if you can get her to join you in making a commitment to not add anything new to either of your schedules, unless it replaces something else.

You can follow that up with a conversation about scheduling an activity together, such as:

- ◆ A Field trip – anything from a trip around town to run errands, to visiting a relative or friend. One of my favorite choices is to go someplace that ties in with what she's studying in school.

- ◆ Laundry and a Movie Marathon – Use a Venn Diagram to select a movie. Pause it when you have to tend to the machines, and keep going until you put away all of the laundry together.

- ◆ Shared Quiet Time – She works on homework while you work on the exercises in this book in the same room.

- ◆ Volunteer time – Teach your daughter to be a citizen of the earth by finding an activity where you can volunteer together.

There, that wasn't so hard. You can see the benefits of making positive changes like these. Small steps can add up to big impacts on your relationship… and without your usual trimmings of guilt/self-blame regarding what you did, or didn't do. You only need an objective assessment of where your relationship is now to design solutions like these, solutions that will work for both of you.

In addition to strengthening your Mother-Daughter Bond, these feel-good encounters are heart-healthy. Spending quality time together makes the happy hormones, like serotonin, flow, and decreases the negative chemicals in your bodies. More happy chemicals mean making you feel happier, calmer, and less hungry, *and* it means a reduction in the levels of your stress hormone, cortisol.

Lowering your stress also lowers feelings of impatience, irritability, and anger (which can't compete with happy feelings), and therefore decreases that familiar by-product of negativity, the drain on your energy. Cutting your stress levels will also lead to improved physical and mental health, better memory, and enhanced focus.

Wow! All those healthy benefits, just from walking the walk, and talking the talk! Small steps really do add up to big impacts on your relationship. Who knew, right?

Be proud of the fact you're seeking alternatives. Who needs repetitive cycles that trap you both in a negative loop of distrust and resentment? Not you two. Actively stay centered, and remain free of guilt and self-blame, and teach her to do the same.

Models, MEDIA, and Belly Rolls: Media's Influence On Her

Wouldn't it be great if the positive influence of your household dominated your daughter's life?

Yeah, well, good luck with that once she discovers electronic media. From commercials that target preteens, to social media demands, your daughter's self-concept is being molded by companies trying to make her crave their products.

> Your daughter's self-concept is being molded by companies trying to make her crave their products.

As your daughter gets older, the media will continue to color her outlook and philosophy. TV shows, movies, videos, commercials all subtly teach her what her beauty standard should be, simply by the models they choose to showcase. Back in the 1960s when the models were flat-chested and rail thin, voluptuous girls hated their curves. When the modern supermodels (enhanced with media alterations and surgery) became popular, the average girl despaired.

Obviously, you have to address the negative perceptions the media has already established in your wonderful daughter. One of the ways to circumvent the insecurity the media causes is to emphasize the wonderful blend she is between her two parents. "You have daddy's beautiful dark hair, and you have my gorgeous smile."

Another way is for her daddy to compliment her. That kind of attention conveys to her that she must be attractive if he thinks she is, no matter who she takes after.

Meanwhile, how can you help your daughter fend off the negative influence of the media trends, especially when they affect you as well? Get some help. There are a myriad of ways to cope with stress, and the impact that stress manifests in your life:

Acupuncturists
Chiropractors
Counselors
Energy Practitioners
General Practitioners
Meditation Groups
Naturopaths
Nurse Practitioners

Nutritionists
Personal Trainers
Physiotherapists
Psychologists
Social Workers
Support Groups
Therapists
Your Clergy

> I was able to kick Lyme disease without using antibiotics.

Personally, I worked with a Naturopath and an Energy Practitioner who helped me when I was struggling with Lyme disease. Energy Practitioners identify and correct different imbalances in a person's energy field. These imbalances cause all kinds of physical and emotional problems. Correcting underlying imbalances makes conditions right so the body can heal itself.

With their help, plus exercise and a strictly clean menu (no GMOs, gluten, soy, corn, dairy, sugar, or canola), I was able to kick Lyme disease without using antibiotics. In the process, the health protocols they had me follow also:

♦ eliminated my gastrointestinal difficulties

♦ cleared up my skin

♦ gave me healthy, strong nails and hair

♦ boosted my immune system

♦ normalized my cholesterol and thyroid

Although I include the clean menu I used in the *Answers at the Back of the Book*, I'm not sharing the various tinctures, supplements and teas specific to the protocol I was prescribed because this is not a quick fix. Everyone's body is different, and we all have different stressors in our lives. That makes the journey to physical/emotional well-being personal and unique for each individual. I do, however, want to encourage you to find a professional to help you along your journey.

My girlfriend, Chelsea, was a mom with constant abdominal issues. I suggested she visit the Energy Practitioner who had helped me with my Lyme disease. As I mentioned, the protocol I followed was multifaceted and included significant changes in my menu and physical activity. But it also included affirmations and other emotional and well-being exercises.

Chelsea had a similar positive experience regarding her own health issues. Here is a simple exercise she began to follow, and one you can start right now:

☑ Do This: Repeat After Me

Post one note on your refrigerator, and another on your bathroom mirror that says:

**I deeply and completely love
and appreciate myself.**

Repeat it aloud every time you notice it (hence, the two locations). Go ahead. Say it loud and proud. *Right now.*

Chelsea was reluctant to try this *Repeat After Me* exercise because it felt silly and worthless. Of course she loved herself, so what was the point? But she did it anyway. About a month later she shared this story with me:

However skeptical she felt, Chelsea dutifully posted the phrase on bright yellow sticky notes. Just before she left the room, she remembered she was supposed to recite it aloud. With a sigh, she began, "I deeply and completely—"

Embarrassment flooded her. She checked over her shoulder to make sure no one was watching. She began again, hurrying through the first words, but this time she stumbled on the word "love."

Frustrated, she planted her hands on her hips. Why was this so difficult? She started once more, this time focused and determined to succeed. "I deeply and completely... I deeply and completely love... I deeply and completely love and, and... I deeply and completely love and appreciate myself! *Hah!*"

"Well, it's about time!"

Mortified, she spun around at the sound of her daughter's voice.

"Just so you know," the teen said as she wrapped her arms around her mother's middle, "I deeply and completely love and appreciate you, too." She grinned up at her. "I think you need to practice saying it, don't you?"

A few weeks later, Chelsea paused in front of the yellow square adorning her mirror as she realized not only had the phrase rolled right off her tongue, but it had been doing

> so for a while. She repeated the words, this time focused on the feelings they evoked. "I deeply and completely love and appreciate myself."
>
> She did. She really did. She deeply and completely loved and appreciated herself, and now she was comfortable saying it aloud.

Personally, I had the same initial reaction when I started this task, which is why I'm so tickled by Chelsea's story. The question is, why did it feel so awkward for us to say the affirmation aloud? Here's my theory on one contributing factor.

As much as we'd like to establish that *it's not what's on the outside that matters, it's what's on the inside that counts*, the reality to a little girl is her looks do matter. As she gets older, she may be able to put it into better perspective, but the media does its best to make sure we remain discontented with ourselves so they can sell us improvement products (makeup, exercise equipment, clothes, etc.). After decades of the media telling us we needed to improve, it felt awkward to declare that we were pleased with ourselves.

I deeply and completely love and appreciate myself.

Like Chelsea, it now feels normal to reaffirm that *I deeply and completely love and appreciate myself*. Again, the question is, why does it take so much effort to make the statement feel normal?

We can use our thoughts to make ourselves sick, or to heal ourselves.

We all have the power to program our minds into believing a concept of our choosing. We can use our thoughts to make ourselves sick, or to heal ourselves. With positive affirmations, every time we say the phrase aloud, it helps us to focus on how we want to feel about ourselves. Sometimes we think about the words. Sometimes we chant them absentmindedly. Regardless, each and every time the vibration of our voices penetrates the depth of our unconscious minds, and the power of the words takes root there. Eventually, the awkwardness melts away, leaving a positive wake behind.

The added bonus? Chelsea's daughter also read the phrase aloud every time she visited the refrigerator. It had the same positive effect on her.

Along with the daily affirmations, Chelsea's protocol also included cleaning up her menu (no GMOs, gluten, soy, corn, sugar, dairy, or canola), which helped to clear up her abdominal issues. That, plus other specific exercises, helped Chelsea refocus her energy in a constructive direction. Her positive changes came with a bonus ripple effect: the new food she brought into the house contributed to her daughter's improved nutrition, providing her with the associated benefits as well. (Of course, there's no way to keep track of the media-enticing junk food her daughter ate once she left the house.)

Models, Media, and **BELLY ROLL**

Lobster Rolls or Jelly Rolls, they all contribute to our Belly Rolls, a.k.a., the Spare Tires of fat circling our abdomen. Obesity is at epidemic proportions in the United States. *Thirteen million* American children are already dealing with this health problem. Most girls have issues with their body images, but for overweight girls, it can be so much worse. Insecure kids with low self-esteem are more likely to make bad choices in pursuit of the all-important quest for popularity.

Obesity is a health problem, not a judgement.

If you tell little girls, tweens, or teens they have a heightened risk of diabetes, they may worry about their health, but they won't feel embarrassed or judged. However, discussions about the extra pounds they carry (the reason they have a heightened risk of diabetes) make them feel insecure and unattractive; they feel judged and inadequate. Yet, the term *diabetes* doesn't make them feel that way. It's a double-standard because obesity should not be about making a judgment call.

Society's thinking needs immediate adjusting. **Obesity is a medical issue, not a cosmetic problem.** Obesity is a reversible medical condition. If you remain obese, eventually your daughter will be sentenced to years of sitting by your hospital bed as your poor health diminishes your ability to move around… in addition to struggling with her own health problems. If you allow your daughter

Obesity is a medical issue, not a cosmetic problem.

to remain overweight, you are sentencing her to a future filled with chronic illness and health emergencies.

If, on the other hand, the two of you can get your nutrition and fitness under control, by this time next year:

♦   Her self-confidence will soar, as will yours.

♦   You will feel powerful for having conquered such a difficult obstacle, as will she.

♦   You will both have someone to whom you are accountable.

♦   You will have a workout buddy, whether you exercise together or not.

♦   Your environment will change because neither of you will bring sabotaging foods into the house, thereby increasing your chances for success.

♦   You will be working in tandem to achieve your S.M.A.R.T. Goals.

♦   You will enhance your mother-daughter relationship in so many ways!

To open the dialogue, begin with you and your nutrition choices. Find a recent article about the obesity epidemic in our schools. The American Heart Association has a great article called *Understanding the American Obesity Epidemic*. Here's an excerpt from their website:

> *"Body organs like the stomach, intestines, fat and pancreas send signals to the brain that trigger hunger and make you want to eat. While you're eating, signals tell the brain that you're full and to stop eating… [But when] you see or smell appealing food, it can trigger the desire to eat whether or not you're hungry…*
>
> *Recent studies show that obese individuals have less ability to resist food cues. Stress, mildly low blood sugar and other factors also play a role."*
>
> American Heart Association

☑ Do This: Share an Article

If you search, you can find a new article on the Obesity Epidemic literally every week. You'll find more resources in the *Answers at the Back of the Book* in the *Bibliography.* Select an article to share with your daughter.

Say This: "I saw this article and it got me thinking about how it applied to us. Five years ago, I weighed _____. Right now I weigh about _____ . At the rate I'm going, in five more years, I'll weigh _____. That's not very healthy, is it? You eat what I eat, and I want a healthy future for you. Let's make some changes so we can have a healthy future together."

Then brainstorm about how you can change the course of your lives. She is more likely to buy into change if she helps create it.

---

7 Ways to Tame the Obesity Beast

You might want to go back to *Kick the Bad Habits and Change the Course of Your History* section in the *History Class* chapter to review the formation of good habits. Meanwhile, here are seven starter suggestions. Pick one to start (that's why they are called starter suggestions).

Let's start with the obvious:

1. **Do not go on a diet**. *Diets* are about denial and temporary fixes. They tear things down instead of building them up. **Do not go on a diet**.

   Instead, plan how to form new nutritional habits one at a time. If you and your daughter can embrace the positive modifications together and support each other, the change will become an expected behavior in about two or three months, a.k.a., almost a habit. It may take a bit longer to reach actual habit status, like brushing your teeth, but you will be well on your way. But, whatever you do, **don't go on a diet**.

Do not go on a diet!

2. **Increase the frequency you eat to six times a day.** People make the mistake of decreasing how much food they consume when they want to lose weight. That creates hunger, which messes with your food cues and your blood sugar levels. You'd find more success if you can fit in food five to six times a day. Six smaller meals insure you don't get hungry, your blood sugar levels will be more stable, and your cravings will diminish. Basically, I eat all day so I can stay slender. If I skip a meal, or forget to bring a snack with me, I end up heading straight for the suddenly-irresistible candy bars. When I eat six times a day, I have no cravings, and my energy stays elevated.

3. **Add green veggies to your menu until you are eating 4 cups a day.** It's a lot easier than it sounds. Scramble a cup of veggies (onions, tomatoes, spinach, etc.) with your eggs for breakfast. Have 2 cups of salad for lunch. Sauté some summer squash with a little olive oil and garlic to accompany your dinner. When the weather turns cold, substitute a cup of vegetable soup for a cup of the salad.

    Start slowly by adding a single veggie serving to one meal. After a while, you can add the rest. If you eat 4 cups of veggies a day, they will fill you up so you will eat less of the other stuff *without denying yourself anything*. They will also keep your GI track healthy.

    You must take care of you first.

    New habits are best formed by substituting them for existing habits. For example, an average cup of beef chili has 256 calories, but who eats just 1 cup? Most people grab a bowlful. If you don't measure out each serving, then you might be consuming as much as 2-3 cups for each serving.

    So, here's a thought: There are 12 calories in 1 cup of salad, plus 119 calories for a tablespoon of olive oil dressing, or a total of 131 calories.

    Now, let's say you have just 2 cups of chili for dinner every Friday night (and don't go back for more). You will be consuming 512 calories for that meal. But, if you switch it up to have 1 cup of chili plus 1 cup of salad, you'll take in only 387 calories. That's a difference of 125 fewer calories per week. Over the course of 1 year, it comes to 45,625 fewer calories, which translates into dropping about 13 pounds of fat in 1 year... simply by replacing that second cup of chili with a cup of salad. Personally, I love chili, but I use the salad and veggies to keep me full so I reduce the urge to overindulge.

☑ Do This: And the Survey Says…

Remember what I said in *Chapter 4: Math Class*, Math is your friend. But, rather than share these specific numbers with your daughter, use the information as a foundation to begin implementing healthy changes in your menu planning.

> Math is your friend.

Meanwhile, casually survey your family about their health, mood, and sleep patterns. Make sure you keep track of what they share.

Then, work on substituting healthier menu options, a half-cup at a time, without any fanfare. Most kids won't notice. The transition will be painless, and after a couple of months, their food group proportions will look quite different.

At that point, survey your family again about their health, mood, and sleep patterns. Are any benefits noticeable yet? Tell them about the menu changes you've instituted and ask for suggestions for upcoming modifications.

Aren't new habits awesome?

———◆———

Homework: Nutrition by the Numbers

Look up the number of calories in your favorite go-to guilty pleasure, then fill in the blanks. I used my guilty pleasure, vanilla ice cream, as an example.

Example: **Vanilla ice cream** has **137** calories per ½ cup serving.

Multiply that by the number of servings you have each time:
137 calories / ½ cup serving x **3** servings = **411** total calories each time

Multiply that by the number of times you have it:
2 per week x **411** calories each time = **822** total calories/week
8 per month x **411** calories each time = **3288** total calories/month
96 per year x **411** calories each time = **39,456** total calories/year

There are 3500 calories in a pound of fat, so divide the total calories by 3500 to see how many pounds you could drop by eliminating your guilty pleasure food.
    "I could be **11** pounds lighter if I stopped eating **ice cream** for one year."

Now, you try it:

My food _____ has _____ calories per _____ serving.

Multiply that by the number of servings you have each time:
_____ calories/serving x _____ servings = _____ total calories each time

Multiply that by the number of times you have it:
_____ per week x _____ calories each time = _____ total calories/week
_____ per month x _____ calories each time = _____ total calories/month
_____ per year x _____ calories each time = _____ total calories/year

There are 3500 calories in a pound of fat, so divide the total calories by 3500 to see how many pounds you could drop by eliminating your guilty pleasure food.

How many pounds is that in 1 week? _____ 1 month? _____ 1 year? _____

"I could be _____ pounds lighter if I stopped eating _____ for one year."

In my example, a cup and a half of ice cream adds up to about an extra pound a month, just from ice cream… that's approximately **11** pounds worth of yearly "weight creep" I have to struggle to keep off. As I'm writing this, I'm thinking, *Okay, the ice cream's gotta go.* Will I miss it? Not really. I think I'll replace it with an evening walk with someone I love. Actually, I'll enjoy that more.

After all, I could be 11 pounds lighter if I stop eating ice cream for one year… *IF* I don't replace it with a sweet something, or an artificially sweet something.

4. **Save the dinner plates for company**. Serve your family on small plates. Don't pile the dishes high with food. You can go get seconds when you finish. Emptying your dish will contribute to the feeling of being full and satisfied. Now, *that's* an easy fix!

5. **Go for a five-minute stroll with your daughter after your meals**. If you usually have a dessert, take it with you while you walk. Walking will:

    ♦ increase your metabolism

    ♦ massage your organs

    ♦ move your lymphatic fluids

    ♦ increase your oxygen intake

    ♦ stimulate your brain

    ♦ burn a few extra calories

    ♦ exercise your heart

    ♦ increase the circulation in your legs

♦ produce the happy hormones for your body

♦ give you five minutes of unstructured time with your daughter while her brain is producing happy chemicals.

Not bad for a mere 5 minutes, eh? And, if you walk for 5 minutes after every meal, you will be fitting in 15 minutes of exercise every day… without even trying. If the conversation should stretch a 5-minute walk into 10 minutes, then so be it.

6. **Use the Powerful Venn Diagram to agree on food choices.** In Circle A, write your favorite foods. In Circle B, write the healthy foods you should eat. In the magical Section C, list the foods that you love that are also healthy options. These are the foods you want to make sure are included in your meals because you *love* them, and they are *good* for you. That prevents the resentment that dieters feel since these choices mean you are getting more of what you want.

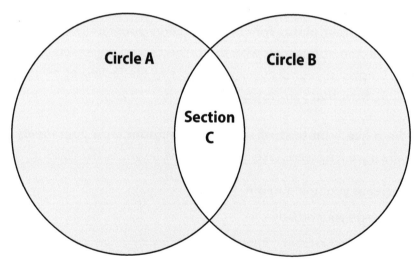

Also, use the Great and Powerful Venn Diagram for selecting foods with your daughter to draw her into the process. In Circle A, write your favorite healthy foods. In Circle B write her favorite healthy foods. In the magical Section C, list the foods that you both love, and *Boom!* You have tonight's dinner options!

7. **Make tap or filtered water your go-to beverage.** Replace your other drinks, including juice, milk, coffee, and alcohol, with water, but avoid plastic bottles if you can. The plastic leaches into the water and its EDCs wreak havoc with your endocrine system and liver. I use a glass bottle and refill it all day.

Your body needs water. It's made up of about 80% water, which needs to be cycled throughout your system, and flushed out by drinking and urinating (in one chute, and out another).

Think about what you crave after your workout. Not milk. Not coffee. It's water. Your body is telling you what it needs. There's nothing like a cool glass of water on a hot summer day. Ignore the beverage advertisements and listen to your body.

> *Endocrine disrupting chemicals (EDCs) are defined as exogenous chemicals, or mixtures of chemicals, that can interfere with any aspect of hormone action… EDCs are demonstrated contributors to infertility, premature puberty, endometriosis, and other disorders. Recently, EDCs have been implicated in metabolic syndrome and obesity. Adipose [fat] tissue is a true endocrine organ and, therefore, an organ that is highly susceptible… [The] "obesogen" [EDCs alter the] programming of fat cell development, [increase] energy storage in fat tissue, and [interfere] with neuroendocrine control of appetite and satiety.*
> Department of Developmental and Cell Biology, University of California

I like being on the safe side when it comes to my family's health, so I've switched us all to using glass and metal containers (instead of plastic). Do I care if these biological concerns prove to be incorrect, and I've been cautious for nothing? Nope, not at all. However, if they do prove there really is a direct link between plastic chemicals and obesity, I'll be doubly glad for my precautions. Besides, for the record, I prefer the taste of water fresh from the tap over water stored in a plastic bottle.

☑ **Do This:** The Milk for Her and Wine for You Challenge

This challenge is modified into two versions, milk and wine, so you can share it with your daughter. If you don't drink milk or wine, substitute soda or juice.

Milk and wine have about the same number of calories, 120ish per cup. If she usually has a daily glass of milk, or if you down a glass of wine daily, you both consume about 143,800 calories each over 365 days. If you were to switch that single daily drink to water, you would each save yourself 143,800 calories over the course of the year. Reducing your calorie intake that much is enough for each of you to lose 12 pounds of fat over this next year... just by substituting 1 drink a day for a glass of water. Hmmm... Is water looking more appealing yet?

———◆◆◆———

By the way, it will take a while to get used to drinking water, especially if you consume a lot of caffeine (coffee, tea, hot chocolate, soda, energy drinks, etc.), so begin by trading just 1 drink a day for an 8-oz glass of water. **Note**: Withdrawing from caffeine can cause headaches and vomiting, so reduce your daily amount slowly.

☑ **Do This:** Pick a Starter Strategy

Why not get started right now? Pick one of the 7 Starter Strategies, and get started. To recap the 7 ways to tame the obesity beast:

1. Don't go on a diet.

2. Increase the number of times you eat to five or six times a day.

3. Add green veggies to your menu until you are eating 4 cups a day.

4. Save the dinner plates for company.

5. Go for a five-minute stroll with your daughter after your meals.

6. Use the Powerful Venn Diagram to agree on food choices.

7. Make tap or filtered water your go-to beverage.

Which one are you going to start with tonight?

Your Own Mini-Pep Rally

Now that you've had a few reminders about how vital a healthy approach is to keeping you and your daughter awesome, you can implement small enhancements to your lifestyle a few at a time. The ripples from your choices reach your daughter, so *you must take care of you first.*

Approach the changes you want to realize with baby steps. Congratulate yourself every morning for embracing life in a positive healthy manner. Don't waste any time chastising yourself for any past lapses in judgment. The future is what matters, so kick that irrelevant guilt to the curb. Your relationship with your Terrific Tween/Teen is going to be more awesome than ever!

You know the drill by now. Stand up and yell so we can rock this party!

 Your Awesome Mom is back,
And here to say hello!
I'm so fired up,
And I'm gonna let it show!

How Did You Do?

To reflect how you feel about the outcome, put one of the following emojis next to each task you undertook.

Assigned Task	Results	Assigned Task	Results
Share the Stats		Share an Article	
Count to 10		The Milk for Her and Wine for You Challenge	
Assessing Your White Stuff		And the Survey Says…	
The Best of You		Nutritional by the Numbers	
Repeat After Me		Pick a Starter Strategy	

Chapter 7

After Final Exams:
20 Ways to Factor in Fun

The 3 R's… Reflection. Recreation. Reexamination.

- ◆ **So Far, So Good: Let's Review**
- ◆ **The Fun Factor**
- ◆ **Final Exams: (The *After* Part Of Before-and-After)**
  - ◆ Homework: Awesome Daughter Post-Assessment
- ◆ **Your Own Mini-Pep Rally**
- ◆ **How Did You Do?**

The objective of this book, and perhaps the reason why you picked it up, is to help you make your way to a loving, healthy, productive relationship with your daughter. Simply wanting a better relationship is about as effective as wishing on a star. Instead, you've chosen to be proactive by exploring strategies and solutions that could benefit you and your daughter. That's what makes you an Awesome Mom, even on the days when you don't feel so awesome.

I've packed a huge amount of information into this book, but the one point I will continue to emphasize is that you never had to be a perfect mom to be one of the Awesome Moms. You *are* an Awesome Mom. You continuously try to make positive changes, to implement the best strategies for you and your family, and to resolve the issues straining your relationship with your special girl. That's why you're awesome!

> You constantly have to adjust to each other, to new rules, to fluctuating hormones, and to the pressure from the outside world.

No one in a relationship is perfect, even under the best circumstances. You constantly have to adjust to each other, to new rules, to fluctuating hormones, and to the pressure and angst you each bring in from the outside world as different people affect your lives.

Did I mention Awesome Moms aren't perfect? I did? Well, we're not. But we're Awesome, and that's way better.

Now, complete this sentence:

Awesome Daughters aren't _____ .

(I'll give you a hint. It begins with "P".)

You guessed it! They aren't perfect, either. They're Awesome. And you knew that she was awesome the day she was born.

Relationships have to be maintained for them to blossom and grow. A strong healthy relationship is a moving target, dynamic in nature. What works today may not work tomorrow. They don't become static until you give up on them.

But you're not going to give up on your relationship with your adorable adolescent, no matter what, because you're awesome, and because she needs that relationship. And, she needs you—healthy, vibrant, and moving along your continuum of life. Living within a healthy relationship will teach your growing girl how to have a healthy relationship with someone else. Remember, she watches everything you do and say, and models her behavior after you. Why? Because she knew you were awesome the first time she opened her eyes and gazed into yours.

"A strong, healthy relationship is a moving target, dynamic in nature."

So Far, So Good: Let's Review

Let's review what we've covered in our Awesome Mom "school day" together. You began with a Pre-Assessment of your relationship, which will be used later to mark the changes in your journey since you started this book. From there, you examined pressures affecting the two of you, and subsequently impact your relationship. If you tried all the activities, here are some of your key takeaways:

♦ The illusions of the **Guilt Myth,** the **Supermom Myth**, and the **Plenty Of Time Myth** have been dispelled.

♦ You and your daughter understand about how the undeveloped teenage brain impacts your interactions.

♦ You now have a couple of quick stress release methods, and are incorporating them into your daily routine.

♦ As you went through the chapters, you collected strategies—against peer pressure, to help self-image, for healthy lifestyle changes, for compromise and negotiating—and in the process, you've gathered lots and lots of Conversation Starters to help you approach your daughter.

♦ You held up a mirror to your lifestyle, and in the reflection, you are analyzing the example that you are setting for your developing daughter *without guilt or self-blame.*

♦ Patience has replaced negative perceptions as you now recognize the importance of taking baby steps when forming good habits, and the importance of setting and enforcing limits, because of their long-term impacts. You've stopped sprinting and are now developing a pace more fitting for the marathon.

♦ The steps you've taken to shield you and your daughter from the toxicity of chemical food additives, white sugar/flour in processed foods, caffeine, cigarettes, alcohol, and drugs, are beginning to improve both your bodies and minds, and are positively impacting your relationship.

Most importantly, the lines of communication are expanding between the two of you. If you have gone through the homework, your glorious girl is starting to perceive you differently. Her faith in you is on the rise, and the pressures on your relationship are decreasing. Perhaps it's a little easier to engage her in conversation, or maybe her outbursts are less intense. In whatever manner the difference is being expressed, you and your touchy teen are acting like a team more often, and find yourselves on opposing sides less frequently.

Wow! You go, Girl!

It's time to add the Fun Factor to all that hard work. You both deserve it.

The Fun Factor

Let's take a break and have some fun before your **Final Exams**! Think back to an activity you used to do together that your dauntless daughter loved when she was younger. Who initiated those good times? It was awesome you! It's time for you to pick up the gauntlet again. Take a break from all this learning and go have some fun!

The objective here is to pick something *you* have never done before so both of you will be a little unsure and inexperienced. Shared vulnerability has a better chance of creating a judgment-free zone where the outcome has nothing weighing in the balance.

Time to initiate another conversation.

Say This: "Remember when we used to ___________________ ? I sure enjoyed having fun with you. What do you say we take off, just the two of us? We should try something neither of us has ever done before. I have a great idea …"

☑ **Do This:** Try It. You'll Like It!

In case you don't actually have a great idea, here's a dozen you can use:

1. Visit an aquarium, a butterfly farm, or interactive science museum.
2. Try an escape room or a puzzle room. They put you in a room filled with clues. You race against the clock to see if you can figure the way out before they open the door.
3. Challenge yourself at a zip line adventure park or an obstacle course.
4. Attend a Renaissance Faire. They hold them all over the country. Don't forget your costume.
5. Take a cooking class at *Sur La Table*. Some are specifically designed for kids.
6. Join a 1-day art class. They teach you how to create one masterpiece, which you take home at the end of the class. Choose your medium: paint, clay, etc.
7. Get a recipe for a completely foreign meal and prepare it together.

8.   Choose a new bike trail and see the world up close and personal.

9.   Take a drumming class, or Zumba, or dance fitness class together (so much fun!)

10. iPhone photography – Pick a theme and collect pictures on your phone. I have a friend who takes pictures of "lone" gloves. I have another friend who takes pictures of unique teacups she finds in thrift stores. I take pictures of bunches of random red cars parked next to each other (for no particular reason).

11. Find a uniquely themed restaurant. The staff at the Victor Café in Philadelphia consists of all opera singers who burst into song throughout the evening. The Medieval Manor in Boston provides a romp through the Dark Ages with a six-course meal. The Vienna Restaurant and Historic Inn in Southbridge, MA is an entirely Bavarian setting. The Crop Bistro & Bar is in a converted bank in Cleveland. Find something in your area by researching "themed restaurants."

12. Volunteer at the pound to walk dogs or help groom them. See if you can help them find homes. Many people who can't own a dog or cat full time opt to foster them for a while in their homes.

Now, don't just read about it. Go have some fun! Schedule something with your cheeky cherub right now!

—————◆—————

Your teachable teen needs help along her journey. The question is, from where will that help come? From you? From her teenage world? How about from both?

What better way to connect than to have fun together? All those good times you remember sharing with your daughter had something in common. Do you know what it was?

You weren't fighting.

Set your intention to create pockets of time where you can explore fun activities together, and if you avoid conflict along the way, so be it.

Don't forget to include your Support Team in the fun. Here are some group suggestions.

☑ Do This: Not Your Every Day Hangout

1. Create a graphic novel with a group of friends. You will need an artist, a writer, a designer, and an organizer.

2. Spray paint or mow the lawn like a chessboard layout, and then gather the neighborhood for a game of chess/checkers where people are the playing pieces. Not your game? How about Chutes and Ladders, Monopoly, or Twister?

3. Conduct a Scavenger Hunt around town, focusing the clues around a theme (like Summer Movies, *Twilight* series, *Harry Potter*, *Avengers*, *X-Men* … you get the idea). Or set up a Library Scavenger Hunt using your favorite books.

> HEY! If you have a great idea that does not appear on this list, send me a description of your idea so I can share it with others at info@DeborahAnnDavis.com.

4. Earth Hour – shut off the electricity in the house for an hour and go outside. Celebrate Earth Hour, on the last Saturday evening in March, with a campfire and Charades. Or, hold an old-fashioned cookout, complete with croquet, badminton, and horseshoes.

5. String lights across a volleyball net for VAD (Volleyball After Dark). Put glow sticks in water-filled plastic bottles for night-time lawn bowling in the dark. Pair that up with some fruit grilled over a campfire for a perfect event.

6. Play Capture the Flag, Zombieland version, at a local park … One Human team; One Zombie team. Create a Zombies Versus Humans competition, set up teams and rules, and go at it.

7. Invite your friends and neighbors to Weekend Recess at an elementary school. Play Dodge Ball, Kick the Can, Hopscotch, Four Square, Double Dutch, Tag, Hide–and-Seek, Simon Says, Red Light, Horse, etc. It will be a whole new experience with older players.

8. Hold a Mother/Daughter Spa Day with your friends and their girls. Hair. Nails. Yoga. Exotic Teas. Hot Towel Treatments. Candles. New Age Music. Meditation Videos. The works!

9. Go get your own food: hunting, fishing, crabbing, clamming; pick your own berries and apples at orchards and farms; get a plot at a community garden.

10. Try Geo-Dashing, Geo-Caching, Letter-Boxing, Orienteering, Laser Tag, or Scavenger Hunting. Many states have competitions that anyone can join. Some activities allow you to go at your own pace, while others have deadlines. It's your choice.

Final Exams (The *After* Part Of Before-and-After)

NOTE: Do Not Go Back And Look At Your Pre-Assessment Before You Do Your Post-Assessment.

Pre-Assessments and Post-Assessments are used to document progress by recording and comparing where you were when you began (Pre-Assessment), and where you are now that the endeavor is completed (Post-Assessment). At the beginning of this *Awesome Mom Handbook*, you and your daughter filled out a **Pre-Assessment** to identify a starting point for your relationship. Over the course of reading this book, you completed the assignments, practiced the things you learned, and enjoyed time spent with your daughter.

Now, it's time for both you and your daughter to fill out the same questions again in the **Post-Assessment**, which describe your relationship, as it exists today, after the work you've put in to strengthen the bond between you.

Are you ready for this?

Awesome Mom Post-Assessment   Today's Date:

Note: Do Not Review Your Pre-Assessment before completing this assessment.

DIRECTIONS: Answer the questions privately.

How Do You Describe Your Relationship With Your Daughter?					
Write 5 words that describe your daughter.					
Write 5 words that describe your relationship.					
Write 5 words that describe how you feel about your daughter.					
Write 5 words that describe how you feel about the relationship.					
Write 5 words that describe how you treat your daughter.					
Write 5 words that describe how your daughter treats you.					
Why do you think things are the way they are between you?					
How does she contribute to the way things are between you?					
How do you contribute to the way things are between you?					

AFTER you complete the Post-Assessment form, dig out the *Awesome Mom Pre-Assessment* you filled out at the beginning of this *Awesome Mom Handbook*. Go sit somewhere private and compare your before-and-after responses. Once you recognize the positive changes you've both achieved through your hard work, you will be able to identify the areas you should continue working on.

Additional Reactions, Reflections, and Ruminations:

How have things changed?

_____

_____

_____

_____

_____

_____

_____

_____

_____

_____

_____

_____

_____

_____

_____

_____

_____

Homework: Awesome Daughter Post-Assessment

Schedule time with your daughter to sit down and answer the questions, but have her fill out her form privately.

Download the free **Awesome Daughter Post-Assessment** at http://DeborahAnnDavis.com/relationship-post-assessment, and print out a copy for your daughter.

Say This: "It's time to take a look at that project I've been working on, and I need 30 minutes of your time. I know you're really busy with school and (homework; sports; work; friends), so would it be better to do this with me today or tomorrow?" (Remember: Don't ask a question that can be answered with 'Yes' or 'No'.)

Then, show up prepared (pen, printed self-assessment, tall glass of herbal ice tea). Have your daughter fill out her *Awesome Daughter Post-Assessment* while you do yours, but again, fill them out privately. Tell her to answer the questions honestly since she will be the only one who sees them.

That's right. If you want her responses to be open and honest, you have to promise not to read them. That doesn't mean you can't discuss them …

When she is done, have her dig out her *Awesome Daughter Pre-Assessment*. Give her some time to compare the two before you ask her to chat about the changes in your relationship.

Good to Know

Don't be surprised (or offended) if your daughter doesn't want to share what she actually wrote. It's private, and that needs to be respected. You can still have the discussion about what has changed, what's trending, and what still needs changing, without actually having to share her words.

☑ Do This: Do You See What I See?

You've looked at your journey, and she's looked at her journey. Pick her favorite place to sit and talk with you to discuss your progress, what you want to work on next, and where you would like to see the relationship go from here. You could very well be creating a memory she'll cherish for a long time.

—◆—

Note: All relationships are dynamic and ever-changing by nature. These assessments merely represent a spot on your relationship continuum.

They're not good.
They're not bad.
They just are.
What matters is in which direction you are moving.

> To illustrate this point, suppose your blood pressure reads 145/95. Is that good or bad? Actually, you can't tell. That reading by itself does not give a complete story. However, comparing it the previous reading does. If it was lower before, 145/95 waves a major red flag because your blood pressure is on the rise. But if the previous reading was higher, 145/95 is good news, an indication your blood pressure is coming down.
>
> Just like with your blood pressure readings, what always matters in your relationship is the direction in which you are moving.

Besides highlighting the changes in your relationship, these assessments are a great stimulus for getting you started on the next phase of your journey. Together, you and your daughter are going to be even more Awesome than ever!

☑ Do This: Everything Old Becomes New Again

It doesn't have to stop here. You can use copies of these forms to track the progress in your relationship from this point forward. For the next leg of your journey, all you have to do is designate today's **Awesome Mom Post-Assessment** as your new **Awesome Mom Pre-Assessment**, and *Presto Change-o!* Today's assessment becomes your new starting point. Print out additional copies of the Pre- and Post-Assessments on my website at:

- ◆   http://DeborahAnnDavis.com/Awesome-Daughter-Pre-Assessment/

- ◆   http://DeborahAnnDavis.com/Awesome-Daughter-Post-Assessment/

☑ **Do This:** Be S.M.A.R.T. About What's Next

Awesome Moms need Awesome Goals. To propel yourself forward, set one new S.M.A.R.T. Goal for yourself for each of the following:

- ◆   your personal development

- ◆   your relationship with your daughter

- ◆   for fun

While you're at it, help your daughter set her own three S.M.A.R.T. Goals because Awesome Daughters need Awesome Goals, too.

Success builds more success, so you got this! Pick any aspect of your life, as long as:

- ◆   you make your new goals S.M.A.R.T.

- ◆   you design goals for the marathon, not for a quick-fix sprint

- ◆   you find the outcome for the new goals exciting

S.M.A.R.T. Goal For My Personal Development:	
S.M.A.R.T. Goal For Helping Our Relationship:	
S.M.A.R.T. Goal For Adding Fun Into My Life:	

Post your goals around your house, in your car, at your workplace, etc. to keep them in the forefront of your mind, and to keep you accountable.

Are you excited yet? You should be!

Your Own Mini-Pep Rally

Congratulations on completing your *Final Exams*!

I'm sure you've figured out by now this book is not about adjusting your relationship to a more pleasant level just to get you through this week. That would be like using a Band-Aid to treat pneumonia.

It is also not about making sure you have a peaceful month with no tantrums disrupting your life. That would be a short-sighted sprint whose benefits quickly fade.

> This handbook is, and always has been, about training for the relationship marathon.

This handbook is, and always has been, about training for the relationship marathon, for fashioning the type of Awesome Mother-Daughter bond that will be loving, supportive, and constructive, and will endure *for the rest of your lives*.

Enjoy your Mother-Daughter relationship. You've got some wonderful years ahead of you.

Awesome Moms are back,
and better than before.
You thought you'd seen the best?
We're here to show you more!

How Did You Do?

To reflect how you feel about the outcome, put one of the following emojis next to each task you undertook.

Assigned Task	Results	Assigned Task	Results
Try It. You'll Like It		Do You See What I See?	
Not Your Every Day Hangout		Everything Old Becomes New Again	
Awesome Mom Post-Assessment		Be S.M.A.R.T. About What's Next	
Awesome Daughter Post-Assessment			

I hope you keep the reflections you journaled throughout these exercises, and the Pre/Post-Assessments, and refer to them occasionally. They are a loving reminder of your growth, a testament to your determination and grit, and definitive proof of your Awesomeness. Besides, your Awesome Grandkids will find them *very* interesting as they enter their own tween/teen years.

May you look back on this year and say,

"This was the best year I've ever spent with my daughter!"

… so far …

One More Gift For You

The 3 R's… Recap. Reaffirm. Rekindle.

Write A Letter To Your Mother

You are the sum total of everything you have experienced thus far, including how you were raised by your mother, and the good/bad points about your relationship with her. As you work on your relationship with your daughter, everything—the ideas, the decisions, the feelings, the reactions—are all touched by your mother's influence, or lack thereof.

The work you did in **History Class** helped you take a look at where your mom was when you were your daughter's age. Go back and review your responses to **Where She Stops and Where I Begin** and the **Me and Mom** tasks. Embrace all that was good in the way your mother parented you when you were a teenage girl, and let go of any negativity in the past. It's time to move forward unencumbered.

Now that you and your daughter both have taken the **Post-Assessments**, compared them to your **Pre-Assessments**, and discussed the before-and-after changes in your relationship, what do you think life would be like if your mother had done these exercises with you when you were a teen? How would they have impacted your relationship and your life? How would they have impacted your motherhood?

The last task you did was to decide on new S.M.A.R.T. Goals for enhancing your future, but I have one more job for you. Your final task is to share your new plan with your mother… in a letter.

Compose the letter for *your* sake.

You are not actually going to give her the letter to read. That will allow you to write freely. Write the letter regardless of the type of relationship you have, regardless if she is still with you, regardless if you are on speaking terms. Compose the letter for *your* sake.

☑ **Do This:** Write a Letter

1. Share with her what you want to do, and why you are doing it.

2. Describe the goals and hopes you hold for you, for her, and for your relationship with your daughter.

3. Discuss the positive things she did that made you the Awesome Mom you are today.

4. Recall her habits and any events you have strived to keep out of your relationship with your daughter, and why.

5. They say teaching is the best way to learn, so teach your mom how to avoid self-blame and guilt. Explain the advantages of objectively examining a situation for a better solution.

6. Describe how you want your ideal relationship with your mom to look three, six, and twelve months from now.

———◆———

Add anything else you feel moved to add. When you are done writing the letter, sign it. That's an informal way of claiming what you wrote, even if it's never delivered.

Writing the letter will have a cleansing and uplifting effect on you. It will clarify how you view your mother, and how you view yourself as a daughter. By examining your history, your present-day path will become more defined.

When you are done, share your epiphanies with your daughter. Talk to her about how you were raised, and how that background affects her… the good, and the not-so-good. Describe the most humbling parts of your relationship with your mother as compared to your relationship with your daughter.

Save the letter so you can revisit it in a year. Put a reminder on your calendar. It will be interesting to see if your views have changed after another year of parenting.

Always remember that YOU are an Awesome Mom.

May the universe always smile down on you, Awesome Mom.

ANSWERS AT THE BACK OF THE BOOK

The 3 R's… Resources. Recommendations. References.

- ◆ **Cleaning Up Your Menu**
- ◆ **Pop Quiz Answers: What Does Your Face Say?**
- ◆ **Examples of School Forms**
- ◆ **Book and Video Resources**
- ◆ **Intervention Telephone Numbers**

Cleaning Up Your Menu

When I had Lyme disease, this was the cleaned-up nutrition protocol I was on. I am not saying all of these foods are safe for everyone, so pay attention to your body. This was all I was allowed to consume:

- ◆ Organic green veggies, including herb seasonings
- ◆ Organic carrots
- ◆ Organic onions
- ◆ Organic garlic
- ◆ Extra virgin olive oil (preferably not imported due to purity concerns)
- ◆ Organic brown rice (not imported due to arsenic concerns)
- ◆ Wild-caught fish (not shellfish or filter feeders)
- ◆ Organic fowl (chicken, turkey, duck, etc.)
- ◆ Filtered tap water (No plastic bottles allowed due to plastic leaching into the water)

Absolutely no GMOs, gluten, wheat, corn, soy, canola, or dairy. Absolutely no fruit, juice, sugar, sweeteners, stevia, artificial sweeteners, vinegars, red meat, processed foods, or white stuff (potatoes, rice, breads, etc.).

Eat organic whenever possible. When grocery shopping, skip anything that has more than 3 ingredients, and avoid any ingredient you can't pronounce.

When I ate out, I usually ordered grilled chicken on romaine lettuce, dressed with olive oil, salt and pepper.

The idea is while your body is fighting something, or trying to fix itself, you don't add any additional problems for it to handle. By cleaning up your menu, your body can devote 100% of its resources to addressing your health problem.

The big bonus? I could eat all I wanted, when I wanted, *and* I lost weight.

Pop Quiz Answers: What Does Your Face Say?

Ekman and Friesen's facial expressions used to determine emotions:

Fearful	**Angry**	**Sad**
Happy	**Disgusted**	**Surprised**

From the article, *Can Children See Emotions in Faces?* by Lawrence K, Campbell R, and Skuse D (2016).

Examples of School Forms

Sample Letter #1: Requesting Homework Info For Absences

Whether you use this letter, or modify it to better suit your purposes, communication with your daughter's teachers is one of the best tools at your disposal.

Dear _____,

My name is _____ and I'm _____ 's mother. She will not be in school on [DATE] due to a [field trip/funeral/family matter/illness]. Can you please tell me what work she will be missing, and what is the best way I can support her catching up in your class?

  Also, how is she doing in your class overall?

  How are her grades?

  Is her work being turned in on time?

  Is she focused or distracted in class?

  Do her tests show that she is mastering the material?

  Do you have any suggestions for me?

  I would be more than happy to meet with you, or have a phone conference at your earliest convenience. You can call me at 123-456-7890, or email me at xxx@xyz.com.

  I look forward to hearing from you.

  Best regards,

  _____

Sample Letter #2: Weekly Progress Report Request

To the teachers of _____

   It's Friday again. I realize how busy you are, and really appreciate you taking the time to fill this out. How did my daughter do this week? Please fill this out and sign it in the subject box.

   Sincerely,

_____ 123-456-7890 or email at mommy@xyz.co

Subject and Signature	Behavior	Grades	Homework
English			
Science			
Math			
Social Studies/ History			
Foreign Lang.			
PE or Health			
Other			

Books, Videos, etc.

Dialing Down the Drama by Colleen O'Grady

Dove Legacy | A Girl's Beauty Confidence Starts With You or watching it here: **https://www.youtube.com/watch?v=qzL8JbhEOyo**

How To Get Your Happy On by Deborah Ann Davis

How to Grow Courageous Girls by Priscilla Wainwright

Energy Medicine for Women: Aligning Your Body's Energies to Boost Your Health and Vitality by Donna Eden

"Now What?" Transformation™ Clarity Card Deck by Brenda Kline Reynolds

TBD-To Be Determined: Leading With Clarity and Confidence in Uncertain Times by Brenda Kline Reynolds

The Energies of Love: Keys to a Fulfilling Partnership by Donna Eden and David Feinstein

The Mom Happiness Project by Naomi Haupt

The Story Of Stuff: **http://StoryOfStuff.org/movies/story-of-stuff/**

Intervention Telephone Numbers

- AIDS Hotline (800) FOR-AIDS

- Alcohol Hotline (800) 331-2900

- Al-Anon for Families of Alcoholics (800) 344-2666

- Alcohol & Drug Abuse Hotline (800) 729-6686

- American Association of Poison Control Centers (800) 222-1222

- Child Help USA National Child Abuse Hotline (800) 422-4453

- Crisis Call Center (800) 273-8255

- Crisis Call Center Hotline (775) 784-8090

- Eating Disorders Awareness and Prevention (800) 931-2237
  https://psychcentral.com/disorders/eating_disorders

- Families Anonymous (800) 736-9805

- Help for Domestic Violence? (800) 799-7233 **(SAFE)**

- National Domestic Violence/Child Abuse/Sexual Abuse (800) 799-7233

- National Help Line for Substance Abuse (800) 262-2463

- National Runaway Switchboard (800) 231-6946

- National Suicide Prevention Lifeline (800) 273-8255

- Teen Help Adolescent Resources (800) 840-5704

Glossary

Adolescent 13-19 years old; a teenager

A.K.A. Also Known As

Amygdala lower interior section of the brain responsible for gut reactions, triggering fear, defensive behavior, and instant gratification

BFF Best Friend Forever

CDC Center for Disease Control

Cortisol a hormone secreted in response to stress; with continued elevated stress, it decreases your immune response, making it easier to get sick

Energy Practitioners professionals who identify and correct different imbalances in a person's energy field (which cause all kinds of physical and emotional problems) and thereby makes conditions right so the body can heal itself

Forebrain the center for logic and reasoning located behind the forehead, capable of good decision-making despite the good-natured pressure from friends

Frontal Cortex area behind your forehead responsible for reasoning, logic, planning, and detecting subtlety

GMO Genetically Modified Organisms; foods that have been genetically altered, and inserted into our food production, but have not been tested for the long term effects on the human body (wheat, soy, corn, sugar beets, canola oil, potato, zucchini, tomato, papaya, pineapple, apple, rice, etc); non-organic food

GI Track Gastro-intestinal system that includes organs, such as the esophagus, stomach, small intestines and large intestines

Habit behaviors so ingrained in one's very existence, that they are conducted without being noticed

Health Education the teaching of personal hygiene, cleanliness, exercise of body and mind, good menu, care of the skin and hair, and the avoidance of hazards such as smoking, excessive drinking, and the abuse of drugs

History the whole series of past events connected with someone or something

Lyme disease a potentially fatal inflammatory disease caused by the bacterium *Borrelia burgdorferi*, transmitted to humans by deer ticks; symptoms include fever, headache, fatigue, bulls-eye skin rash, cardiac and memory issues, etc.

Lymph the almost colorless fluid that travels through the lymphatic system, carrying white blood cells that help fight infection and disease

Lymphatic System a set of circulatory vessels that help rid the body of toxins, waste and other unwanted materials; the tissues and organs, including the bone marrow, spleen, thymus, and lymph nodes, which produce and store cells that fight infection and disease

Madness doing the same thing over and over again, but expecting a different outcome

Math the science (Yay, Science!) of numbers and their interrelations, combinations, and generalizations

MRI Magnetic Resonance Imaging; a diagnostic technique that uses magnetic fields and radio waves to produce a detailed image of the body's soft tissue and bones

Neuron nerve cell

Pep Rally a meeting aimed at inspiring enthusiasm, and providing encouragement and support

Pressure the use of persuasion, influence, or intimidation to make someone do something

Serotonin a chemical produced in the brain that affects the way you feel, making you feel happier, calmer, and less hungry

S.M.A.R.T. Goals setting goals that are Specific, Measurable, and Accountable, with Reminders and a Timeframe

Teenager 13-19 years old

Tween 10-12 years old

Venn Diagram a graphic representation used to clarify differences and similarities

Bibliography

"About." *Free to Be Me*, edited by Dove Self-Esteem Project and World Association of Girls Guides and Girl Scouts, 2017, **free-being-me.com/about/**.

American Diabetes Association. "National Diabetes Statistics Report, 2017." *CDC.gov*, 2017, **www.cdc.gov/diabetes/pdfs/data/statistics/national-diabetes-statistics-report.pdf**.

Aubrey, Allison. "Moderate Drinker Or Alcoholic? Many Americans Fall In Between." *NPR*, NPR, 20 Nov. 2014, **www.npr.org/sections/thesalt/2014/11/20/365500037/moderate-drinker-or-alcoholic-many-americans-fall-in-between**.

Barbalich, Andrea. "Moms on Drugs: The Prescription Pill Epidemic." *Parents Magazine*, Meredith, Nov. 2011, **www.parents.com/parenting/moms/healthy-mom/prescription-drug-addiction/**.

Binns, Corey. "How Long Can a Person Survive Without Water?" *LiveScience*, Purch, 30 Nov. 2012, **www.livescience.com/32320-how-long-can-a-person-survive-without-water.html**.

Breuning, Loretta. "Boost Your Natural 'Feelgood' Chemicals." *Psychologies*, Kelsey Media, 14 Mar. 2017, **www.psychologies.co.uk/self/how-to-boost-your-natural-feelgood-chemicals.html.**

"Caffeine in Food." *Caffeine Informer*, 2017, **www.caffeineinformer.com/caffeine-in-candy**.

Cali. "Can't Lose Weight." *Weight Loss Performance*, 26 May 2016, **www.weightlossperformance.com/health-and-fitness/cant-lose-weight/**.

Campbell, Susan. "The Mother-Daughter Bond." *Psychology Today*, Sussex Publishers, 1 May 2001, **www.psychologytoday.com/articles/200105/the-mother-daughter-bond**.

Canizaro, Mark. "Chocolate Does Not Contain Caffeine." *All about Chocolate – No Caffeine*, **www.xocoatl.org/caffeine.htm**.

Carroll, Linda. "Kids and Caffeine May Be a Dangerous Combination, New Study Suggests." *Today*, 16 June 2014, **www.today.com/health/ kids-caffeine-may-be-dangerous-combination-new-study-suggests-1D79801666**.

Clear, James. "5 Common Mistakes That Cause New Habits to Fail." *James Clear*, 18 Sept. 2017, **jamesclear.com/habits-fail**.

Daily Mail. "Duke University Scientists Find Women Need More Sleep Than Men." *NewsComAu*, News Limited, 20 Dec. 2013, **www.news.com.au/lifestyle/health/duke-university-scientists-find-women-need-more-sleep-than-men/news-story/145ac5019468614c170432eb a0a78977**.

Dean, Signe. "Here's How Long It Takes to Break a Habit, According to Science." *ScienceAlert*, 2015, **www.sciencealert.com/here-s-how-long-it-takes-to-break-a-habit-according-to-science**.

Department of Developmental and Cell Biology, University of California, Irvine, Irvine, California; Department of Pharmaceutical Sciences, University of California, Irvine, Irvine, California. "Obesogens: An Emerging Threat to Public Health." *PubMed.gov*, National Center for Biotechnology Information, U.S. National Library of Medicine, 29 Jan. 2016, **www.ncbi.nlm.nih.gov/pubmed/26829510**. Accessed 17 Nov. 2018.

DiscoveryHealth.com Writers. "Our Mothers, Ourselves: Mother-Daughter Relationships." *HowStuffWorks*, HowStuffWorks, 25 May 2005, **health.howstuffworks.com/wellness/women/general/mother-daughter-relationships4.htm**.

"Dove Legacy." *Dove*, Unilever, 2017, **www.dove.com/us/en/stories/campaigns/legacy.html**. Accessed 9 Nov. 2017.

"Downloadable Parent Resources." *DrugFree.org*, Partnership for Drug-Free Kids, 2017, **www.theantidrug.com**.

Ekman, Paul. "Facial Expressions of Emotion – Stimuli and Tests (FEEST)." *www.researchgate.net*, edited by Thames Valley Test Company, v. 1.0 ed., Boag Associates, Jan. 2002, **www.researchgate.net/profile/Reiner_Sprengelmeyer/publication/252068424_Facial_expressions_of_emotion_Stimuli_and_tests_FEEST/links/02e7e5315a1722136d000000/Facial-expressions-of-emotion-Stimuli-and-tests-FEEST.pdf**. Accessed 14 Nov. 2018.

Ekman, Paul. "Pictures of facial affect." *Consulting Psychologists Press* (1976).

"Equation." *Https://Www.collinsdictionary.com*, Collins Dictionary, **www.collinsdictionary.com/us/dictionary/english/equation**.

ETR. "Join Our Email List!" *ReCAPP: Statistics: Sexual Activity*, **recapp.etr.org/recapp/index.cfm?fuseaction=pages.StatisticsDetail&PageID=555**.

Gregoire, Carolyn. "5 Amazing Things Your Brain Does While You Sleep." *Huffington Post*, HuffPost Lifestyle, 28 Sept. 2014, **www.huffingtonpost.com/2014/09/28/brain-sleep-_n_5863736.html**.

"Health Education." *Collins Dictionary of Medicine*. 2004, 2005. Robert M. Youngson 7 Nov. 2017. **https://medical-dictionary.thefreedictionary.com/health+education**.

"Helping Children and Adolescents Succeed Socially!" *Social Skills Place*, Susan Stern, Mar. 2008, **socialskillsplace.com/archive/0408.newsletter.html**.

HHS. "About the Epidemic." *HHS.gov*, US Department of Health and Human Services, 21 Dec. 2017, **www.hhs.gov/opioids/about-the-epidemic/**.

Hopkins, Kiernan. "25 Shocking Distracted Driving Statistics." *Distracted Driver Accidents*, 30 Oct. 2015, **distracteddriveraccidents.com/25-shocking-distracted-driving-statistics/**.

Kandel, Denise D., et al. "Intergenerational Patterns of Smoking and Nicotine Dependence Among US Adolescents." *ADPH*, American Journal of Public Health, Nov. 2015, **ajph.aphapublications.org/doi/abs/10.2105/AJPH.2015.302775**. Accessed 2 Mar. 2018.

Klein, Sarah. "12 Surprising Sources of Caffeine." *Health*, Health Media Ventures, 8 Apr. 2015, **www.health.com/health/gallery/0,,20313656,00.html#perky-jerky**.

Laurance, Jeremy. "Girls More Likely to Smoke than Boys." *The Independent*, Independent Digital News and Media, 22 Sept. 2004, **www.independent.co.uk/life-style/health-and-families/health-news/girls-more-likely-to-smoke-than-boys-547339.html**.

Lawrence, Kate, Ruth Campbell, and David Skuse. "Age, gender, and puberty influence the development of facial emotion recognition." *Frontiers in psychology,* 6, 2015.

Lawrence, Kate, Ruth Campbell, and David Skuse. "Can Children See Emotions in Faces?" *Frontiers for Young Minds*, 25 Aug. 2016, **kids.frontiersin.org/article/10.3389/frym.2016.00015**.

"Learning Style Inventory." *Georgia Department of Education*, **www.gadoe.org/Curriculum-Instruction-and-Assessment/Special-EducationServices/Documents/IDEAS%202014%20 Handouts/LearningStyleInventory.pdf**. Accessed 2 Mar. 2018.

Lee, Dawn. "Single Mother Statistics." *Single Mother Guide*, edited by Dawn Lee, 29 Sept. 2017, **singlemotherguide.com/single-mother-statistics/**. Accessed 2 Nov. 2017.

Lehman, Janet. "Scared of Your Defiant Child? Learn How to Get Back Your Parental Control." *Empowering Parents*, 2017, **www.empoweringparents.com/article/scared-of-your-defiant-child-learn-how-to-get-back-your-parental-control/**.

"'Like Mother, Like Daughter' … Is the Phrase Really True? Are You Destined to Be Like Your Mother?" *Six Wise*, 2009, **www.sixwise.com/Newsletters/2010/April/28/Like-Mother-Like-Daughter.htm**. Accessed 29 Nov. 2017.

Mehrabian, Albert. *Biographical Sketch of Albert Mehrabian*, **www.kaaj.com/psych/bio.html**.

Mehrabian, Albert (2009). "Silent Messages' – A Wealth of Information About Nonverbal Communication (Body Language)". *Personality & Emotion Tests & Software: Psychological Books & Articles of Popular Interest*. Los Angeles: self-published. Retrieved April 6, 2010.

Melemis, Steven. "How to Quit Smoking." *Addictions and Recovery*, 13 Oct. 2017, **www.addictionsandrecovery.org/quit-smoking-plan.htm**.

Onayli, Selin, and Ozgur Erdur-Baker. "Mother-daughter Relationship and Daughter's Self Esteem." *Procedia-Social and Behavioral Sciences* 84 (2013): 327-331.

"Perception Sayings and Quotes." *Wise Old Sayings.com*, Wise Old Sayings, 2016, **www.wiseoldsayings.com/perception-quotes/**. Accessed 16 Nov. 2018.

Preidt, Robert. "How many American teens are still lighting up?" *CBSNews.com*, CBS Interactive, 13 Nov. 2014, **www.cbsnews.com/news/how-many-american-teens-are-still-lighting-up/**. Accessed 2 Mar. 2018.

"Pressures on Today's Teens." *Connecticut Clearinghouse*, **http://www.ctclearinghouse.org/ customer-content/www/topics/pressures_on_today_s_teens_010709.pdf**.

Salzman, C. Daniel. "Amygdala." *Encyclopædia Britannica*, 6 June 2016, **www.britannica.com/science/ amygdala**.

Scientific American. "What Happens in the Brain During Sleep?" *Scientific American*, 2017, **www.scientificamerican.com/article/what-happens-in-the-brain-during-sleep1/**.

"Seventeen Magazine and Kaiser Family Foundation Release New Survey of Teens About Virginity." *Kaiser Family Foundation*, 2 Oct. 2003, **www.kff.org/other/ seventeen-magazine-and-kaiser-family-foundation-release/**.

Sixwise. "'Like Mother, Like Daughter' … Is the Phrase Really True? Are You Destined to Be Like Your Mother?" *Sixwise*, 2009, **www.sixwise.com/Newsletters/2010/April/28/Like-Mother-Like-Daughter.htm**.

Smith, Art. "Half of Americans Take Vitamins Regularly." *Gallup*, 19 Dec. 2013, **news.gallup.com/poll/166541/half-americans-vitamins-regularly.aspx**.

Smith, Cecilia. "Surprising Foods That Have Caffeine and Make You Gain Weight Fast." *Eat This*, Galvanized Media, **www.eatthis.com/surprising-foods-that-have-caffeine**.

"Smoking & Tobacco Use." *Centers for Disease Control and Prevention*, Centers for Disease Control and Prevention, 16 Nov. 2017, **www.cdc.gov/tobacco/data_statistics/fact_sheets/fast_facts / index.htm**.

"Smoking Leads to Disease and Disability and Harms Nearly Every Organ of the Body." *CDC*, 29 Mar. 2017, **www.cdc.gov/tobacco/data_statistics/fact_sheets/fast_facts/index.htm**.

Sophy, Charles, and Brown Kogen. *Side by Side: The Revolutionary Mother-Daughter Program for Conflict-Free Communication*. HarperOne, 2011.

Spinks, Sarah. "One Reason Teens Respond Differently to the World: Immature Brain Circuitry." *PBS*, Public Broadcasting Service, 2002, **www.pbs.org/wgbh/pages/frontline/shows/teenbrain/ work/onereason.html**.

Sitar, Dana. "9 Ways to Get Free or Cheap Therapy When You Don't Have Health Insurance." *The Penny Hoarder*, **Https://www.thepennyhoarder.com/**, 12 Sept. 2017, **www.thepennyhoarder.com/life/wellness/low-cost-and-free-mental-health-services/**.

Swift, Art. "Half of Americans Take Vitamins Regularly." *Gallup.com*, 19 Dec. 2013, **www.gallup.com/poll/166541/half-americans-vitamins-regularly.aspx**.

Thorpe, K. E., A. C. Wisniewski, and G. M. Lindsay. "The burden of chronic disease on business and USA competitiveness." *USA workplace wellness alliance* 2009, **http://www.prevent.org/data/files/News/pfcdalmanac_excerpt.pdf**. Accessed 4 Nov. 2017.

"Tobacco-Related Mortality." *Centers for Disease Control and Prevention*, Centers for Disease Control and Prevention, 1 Dec. 2016, **www.cdc.gov/tobacco/data_statistics/fact_sheets/health_effects/tobacco_related_mortality/index.htm**.

Tone, Erica, et al. "Facial Expression Recognition in Adolescents with Mood and Anxiety Disorders." *The American Journal of Psychiatry*, vol. 160, no. 6, June 2003. *Research Gate*, item10.1176/appi.ajp.160.6.1172. Abstract.

"U.S. Women Hit Milestone for Obesity." *CBS News*, 7 June 2016, **www.cbsnews.com/news/us-women-hit-milestone-for-obesity/**.

Walters, Joanna. "America's Opioid Crisis: How Prescription Drugs Sparked a National Trauma." *The Guardian*, 2017, **www.theguardian.com/us-news/2017/oct/25/americas-opioid-crisis-how-prescription-drugs-sparked-a-national-trauma**.

"What Happens in the Brain During Sleep?" *Scientific American*, 2017, **www.scientificamerican.com/article/what-happens-in-the-brain-during-sleep1/**.

"What's Your BMI?" *NHS Choices*, NHS, 30 Dec. 2016, **www.nhs.uk/Livewell/loseweight/Pages/BodyMassIndex.aspx#waist**.

Whiteman, Honor. "Caffeine: How Does It Affect Our Health?" *Medical News Today*, Healthline Media, 28 Oct. 2015, **www.medicalnewstoday.com/articles/271707.php**.

Williams, Ray. "Why New Year's Resolutions Fail." *Psychology Today*, Sussex Publishers, 27 Dec. 2010, **www.psychologytoday.com/blog/wired-success/201012/why-new-years-resolutions-fail**.

Acknowledgement

Thank you to the Awesome Mom Tribe who told me how much they wish I had written this book back when their daughters were young. A special thanks to Erin Riley, Joanna D'Angelo, Leeza Steindorf, Kate Richards and Catherine Williams, all of whom are responsible for this book becoming a reality.

Dedication

This book is dedicated to my darling daughter, without whom I could not have been an Awesome Mom. I'm so proud of her, and the young woman she has become.

Dear Awesome Mom,

I hope you found dozens and dozens of strategies you can use right away. As a mother, I've been through what you're going through – the heavy sighs, the knocking heads, the unexpected conflict when you offer helpful advice. I want to assure you that you can bridge that chasm… you know… the one that suddenly appeared out of nowhere when your daughter reached double digits.

As a speaker, coach, and educator, I've worked with thousands of people via classes, workshops, and live events, leading them towards solutions to make home life, school life, and everyday life, more manageable. Today, my mission is to help you, Awesome Mom, tap into the tools you already have inside, plus a few extra techniques to help you positively influence your teenage daughter as she develops into a strong, well-adjusted woman.

Enjoy these teenage years. They'll fly by before you know it. You got this, and you don't have to go it alone. I've got your back. Just reach out if you need a little extra help.

Welcome to the Awesome Mom Tribe!
Deborah

Award-winning author and acclaimed speaker, Deborah Ann Davis, is on a mission to help moms create emotionally strong girls who will become emotionally strong women, who, in turn, will raise emotionally strong families. She has met with hundreds of families who were seeking advice to help their kids better navigate middle and high school. Through classes, workshops, and books, Deborah has touched thousands of people, coaching them towards solutions that make school and everyday life more manageable.

Deborah spent 27 years in the classroom, taking six years off somewhere in the middle to have her daughter. Over the course of her teaching career, in addition to successfully raising her own teenager, Deborah drew on her own experience as a former adolescent, and her personal acquaintance with thousands of teens to help her students.

It wasn't until she had been bitten by the Writing Bug that Deborah left teaching—only to discover that she missed the classroom. Her solution? The Awesome Mom Tribe, a series live events for moms and their teenage girls.

Today she provides the benefit of her wisdom and experience, with compassion and humor, in the form of workshops, day-long seminars, and weekend getaways, and through her books, the upcoming *Ultimate Girl Guides* (for teens), and *Awesome Mom Handbooks* (you guessed it... for moms).

Deborah would love to hear from you. You can reach her at **Info@DeborahAnnDavis.com**, or stop by her website **http://DeborahAnnDavis.com** for tips and ideas to help you remember you are Awesome, and sign up for her monthly newsletter, *Merry Meddling*. Once you're there, grab a free copy of *How To Get Your Happy On!*.

How would you like to take your relationship to the next level?

You're not alone. The landscape is cluttered with concerned mothers who are trying to figure out why their darling tween/teen girls snarl at them over minutia. You have an advantage because you have this book.

However, if you want to practice what *How To Keep Your Daughter From Slamming the Door* preaches, come to one of Deborah Ann Davis's live events!

Attend one of the

Mothers Days
All Day Live Events

for moms, with moms, and by moms. Explore tools for navigating and negotiating an edgy relationship with your daughter (who is impatiently waiting for you to figure it all out), away from the distractions of home.

Better yet, spend an entire weekend with your teenage daughter at the

Rx for the 21st Century:
Moms & Teenage Daughters
Weekend Live Event

After a couple of uninterrupted days, you both will gain insights to yourselves, your relationship, and each other!

Visit **www.DeborahAnnDavis.com/Events**,
or send a request for information to **Info@DeborahAnnDavis.com**.